The Modern Prince

The Modern Prince

Charles J. Haughey and the Quest for Power

Justin O'Brien

Published in 2002 by
Merlin Publishing
16 Upper Pembroke Street
Dublin 2
Ireland

www.merlin-publishing.com

Quotations from Niccolò Machiavelli, *The Prince*
(London, Penguin Books, new edition 1999)

ISBN 1-903582-41-5

A CIP catalogue record for this book is available from the British Library.

Typeset by Gough Typesetting Services, Dublin

Printed by Creative Print and Design Group, Harmondsworth

Dedicated to the memory of my father, Jack, who died while I was working on this book, and in celebration of my son, Jack, whose safe arrival ensured that the project, like the circle of life, was completed.

Acknowledgments

Charles J. Haughey has become something of a hate figure. This book is designed to deconstruct the enigma. How could someone so comprehensively vilified dominate the course of contemporary Irish history for so long? Was he a product of his time, a ruthless Machiavellian devoid of moral purpose, or merely better than his internal opponents at reading the mood of Fianna Fáil and the truncated nation it represented? *The Modern Prince* eschews hysteria in favour of political science to demystify the Haughey legend.

I am particularly grateful to Professor Paul Bew and Professor Richard English of the School of Politics at Queen's University, Belfast. They nurtured the project from its origins as a doctoral thesis, generously devoting endless afternoons in the coffee houses of Botanic to rake over the embers of the subject's controversial career. Professor Henry Patterson and Dr Margaret O'Callaghan read through the manuscript and offered many insightful comments that considerably improved the product. Chris Moore and Mike Nesbitt at UTV displayed professional and personal friendship above the call of duty. This book is in part the result of a number of television programmes; to all those involved, from editorial to technical to interviewees, my grateful thanks.

Such is the controversial nature of the subject that some of those interviewed for this book remain reticent about divulging their identities at this time. Their contributions have been of immense importance and are gratefully acknowledged.

Editors are notoriously difficult to edit, and my heartfelt thanks go to Selga Medenieks at Merlin, who took to the project with enthusiasm from the very beginning. Publishing anything that challenges the new orthodoxy about Charles J. Haughey takes courage. It is a mark of the company that it has shown the determination to see this project through.

As always, my warmest thanks go to my wife, Darina, for giving me the dispensation from family commitments to write this book. To her, and my children Élise and Jack, I owe an enormous debt of gratitude.

"The Modern Prince" is a phrase coined by Antonio Gramsci in *Selections from the Prison Notebooks* (London, 1971).

Justin O'Brien

Belfast, July 2002

As a prince is forced to know how to act like a beast, he must learn from the fox and the lion; because the lion is defenceless against traps and a fox is defenceless against wolves. Therefore one must be a fox in order to recognize traps, and a lion to frighten off wolves.

– Machiavelli, *The Prince*, p. 56

Contents

Introduction

Deconstructing the Enigma

Everyone sees what you appear to be, few experience what you really are.

– Machiavelli, *The Prince*, p. 58

On 30 January 2002, Johnny Silvester, a thinly disguised facsimile of Charles J. Haughey, appeared on stage at the Abbey Theatre to ruminate on the vagaries of Irish political life. The timing of the opening of *Hinterland* by Sebastian Barry, a decade to the week from Haughey's ignominious fall from grace, was like the work itself, a somewhat vulgar attempt to cash in on the public fascination with the Modern Prince. Now ensconced in his Georgian estate, pilloried by wider society, forlornly attempting to stave off judicial tribunals while cancer destroys him from within, the representation of Haughey in *Hinterland* was little more than vaudevillian farce dressed up as social realism. The flotsam and jetsam of a controversial life provided the backdrop: the spurned wife, the expensive shirts, the gossip-columnist mistress, the self-personification of the protagonist with the nation. Fragments of speeches that defined the times littered the dialogue; the staccato delivery of Johnny Silvester's lines mimicked the distinctive Haughey style.[1] As theatre the play was deeply flawed. The legacy of the most controversial leader in the history of the State was traduced to compromised and inadequate caricature. Its insights into the protagonist's failed marriages, both political and personal, were both vulgar and unnecessarily vindictive. The ghost of a political colleague betrayed, visiting the ageing former Taoiseach to declare him responsible for his untimely death, is an amateur approximation of Brian Lenihan. To reinforce the guilt-laden message, the spectre alerts Silvester that the fires of hell are being stoked in anticipation of his own mortality. Silvester's wife, a character presented as the progeny of a previous Taoiseach to reinforce parallels with Haughey's own marriage to the daughter of Seán Lemass, delivers an even harder message.

[1] For critical review see Eileen Battersby, 'Poor drama and bad manners', *Irish Times*, 9 February 2002. For a more sympathetic reading see Fintan O'Toole, 'Portrait of Haughey as Macbeth at bay', *Irish Times*, 2 February 2002. The play clearly divided audiences. For a somewhat astounded reaction to the criticism from the actor who played Silvester see Patrick Malahide in Daniel Rosenthal, 'Charles Haughey, I presume?', *The Independent*, 27 February 2002.

> I can see you in this house in ten years' time, when old age has got a proper grip of you. When it will finally have sunk in, what you are, what you have done. The great iron hammer of guilt that will smash down on your despicable, eternal self-regard. And you will be a nightmare figure in this ruined house. With filthy hair and withered body, the lonely pooka-man of Ireland. And not one moment of pity for you will register in the annals of humankind. You have earned all our contempt and hatred. God Himself will reject you. Even the devil may scorn to have you in his fearsome halls![2]

The playwright was struck by the negative reaction the work received. In his defence he told the *Guardian* newspaper:

> My horrible thesis is that these people [corrupt politicians] are part of us... It is not possible to step away from them now that they are disgraced. Even as a principle of self-preservation, we should realise we're shooting off a part of our own body. The thing has to be healed rather than cut off... A character like Johnny Silvester, so completely condemned by society, provides a sort of laboratory for these big questions.[3]

The problem was that the mechanism chosen obviated the very reason why Haughey was successful: his profound understanding of the mechanics of modern Ireland. Nowhere in the text did Barry provide a convincing rationale that might render understandable the extraordinary resilience and drive of the politician. Instead, Haughey is presented as petulant, self-serving and raging in an intellectually incoherent fashion.

> I made this country, whether they like it or not. They all voted for me when they thought it was to their advantage. How did those mealy-mouthed bastards and biddies get so high up they were heard and listened to? It's like the Salem witch trials, the McCarthy era, the last years of Tsarist Russia, the Third Reich, Kristallnacht, is anyone safe? They will not give me my due now. I am to be ritually disembowelled in my own country, by my own countrymen. That is my fate now! That is my fate now![4]

As the above passage demonstrates, the protagonist in *Hinterland* is unable to comprehend attempts to analyse the dynamics that drove him and the process that led to the creation of tribunals of inquiry. In truth, a strategist of Haughey's calibre would well understand the rationale behind removing the current investigations from the political to a judicial sphere, thereby minimising the destabilising effect of the disclosures. His doppelgänger in *Hinterland* is reduced to a lesser person, an other-worldly phantom that must be exorcised. Barry, like

---

2 Sebastian Barry, *Hinterland* (London, 2002), p. 81.

3 Quoted in Fiachra Gibbons, 'Ireland's villain recast in a new light: Satire based on Haughey's notorious career divides Dublin', *Guardian*, 16 February 2002.

4 Sebastian Barry, *Hinterland* (London, 2002), pp. 16–17.

Conor Cruise O'Brien before him, requires a clove of garlic to protect him from the spell of the Modern Prince.

> I will outlast you, turning your admired middle age into the addled decrepitude and loneliness of the old! I will live, I will live for ever, like a fucking vampire![5]

The real complexity of Haughey's character and his ability to invoke adoration and excruciation in equal measure is simply lost. By failing to demonstrate the sheer resourcefulness of the man as a political strategist, the internal dynamics of the play are skewed from the outset. So, too, is the capacity of the drama to articulate the wider implications of Haughey's decline and fall for Irish politics in general and for Fianna Fáil in particular.

It is important to disentangle fact from illusion in order to assess the overall impact of Haughey on Fianna Fáil and, by extension, on wider Irish society. That society was a mono-cultural construct defined by Fianna Fáil's conception of the nation, which remained largely unchanged until the Good Friday Agreement and the influx of migrants occasioned by the Celtic Tiger economy, both developments occurring after Haughey's departure from public office. It is imperative, therefore, that in assessing his legacy we do so with reference to the political realities which he faced rather than those pertaining today.

What made Haughey unique in Irish politics was the combination of intellectual prowess and political acumen which he was able to communicate to the Fianna Fáil organisation as a whole and to the Irish people in general. Despite the gap in lifestyle that separated Haughey from his constituents in inner-north Dublin, he instilled in them a loyalty that remained undiminished despite, and perhaps because of, the attempts to hasten his political demise. His charisma, a key part of the Haughey enigma, and public rejection of the conservative, diffident and comparatively Spartan lifestyle adopted by his political contemporaries, guaranteed his centrality in a new media discourse as Ireland moved away from the social straitjacket of the 1950s. The inevitable irony is that, with that discourse challenged on both ideological and pragmatic grounds, it is now Haughey himself who stands accused of corrupting its very nature.

Throughout his career Haughey displayed administrative brilliance, revealing not only a keen appreciation of the need to energise a slow and

---

5 *Ibid.*, p. 83. The reference is to one of the most damning assessments of Haughey ever penned, by Conor Cruise O'Brien. Writing just before Haughey's resignation in 1992, O'Brien observed caustically:

> I wrote some years back, during one of Mr Haughey's earlier political crises, that I would not believe him to be politically dead until I saw him buried at midnight at a crossroads, with a stake driven through his heart. That rendezvous at the crossroads is now not far off... In the meantime, whether it be of days or weeks, I am still wearing that clove of garlic around my neck.

See Conor Cruise O'Brien, 'Don't write him off just yet', *Irish Independent*, 25 January 1992, and also 'Diary: Clove of Garlic', *The Times*, 24 January 1992.

somewhat cumbersome bureaucracy but also the mechanisms required to unleash its potential. Capable of a prodigious workload, Haughey worked and played hard, expecting total commitment from his civil servants, pushing them to the limits of their ability and infusing a professional work ethic. This mantra was accompanied by an incisive and sometimes vicious temperament, which he deployed to cutting effect on those who failed to make the grade. Haughey was a tough taskmaster, determined to make his mark on Irish politics and society. Peter Berry, the respected Secretary of the Department of Justice, regarded him as the most able minister with whom he had ever worked.[6] This was quite a compliment, given the fact that Berry, one of the most influential civil servants in the history of the State, had served with every Minister for Justice since Kevin O'Higgins in the 1920s.

The strengths that singled out Haughey for early advancement in the 1960s also necessitated his return to the front benches (after serving his penance for the daring challenge to Lynch during the Arms Crisis). The paradox was that the very skills that differentiated him also nurtured the seeds for his downfall. He proved incapable of delegating power, interfered in the work of ministers and stored up resentment.[7] The deleterious effects of these traits were magnified precisely because of the interminable attempts to undermine his leadership from within the party. Haughey, like Lynch before him, retreated to a coterie of advisors. These were occasionally retained and sometimes promoted beyond their ability solely because they displayed the requisite loyalty so obviously missing in others more determined to pursue their own advancement than row in behind the party leader.

Haughey's entire career was informed by two consistently and cogently articulated themes. These were each designed to complement the other and formulated to enhance his own standing within Fianna Fáil and copper-fasten his leadership: the need to generate income by reducing the tax burden on business and the need to develop a distinctive position on the national question in order to differentiate himself from his rivals. A failure to give equal credence to both formulations risks misdiagnosing the enigma that is Charles J. Haughey, Ireland's most controversial leader.

He was a man with a clear sense of his own destiny, using his maiden speech in the Dáil in 1957 to advocate tax reductions. Married to Maureen, the

---

[6] Berry made the claim in evidence to the Committee of Public Accounts investigation into the Arms Crisis: recounted by Garret FitzGerald and cited in Justin O'Brien, *The Arms Trial* (Dublin, 2000), p. 220.

[7] Attendees at Haughey's first press conference of the 1982 general election observed his unwillingness to delegate first-hand. When Frank Wall was asked if the party was short of money, Haughey infamously cut in: "I'll answer that." A few days later, when Desmond O'Malley was finishing a response to an awkward question on the subject of Knock airport at another press conference, Haughey took the microphone from him and hissed: "*Say yes!*": Gene Kerrigan and Derek Speirs, *Goodbye to all that: A souvenir of the Haughey Era* (Dublin, 1992), pp. 40–42.

daughter of Seán Lemass, he took seriously his father-in-law's famous 1926 admonition that Fianna Fáil needed to 'forget all the petty conceits which bedeck us, like rouge on the face of a corpse, and face the facts, the hard facts which we must overcome'.[8] As he continued his rise through the ranks of Fianna Fáil Haughey became synonymous with the Mohair generation, thrusting individuals who were convinced not only of their own self-worth but also of the power political stability gave them to challenge old shibboleths.[9] In essence, Haughey and his political associates behaved in a similar fashion to the New York stockbrokers so savagely parodied by Tom Wolfe a generation later as 'Masters of the Universe'.[10] But beneath the public flaunting of wealth was a very serious political project: control of Fianna Fáil and, with it, the levers of Irish society.

When Lemass stepped down in 1966, Haughey had positioned himself to challenge for the leadership along with George Colley, Neil Blaney and Jack Lynch. Each offered, to varying degrees, a new departure from the revolutionary generation. Colley was an Irish language exponent who, like many in Irish politics, inherited his standing rather than earned it. Blaney's knowledge of the party and its internal politics was as unmatched as it was ruthless. Lynch, a former GAA All Ireland sporting hero, offered the possibility of connecting to voters outside the metropolitan centres. Haughey lacked familial involvement in the revolution, a stain that even marriage into the home of the most important political strategist that the revolution had produced could not overcome. He lacked, too, an acute understanding of the party outside the metropolitan city. Haughey could take Fianna Fáil in new directions but the price would have been the internal unity of the party: 1966 was not Haughey's time.

Like Blaney, Haughey acquiesced in the accession of Jack Lynch to the leadership. Both men clearly regarded Lynch as nothing more than a caretaker and each retained the ambition to succeed. Not for the last time, Colley determined that he read the mood of the party better, forcing a leadership contest in which he was publicly humiliated. Haughey's caution ensured that he was rewarded with Finance, the most important portfolio in government and a key ministry from which to build an alternate power-base. He incorporated into his own political psyche the most useful components of his rivals, particularly their identification with the national question. The question was reduced to simply one of timing and his only real opponent, following Colley's misjudgment in 1966, was the Donegal machine boss.[11] Haughey distilled the schism within

---

[8] Quoted in Richard Dunphy, *The Making of Fianna Fáil Power in Ireland 1923–1948* (Oxford, 1995), p. 68.

[9] For an interesting assessment of Haughey which places the reason for the vituperative criticism at the door of elite snobs who felt the electorate had simply gone mad in supporting him, see Nuala O Faolain, 'Why shouldn't a free-born Irishman do exactly what he wants?', *Irish Times*, 31 January 1992.

[10] Tom Wolfe, *The Bonfire of the Vanities* (London, 1989).

[11] From very early in Lynch's stewardship the cracks and the burning ambition that fuelled it began to show. The leader of Fine Gael, James Dillon, caught the mood in a Dáil debate in which he sympathised with Lynch's predicament: 'There is not an hour, or a day, or a week until they

Fianna Fáil, according to an authoritative source, 'to personal ambition alone. It was not based on ideological or policy divisions. All wanted power'.[12]

When the Troubles began to break out in 1969, Haughey demonstrated just how much he wanted that power and what he was prepared to sacrifice in order to maintain it. Content to allow Blaney to make the public challenge, his covert financing of the Provisional IRA demonstrated a key awareness that the instability occasioned by the violence in the North offered an opportunity to assert his own republican credentials. Never again would Haughey allow himself to be exposed on the republican flank. His sacking by Lynch in May 1970 and subsequent trial in the very Four Courts building that his father-in-law had attempted to blow up in 1922 (sparking the Civil War), ensured that the whiff of cordite became part of the Haughey armoury. Crucially, a decade later it allowed Haughey to tap into the wider republican zeitgeist.

Haughey never lost his sense that he was destined to rule. His determination to return to power was further strengthened by years spent in the political wilderness after his acquittal at the second Arms Trial. He bought an island home, Innishvickillane, off the western seaboard and internalised the mystique of the Great Blasket Islands, in the process challenging the assumption that he was an effete dilettante.

> We bought the island from the last people to live here. They were the O'Donnelly brothers and they taught us about island life. How to judge the weather, to understand the moods of the sea and tides and currents. About the puffins, the storm-petrels, the black beaded seagulls, the seals, where to put down our lobster pots and where to catch a fine big mackerel.[13]

By 1975 the paucity of talent at the top echelon of Fianna Fáil meant only vindictiveness could have prevented the rehabilitation of Haughey. Once back in the political mainstream, he began the process of securing the leadership by ingratiating himself with the new raft of TDs elected in the 1977 landslide. As the economic consequences of the 1977 manifesto became apparent, Haughey stepped aside from collective responsibility in order to sow the seeds of dissent. He also reaped the benefit of electoral insecurity within the parliamentary party occasioned by a dismal showing in the 1979 European elections.

The deteriorating security situation within Northern Ireland, which the government appeared powerless to affect, served to further undermine the Lynch administration. The killing of Lord Mountbatten at Mullaghmore, a County

---

break his heart, that the clash of knives will not be heard in the corridors of Fianna Fáil.' Dillon regarded Lynch as an honourable figure hopelessly compromised by the ambitions of ministers who 'are now sharpening their knives and whirling their tomahawks, not only for their enemies but for one another': *Dáil Debates*, 11 November 1966, vol. 225, col. 916.

[12] Confidential source, interview with the author, Dublin, 24 July 2002.

[13] *Charles Haughey's Ireland*, Channel 4, 15 January 1986.

Sligo resort, in August 1979, and a devastating IRA attack on a group of soldiers on the outskirts of the Northern village of Warrenpoint on the same day seemed to herald an intensification of the Northern conflict. Once again the stability of the Republic was threatened. Britain was demanding the right to follow targets across the border. However reasonable a request, to the guardians of de Valera's vision of a sovereign Ireland, this amounted to unwarranted interference.[14]

The crisis grew when a junior TD invoked her grandfather's name to buttress the charge. In a calculated rebuke, deep in the Munster heartland where Lynch had built his own power-base, Síle de Valera condemned what she termed the forsaking of traditional Fianna Fáil policy. The ideological basis for her challenge was brought pointedly to the fore through being delivered at a commemoration in honour of Liam Lynch, the Anti-Treaty commander whose seizure of the Four Courts in 1922 started the Civil War. Lynch was under pressure to go. Murmurings of discontent were amplified by the loss of two by-elections within the Cork heartland. Backbenchers, nervous that they would fail to be re-elected to the Dáil if the situation were replicated across the country, began to panic. The Northern question, therefore, provided the final nail in Lynch's political coffin. When a backbencher, Bill Loughnane, used Dáil privilege to accuse the Taoiseach of lying about the extent of security co-operation with the British, the crisis of confidence intensified. Lynch, on a State visit to the United States, demanded Loughnane's resignation but was forced to content himself with a withdrawal of the remarks and not even an apology.[15] The Taoiseach's days were numbered from that moment on, as indeed were Colley's, who showed an inability to control the parliamentary party in Lynch's absence.

Haughey was on the verge of power. He was also perilously close to bankruptcy. Furthering his political ambition came with huge costs. These were eventually underwritten by influential businessmen who viewed his accession to power as the mechanism to preserve their own self-interest. It was a corrosive compact that ultimately served to destroy the credibility of the man who self-consciously portrayed himself as the Spirit of the Nation. Far from the ideal of nobility and idealism, the sordid reality of Haughey's accession to the leadership of Fianna Fáil and the country on 7 December 1979 was the accusation that he was responsible personally for the institutionalised corrupting of Irish politics.

Haughey was a superlative manipulator of emotion within Fianna Fáil, a character trait that was to ensure his reign was challenged by the party establishment. They saw him as a dangerous charlatan and tried to use the media

[14] T. Ryle Dwyer, *Short Fellow: A Biography of Charles J. Haughey* (Dublin, 1999), p. 156.

[15] Bruce Arnold, in his biography of Lynch, places little importance on Loughnane's intervention, whom he described as a 'very marginal backbencher': Bruce Arnold, *Jack Lynch: Hero in Crisis* (Dublin, 2001), pp. 217–218. But the fact that neither Lynch nor Colley had the power to force his expulsion indicated just how little power they actually wielded in Fianna Fáil at that point. For a more balanced view see Arnold's earlier work, *What Kind of Country: Modern Irish Politics 1968–1983* (London, 1984), and Dick Walsh, *The Party: Inside Fianna Fáil* (Dublin, 1986), p. 140.

to destroy his hold over the party. What his critics failed to recognise, however, was that Haughey personified the wider Fianna Fáil organisation. Challenge based on little more than personal animosity was always destined to failure, a fact Haughey recognised and utilised to his benefit, particularly in 1981 and 1982. Fianna Fáil always differentiated itself from its rivals by its commitment to the national question. Haughey's distinct position, even when only articulated as rhetoric, tapped into a visceral feeling within the party that ending partition was an achievable objective. This, in turn, copper-fastened his position and allowed Haughey to dismiss challenges as grounded solely in petulance. The fact that critics attempted to use the national question against him, while accepting the economic policies he enunciated, only added to the futility of his opponents' efforts. Asking Fianna Fáil to move further away from republican certainty by advocating an internal solution on Northern Ireland only served to strengthen Haughey's distinctive position.

Haughey viewed the challengers with disdain. According to a senior source, he judged the putative leaders of the party to be motivated solely by 'vindictiveness and petty vendettas' in which Haughey was to be public enemy number one.[16]

Haughey has been held responsible for the boom and bust economics that hopelessly scarred the Republic during the 1980s but a cogent case can be made that that failure was a systemic one. In many ways it was the decision by Fianna Fáil under Haughey to stick to the spending plans in 1982 that lost him the election. Again, if his administration in 1987 had not forced through stringent cuts, thereby breaking the upward spiral of debt, it is arguable that Ireland could not have benefited from an international economic upturn. Similarly, in the cultural arena, no other political leader in the State paid as much attention to the need to use art as a form of national expression to create and maintain a distinct sense of identity. Critics vehemently opposed the development of Temple Bar in inner Dublin and the creation of the Irish Museum of Modern Art. These were instrumental, however, in steering a cultural renaissance.

Likewise, the restoration of Dublin Castle demonstrated an acute awareness of the political power of the past. The scene was set for Haughey's most important diplomatic triumph: the stewardship of the 1990 European Summit that paved the way for German unification. For Haughey, the Castle was a fitting venue for an appointment with destiny. Basking in the reflected glory of Helmut Kohl, who had demanded unification within the context of a strong unified Europe, and François Mitterand, who had told the Taoiseach that 'Europe must not be a prisoner of its past', Haughey felt that his contribution transcended the squabbles that were already undermining his claim to be personifying the nation. In an ironic twist, it is in those very halls of the Castle that the ritual defenestration of Haughey and his vision is now being played out to an increasingly cynical population. In the process, the central ideological battles for control of Fianna

---

[16] Confidential source, interview with the author, Dublin, 24 July 2002.

Fáil have been downplayed or their significance lost entirely. As a consequence, our understanding of a pivotal period in Irish history is seriously impoverished.

As this book will reveal, Haughey's eventual downfall owes little to the sword so righteously waved by Desmond O'Malley and the Progressive Democrats. Rather, Haughey's eventual vulnerability *within* Fianna Fáil itself stemmed from the failure to translate the rhetoric of opposition into government policy in the period from 1987 to 1992. This is not to suggest that the Northern question was the cause of his downfall, but that the loss of the ideological prop fatally undermined Haughey's claim that only he could ensure Fianna Fáil retained internal cohesiveness as the repository of the revolution's ideals. As a result he was vulnerable, as never before, to the exigencies of electoral fortune. Following the ratification of the Good Friday Agreement, that is the challenge facing Fianna Fáil today. Ceding articles two and three of de Valera's Constitution in return for a crisis-riven process, which has been suspended already twice by the British government acting alone, has demonstrated as never before the inability of the Republic to control the levers of power in the North.

It was a compromise Haughey would never have ceded. A senior source states that he views it as 'inherently unstable, an internal settlement in which the Provisional IRA demonstrates its willingness only to protect the Nationalists within a failed State'.[17] The irony is that this group, the growth of which was expedited by Haughey's adventurism, is now viewed by the Modern Prince as responsible for selling out the dreams of the revolution, presumably in order to achieve short-term improvements in the North. This analysis shows just how far Fianna Fáil has deviated from Haughey's position and also has important long-term implications. Lacking any distinct position on the national question, the internal logic that cemented the organisation has crumbled and with it the primary justification for the party's existence.

It is partly for this reason that Fianna Fáil has attempted to regain its lustre by hooking into select traditions of history. It has presented itself as a technocratic party and used the establishment of tribunals of inquiry in an attempt to convince the electorate that the politics of Haughey represent an aberration of the past. In a recent publication to commemorate the seventy-fifth anniversary of the foundation of Fianna Fáil, Haughey was reduced to bit player. He and his legacy are effectively being airbrushed from the official history of the party. This retraction serves to distort a much more complex and ambivalent reality. Haughey was so successful precisely because of his profound understanding of Fianna Fáil and its revolutionary heritage. He used the goals of the revolution to achieve power and ensure the maintenance of his rule. The ultimate tragedy for the Modern Prince was that in the process he subverted both the revolution and Fianna Fáil's hegemony within it.

More than any other politician in the history of the State, Charles J.

---

[17] Confidential source, interview with the author, Dublin, 24 July 2002.

Haughey, with his mansion, his yacht and his own island off the western seaboard, encapsulated the self-thrusting, post-revolutionary generation of which he was the talisman.[18] His demise ostensibly marks the end of an era, but his final fall also represents a settling of old scores and a concerted attempt to insulate Irish politics from a more systematic onslaught of cynicism. By critically examining the dynamics of his rise to power and the methods used to maintain it, it will be demonstrated that the circumstances of his fall from grace owe less to moral outrage and more to a shift in the paradigmatic structures of internal Fianna Fáil politics.

[18] Despite his undoubted influence in Irish politics, Charles Haughey has been curiously overlooked in academia, in part because of his reluctance to be interviewed since his retirement. The reticence of colleagues still operating at the highest levels of the party can also be advanced as a possible explanation. There is, as yet, no academic biography, although he is the subject of six book-length journalistic profiles: Bruce Arnold, *Charles Haughey: His Life and Unlucky Deeds* (London, 1983); Joe Joyce and Peter Murtagh, *The Boss* (Dublin, 1997); Kevin O'Connor, *Sweetie: How Haughey Spent The Money* (Dublin, 1999); Stephen Collins, *The Haughey File: The Unprecedented Career and Last Years of The Boss* (Dublin, 1992); T. Ryle Dwyer, *Short Fellow: A Biography of Charles J. Haughey* (Dublin, 1999); Sam Smyth, *Thanks a Million Big Fella* (Dublin, 1997). Haughey's tenure as Taoiseach in the 1980s is sketched in J.J. Lee, *Ireland 1912–1985: Politics and Society* (Cambridge, 1989), and Dermot Keogh, *Twentieth-Century Ireland: Nation and State* (Dublin, 1994). Dick Walsh, *The Party: Inside Fianna Fáil* (Dublin, 1986) and Stephen Collins, *The Power Game: Fianna Fáil since Lemass* (Dublin, 2000), assess his impact on party politics.

Chapter One

The Modern Prince

> The only sound, sure, and enduring methods of defence are those based on your own actions and prowess.
>
> – Machiavelli, *The Prince*, p. 79

On the outskirts of Dublin, protected from the ribbon development that has scarred the northern suburban coastline, a discreet, single-lane driveway at Kinsealy meanders out of sight. The lack of ostentatious entrance gates belies the splendour that awaits the visitor as the exquisite mansion at Abbeville comes into view. A single police officer, a clue to the status of the resident, sits nonchalantly outside a hut just as the lane bifurcates. To the right are entrances to a stud farm whose clients have included the famed Italian opera singer Luciano Pavarotti and the Arab sheikh, Prince Fastok. To the left, cannon salvaged from the ill-fated Spanish armada point the way to the former Lord Lieutenant's home in Ireland. With no less than twelve bedrooms, the original seventeenth-century house was redesigned by James Gandon, the man credited with giving the Irish capital a distinct architectural style and whose public commissions included the Four Courts and the Custom House. With both gutted by fire in the maelstrom of the Irish revolution, the ballroom at Abbeville is regarded as 'the finest surviving Gandon interior in the country'.[1]

The current owner has prominently framed over an ornate fireplace an original copy of the 1916 Proclamation of Independence: a subtle and deliberate symbol of the transfer of power from the Anglo-Irish ascendancy to a domestic polity. Yet, in a further ironic twist of historical fate, the proprietor, a man who self-consciously sought to portray himself as the 'Spirit of the Nation',[2] has become a virtual prisoner inside the gilded cage of the Abbeville estate. Both the man and the property exist as metaphors for the impermanence of power in modern Ireland.

Aged seventy-six and dying of prostate cancer, he is quite literally a shadow of his former self. Vilified as a vainglorious scoundrel, his chaotic personal finances have been relentlessly scrutinised. Various tribunals of inquiry continue

---

1 Mary Rose Doorly, *Abbeville: The Family Home of Charles J. Haughey* (Dublin, 1996), p. 2.

2 Martin Mansergh, ed., *The Spirit of the Nation: The Speeches and Statements of Charles J. Haughey (1957–1986)* (Cork, 1986), p. 462.

to systematically examine the corrosive nature of his tenure over Fianna Fáil. The links between his past and present collide in a welter of challenges first exposed during the 1970 Arms Trials and are now reaching a crescendo as the political system itself faces public censure. Not for the first time, the price of stability in the Republic is to be paid with the destruction of one of the shrewdest political tacticians it ever produced. His name: Charles J. Haughey.

Just as in 1970 when, following the failure to convict at the Arms Trial, the political establishment moved to curtail the possibility of Haughey making a comeback, so too from the late 1990s there was a determined effort to insulate the political system from his influence. The media had a veritable feast, gorging on the disgrace of a former Taoiseach who had treated the Fourth Estate with scarcely concealed derision. Most commentators were critical. Typical was the assessment of Peter Murtagh, an assistant editor at the *Irish Times* and co-author of the best-selling Haughey biography *The Boss*. Murtagh described Haughey as 'a political thug… an untrustworthy political hoodlum' who succeeded despite 'the abuses of power and intimidation he had orchestrated within the [Fianna Fáil] party'.[3] Editorials in the paper followed a similar line.[4] The paper's chief political commentator, Dick Walsh, regularly fulminated about the corrosive danger inherent in Fianna Fáil under Haughey.

> Observers, allies and opposition had long recognised Haughey's insatiable appetite for power. Only now are they beginning to realise that it had as much to do with money as with ideology or ambition… In a populist party the only thing more important than daemonic leadership is unquestioning loyalty. The spirit of the party resides in the leader and the spirit of the leader in the party.[5]

The public crisis owes its origins to the attempted suicide of Ben Dunne, an Irish supermarket magnate, at the Hyatt Hotel in Orlando in 1992 following a cocaine-charged encounter with two prostitutes.[6] The resulting power struggle

---

[3] Peter Murtagh, 'Tightening belts for the chancer we knew so well'; http://www.ireland.com/newspaper/special/1999/eyeon20/

[4] See for example, *Irish Times*, 10 July 1997, in which Haughey is deemed to have 'brought shame on the country, on himself, on his family and on Fianna Fáil'. By 17 December 1998 the paper was suggesting in its leader column that '[t]here is a strong argument that the right place for Mr Charles Haughey is in jail'.

[5] *Irish Times*, 3 June 2000. A contrary view was expressed by columnist John Waters in two articles for the same paper, in which he questioned the rationale for the severity of the attacks on the former Taoiseach: 'Laying Bare the Secret behind the Celtic Tiger', *Irish Times*, 14 August 2000; 'Twelve reasons why Charlie should be forgiven', *Irish Times*, 23 October 2000. See also Vincent Browne, 'What has Haughey done to deserve disgrace?', *Irish Times*, 30 December 1998. For a critical analysis from a republican perspective that, ultimately, portrays Haughey as a victim of conflicting political personalities, see Micheal MacDonncha, 'Looking after Number One', *An Phoblacht/Republican News*, 17 July 1997.

[6] A useful summation can be found in Kevin Toolis, 'Troubles of a Taoiseach', *The Observer*, 3 September 2000. The scathing article concluded that Haughey was facing 'a bitter end to an illustrious career. Even Charles Haughey might be forgiven for cursing that Florida police officer,

for control of the Dunnes Stores empire quickly moved from a relatively mundane boardroom battle over the suitability of an acknowledged drug addict to direct the country's largest retail chain to a questioning of the entire political system. Unauthorised payments made by Dunne to political figures in both Fianna Fáil and Fine Gael, throughout the 1980s and early 1990s, seeped into the public domain, exposing an 'inner circle' of political power and patronage long suspected but never proved. The evidence adduced by subsequent tribunals, under the auspices of senior judges Buchanan, McCracken, Flood and Moriarty, have denuded the Irish political establishment. In the process, the dynamics of post-independence politics, based on Civil War divisions, seems increasingly irrelevant. The sordid reality of graft, cutting across both major political parties, is a far cry from the idealism associated with a civil war waged over an ideological debate. The dichotomy between freedom and the freedom to achieve it has been replaced with a perception of common venality.

In short, crises of legitimacy occasioned by the drip feed of revelations from Dublin Castle create the impression of a *fin de siècle*.[7] As Justice McCracken scathingly concluded in his final report into Ben Dunne's payments to Charles Haughey:

> [T]he Tribunal considers it quite unacceptable that Mr. Charles Haughey, or indeed any member of the Oireachtas, should receive personal gifts of this nature, particularly from prominent businessmen within the State. It is even more unacceptable that Mr. Charles Haughey's whole life style should be dependant upon such gifts, as would appear to be the case. If such gifts were to be permissible, the potential for bribery and corruption would be enormous.[8]

It is precisely for this reason that Haughey, the most wilful proponent of a political culture epitomised by greed and betrayal, is being blamed for the institutionalisation of corruption in Irish politics despite the lack of any hard evidence that the former Fianna Fáil leader dispensed favours. Any reference to his illness is seen as a blatant attempt to evade justice. But this justice is of a peculiar variant, not based on actual proof of wrongdoing, but rather the dawning recognition that some of the most prominent business people in the State

far away across the Atlantic, who stopped Ben Dunne, and his secrets, from jumping from the Hyatt Regency's 17th floor balcony.'

7 See, for example, John Drennan, 'The Quick Buck and the Dead', *Magill*, October 2000. For a comparison with European scandals, see the lurid account of the corruption trial surrounding Alfred Sirven, an executive with the French state-owned Elf petroleum company, 'Fugitive takes vacant place in Elf case', *Guardian*, 8 February 2001. For an academic comparison of European corruption that takes a relatively benign view of the Irish case, see Neil Collins, 'Corruption in Ireland: a review of recent cases', in Neil Collins, ed., *Political issues in Ireland today* (Manchester, 1999), pp. 64–88, and Neil Collins and Mary O'Shea, *Understanding Corruption in Irish Politics* (Cork, 2000).

8 Government of Ireland, *Report of the Tribunal of Inquiry (Dunnes Payments)* (Dublin, 1997), p. 51. Hereafter, '*McCracken Report*'.

bankrolled Haughey for unspecified reasons. It is the justice of a society that seeks recompense for believing in the myth created and sustained by a powerful political party. Ultimately, however, it is a catharsis based on the denial of the very reasons that enabled Haughey to command such respect in Fianna Fáil circles in the first place and, more importantly, how the party positioned itself as the dominant force in Irish politics.

Charles J. Haughey's success rested on the dictum of 'loyalty to the party and its leader'. The party's adherence to it enabled him to refashion a political machine into a mechanism designed to foster his own self-interest, an interest he conceived as being conjoined with that of the Irish nation itself. Throughout his public career, Haughey held in abundance that most elusive characteristic: political charisma, a quality that generates enormous respect and hatred in equal measure. His association with violent republicanism, stemming from the position he took during the Arms Crisis, gave the party machine boss a dangerous edge. He self-consciously adopted the persona of vindicated patriot. His charisma, ambition and drive, combined with a messianic ruthlessness, were instrumental in creating a political culture based on unquestioning loyalty.

Under Haughey there would be, as his former press officer, P.J. Mara, once famously remarked: '*uno duce, una voce*.'[9] His sheer resourcefulness in quelling internal critics provides not only interesting gossip but sheds light on the dark arts of political manipulation. Haughey was at the centre of no less than three pivotal crises – the Arms Trial, the telephone bugging of journalists in 1982 (which precipitated his final downfall a decade later when a key participant, Sean Doherty, recanted his previous denials of Haughey's ignorance) and now the unravelling of his personal legacy through the tribunals of inquiry. In a remarkable interview published in December 1984, Haughey himself provided a telling personal insight into the brutal nature of his profession.

> Politics is not the Boy Scouts! It's a bit of a haul. And I think, *per se*, it has to be: you've got to sort of win your spurs and fight your way through... It's a long, hard haul: most of the guys who are at the top have served out a pretty tough, demanding apprenticeship... I *could* instance a load of fuckers whose throats I'd cut and push over the nearest cliff, but there's no percentage in that.[10]

It was, and remains, difficult to provide a neutral assessment of Haughey, a politician who, at the height of his powers, was undoubtedly:

> patently Taoiseach material. Yet, widely admired for his talents, he was also

9 The remark came from a press briefing after Des O'Malley's expulsion from the Fianna Fáil parliamentary party in May 1984 (for criticising attempts to stifle party debate on the options contained in the New Ireland Forum report). Mara allegedly goose-stepped around the room as a prank and proclaimed the legend: 'We are having no more nibbling at my leader's bum.' Cited in T. Ryle Dwyer, *Short Fellow: A Biography of Charles J. Haughey* (Dublin, 1999), p. 291.

10 Emphasis in original. John Waters, 'Personally Speaking', *Hot Press*, Vol. 8, No. 24, December 1984.

> widely distrusted for his use of those talents. He radiated an aura associated in the public mind with a Renaissance potentate – with his immense wealth (discreetly acquired after his entry to politics), his retinue of loyal retainers, his Florentine penchant for faction fighting, his patronage of the arts, his distinctive personality, at once crafty and conspiratorial, resilient and resourceful, imaginative but insecure.[11]

What prompted his desire for office was captured in a 1969 profile in the *Irish Times* that remarked: 'he is a man who wants power. He has everything else.'[12]

Charles Haughey was born in Castlebar in 1926 to parents who had escaped the conflict in the North by moving to Mayo from their native County Derry. Unlike many who reached the higher echelons of Fianna Fáil, Haughey came from unpromising stock. His father had sided with Michael Collins following the establishment of the State and served with the Free State forces during the Civil War. Although a staunch republican, he tired of politics following Collins's death and moved to the Dublin suburb of Sutton. Haughey thus began the slow journey to power with none of the advantages of his school friend and later political rival George Colley, whose familial roots in Fianna Fáil dated back to its inception. A new elite was being groomed by virtue of nepotism rather than merit. Haughey earned his place through sheer intelligence and sporting prowess. He won a scholarship to University College, Dublin, and played in the inter-varsity Gaelic and hurling teams, cementing a relationship with the GAA that was to retain its potency throughout his career.

Upon graduation from the prestigious commerce department at UCD, Haughey became a qualified accountant and barrister, establishing his own accountancy firm with Harry Boland and speculating on real estate. Returned to the Dáil in 1957 and now married to the daughter of Seán Lemass, Haughey began a meteoric journey through the ranks of Fianna Fáil, spurred on by business associates. His maiden speech to the Dáil demonstrated a precocious and imperious manner: he admonished the government for not realising the potential of the country's industrialists. '[T]he trouble with this country,' he intoned, 'is that too many people are making insufficient profits…'[13]

By 1960 Haughey had been appointed Secretary of the Department of Justice. Within twelve months, he was promoted to Cabinet following the

---

[11] J.J. Lee, *Ireland 1912–1985: Politics and Society* (Cambridge, 1989), p. 499. For Lee, Haughey bore close comparison in both temperament and qualities to David Lloyd George. Such generous assessments are now a thing of the past. However, a heart scare on 18 March 2000 which threatened Haughey's life prompted the chairman of Fianna Fáil, Dr Rory O'Hanlon, to comment that history would indeed judge the former Taoiseach as someone who 'did excellent work for the people': 'History will recognise his great contribution to the country, claims FF party chairman', *Irish Independent*, 20 March 2001.

[12] *Irish Times*, 9 June 1969.

[13] *Dáil Debates*, vol. 161, col. 1194, 14 May 1957.

retirement of his boss, the Minister for Justice Oscar Traynor. The ambitious, young Cabinet Minister immediately made a name for himself, piloting through legislation to simplify the legal system. He also demonstrated an acute awareness of the political capital to be made from the disintegrating IRA campaign that had been waged inconclusively along the border since 1956. He authorised the re-introduction of non-jury Special Criminal Courts, while promising amnesty for those disillusioned IRA members who handed over weapons. When the campaign was called off, the Army Council issued a statement denouncing the government for adopting policies that have 'deliberately distracted from the supreme issue facing the Irish people – the unity and freedom of Ireland'.[14] Haughey immediately dissolved the non-jury courts, opened the prisons and claimed responsibility for securing peace.[15]

During his tenure at Justice Haughey demonstrated a liberal approach to criminal and social justice. He removed the death penalty in most cases and ensured, through the Succession Act, legal recourse for dependants to challenge wills that did not cater for their needs. The thrusting and urbane accountant was moved to Agriculture, a pivotal post in 1960s Ireland, when another Cabinet retirement brought him further promotion. Haughey's impatience with the farming lobby brought him into conflict with powerful vested interests. Protests were organised regularly outside the Minister's offices in Kildare Street over his refusal to bail out a bloated, uncompetitive and unreconstructed industry.

But Haughey's desire for modernisation was also linked to the fortunes of Fianna Fáil and to his own advancement. Just weeks before the 1966 presidential campaign, he famously resiled from a commitment not to authorise an unjustified increase in milk quota payments. Haughey had been Director of Elections and recognised that securing the rural vote for Éamon de Valera was critical. Although Haughey argued that modernisation was in the national interest, it was always subservient to power.

A worsening crisis in the farming sector throughout 1966 was accompanied by a deterioration in Haughey's standing. The timing could not have been worse. Haughey's admonition that the farmers must face harsh economic reality was met with sullen resentment as cattle prices deteriorated and the European Economic Community established prohibitive trade barriers. Advocating free trade in a demonstrably protectionist world was not the way to gain a political power base in the rural heartland. Haughey may have had aspirations for the leadership but, at that stage, did not have the necessary support outside the metropolitan area.

---

[14] Cited in Thomas Hennessey, *A History of Northern Ireland 1920–1996* (Dublin, 1997), p. 107.

[15] The campaign was about to be called off anyway but Haughey's public announcements found political capital in the inevitable. Haughey's skill, as T. Ryle Dwyer noted, was in securing an honourable conclusion 'both as a means of facilitating the IRA's desire to end hostilities and as a ploy to score political points for the government in general and the Minister for Justice in particular': see T. Ryle Dwyer, *Short Fellow: A Biography of Charles J. Haughey* (Dublin, 1999), p. 43.

His decision not to contest the leadership following the retirement of Lemass earned him the coveted post of Finance. A relieved Jack Lynch placed Neil Blaney in Kildare Street to negotiate a settlement with the irate farming lobby. Haughey was now one of the most important figures in Fianna Fáil. In charge of overall economic policy and with experience in the three key portfolios of Irish government, he was now in a position to build that alternate base from within the citadel of power. Ensconced in the Georgian splendour of Abbeville and a well-known, even notorious, figure in high society, he had become a political force on all fronts. The *Irish Times* profile that noted Haughey's desire for power, prepared in advance of the 1969 general election, seems, a generation on, to be compellingly prescient.

To Haughey's critics outside Fianna Fáil, the unfolding saga being played out at Dublin Castle tribunals is confirming evidence of a flawed pedigree born out of a desire to own the State. He has been compared to the late Richard Nixon, the disgraced former president of the United States, on more than one occasion.[16] It is, on the surface, an apt comparison. Each man demonstrated political genius in pursuing strategies based on a vulgar articulation of the Machiavellian dictum that the end always justified the means[17] and both were publicly humiliated and survived: Nixon after the defeat by Kennedy in 1960, Haughey in his dismissal from office in 1970. Both rose again to occupy the highest political office by sheer force of will; both were blamed for heralding a crisis of confidence in the political system. Nixon ended his days following Watergate a broken man;[18] Haughey looks likely to suffer a similar fate. Yet, their legacies are at once more complex and more ambivalent than a simplistic reading of Machiavelli would suggest.

---

[16] See, for example, Dermot Keogh, *Twentieth-Century Ireland: Nation and State* (Dublin, 1994), p. 346.

[17] For a more sophisticated reading of Machiavelli, which upholds the use of all necessary means *only* in the context of the fulfilment of a noble objective, see Louis Althusser, *Machiavelli and Us* (London, 1999), pp. 92–93. It was indicative of Haughey's political style that he conflated his own interests with those of the State. This conflation has added significantly to the ambiguity surrounding his entire political career. For Haughey, then, his use of all means necessary to attain and hold power was itself part of the national project. In sworn evidence to the Moriarty Tribunal, Haughey claimed that no wrongdoing could be implied from the decision of friends to help politicians 'because they are engaging in initiatives which are beneficial to everybody, as I think I continually did': see Colm Keena, 'Getting by with a little help from his friends', *Irish Times*, 30 September 2000.

[18] The most detailed examination of the lengths to which the Nixon White House went to assure a second term can be found in Carl Bernstein and Bob Woodward, *All the President's Men* (London, 1974; 1994), the classic account of the Watergate scandal. Republican officials claimed the break in at the National Democratic headquarters, which precipitated the collapse of the Nixon administration, was the work of overzealous campaign staff. The writers concluded, however, that 'the Committee for the Re-election of the President *was* the White House, wholly its creation, staffed by the White House, reporting only *to* the White House' (p. 85). As Deep Throat, Woodward's infamous source throughout the Watergate investigation, revealed: 'fifty people worked for the White House and CRP to play games and spy and sabotage and gather intelligence. Some of it is beyond belief, kicking at the opposition in every imaginable way' (p. 135).

Nixon might have suffered public ignominy but professional politicians continued to turn to him for advice, most famously his ideological rival Bill Clinton. The study of Richard Nixon's presidency reveals the mechanics of modern American democracy, in particular its focus on the negative campaigning and dirty tricks that typified the 1972 campaign. Likewise, a deconstruction of the myths surrounding the rise and fall of Charles Haughey offers key insights not only into the man himself but also the dynamics of modern Irish politics, in particular the consequences of his centralisation of power in the Department of the Taoiseach. This strategy was a mirror image of how the former American Secretary of State, Henry Kissinger, ensured that Nixon's writ went unchallenged, particularly in the realm of foreign policy, with equally disastrous consequences.[19]

The comparison goes deep into the background of each personality. Both were regarded as outsiders, both demanded and were afforded unquestioning loyalty. Both developed a hatred for the media, curtailing access and ensuring servility. Haughey had a volcanic temper with a readiness to use foul, abusive language to reinforce his point, a tendency he frequently displayed to journalists who dared to ask awkward questions.[20] Nixon's Chief of Staff, John Ehrlichman, once noted that there was another side to his public persona, 'that he likened to "the flat, dark side of the moon"'.[21] Haughey ran government like a Medici court, never actively requesting civil servants or ministers to break the law but making it clear that the party and, by extension, he himself must be the recipient of unquestioning loyalty, irrespective of the consequences. To reinforce this, he inculcated a culture based not on subservience but reflex: an ability to read the mind of the Modern Prince gained greater kudos and enhanced the prospects of promotion. For his subordinates it was a high-risk strategy. On at least one occasion, namely the bugging of journalists' telephones in 1982 in order to ascertain who was responsible for leaking Cabinet minutes, this was to bring the party into disrepute. Fianna Fáil continues to pay a heavy price for its fascination with the politics of Charles J. Haughey and the perception that he was responsible for lowering public standards.

Underpinning his credo was a messianic self-belief that a life in politics could make a difference. When eventually cast aside by Fianna Fáil on 11 February 1992, Haughey proclaimed this with a typical flourish.

> The work of Government and of the Dáil must always be directed to the progress of the nation, and I hope I have been able to provide some leadership to that

[19] For an interesting comparison see Tony Judt, 'Counsels on Foreign Relations', *New York Review of Books*, 13 August 1998. Judt argued that despite the myth that grew about the efficacy of the system in the Nixon administration, the result was the implementation of frequently disastrous decisions.

[20] See Stephen Collins's anecdote about being grabbed by Haughey in 1981 in his office in Leinster House and told to 'fuck off': *The Power Game: Fianna Fáil since Lemass* (Dublin, 2000), p. 143. Fintan O'Toole, one of the Haughey's most strident critics, recalled a similar tactic when he requested an interview: Fintan O'Toole, interview with the author, October 1999.

[21] Theodore White, *Breach of Faith: The Fall of Richard Nixon* (London, 1975), p. 163.

> end in my time. I have always sought to act solely and exclusively in the best interests of the Irish people. Let me quote Othello: "I have done the state some service; They know't. No more of that."[22]

This was a classic restatement of Fianna Fáil's core, hegemonic values, a self-conception that Haughey assiduously courted. On another level, however, Haughey's political life and final downfall can be seen as a metaphor of not only the modernisation of Ireland but also how the pursuit of power has led to the unshackling of Fianna Fáil's ideological underpinnings with, as yet, uncharted consequences.

Nationalism defined the twentieth century. The threat of fascism and totalitarianism were never far from the surface as the political boundaries of Europe shifted in pursuit of claims for national self-determination. In the aftermath of the Second World War, the use of the United Nations to guarantee state borders, defined by reference to the tense stand-off between NATO and the Warsaw Pact, provided the illusion of stability. As the century drew to a close, the shibboleth of socialist fraternity fragmented with the collapse of the Soviet Union, re-awakening, in the process, ethnic distrust. The collapse of communism, far from heralding the end of history, has given policy-makers their greatest headache. The assumption that the unifying idea of the European Union – that of integration or post-nationalism – could neutralise the contagion that sparked the bloodshed of two world wars has been sorely tested as ethnic disputes replicate like a virus across eastern and central Europe, and in the mid-East.[23] The wars in Yugoslavia, sign-posted by the West's fateful decision to recognise Slovenia, re-ignited the political debate over nations and nationalism, irredentist logic and the methods used by political parties to solidify their position.

Paradoxically, the break-up of state socialism in Eastern Europe has introduced a new vitality into the study of nationalism. Among its most productive students is Anthony D. Smith, who defined nationalism as 'an ideological movement for the attainment and maintenance of autonomy, unity, and identity on behalf of a population deemed by some of its members to constitute an actual or potential "nation".'[24] Smith did not accept that nationalism can be explained by modernisation alone or merely by the invention of tradition by a manipulative elite without reference to pre-existing kinship ties. Rather, he argued that cultural nationalists must identify with pre-existing ethnic ties if the

---

22 *Dáil Debates*, 11 February 1992, vol. 415, col. 1510.

23 See George Schöpflin, *Nations Identity Power: The New Politics of Europe* (London, 2000); Misha Glenny, *The Balkans 1804–1999: Nationalism, War and the Great Powers* (London 1999; 2000). As Benedict Anderson has pointed out, 'the "nation" proved an invention on which it was impossible to secure a patent. It became available for pirating by widely different, and sometimes unexpected hands': see Benedict Anderson, *Imagined Communities: Reflections on the Origin and Spread of Nationalism* (London, revised edition 1991), p. 67.

24 Anthony D. Smith, *The Nation in History: Historiographical Debates about Ethnicity and Nationalism* (Cambridge, 2000), p. 3.

mobilisation is to be successful, even if it is sometimes based on shadowy and ill-documented reality.[25] For Smith, community cannot only be imagined, but also has to be felt and willed, demanding sacrifices for tangible gain.[26] His approach does not invalidate the proposition that nationalism in its contemporary form is a modern invention; rather it provides a mechanism to establish whether the national project can mobilise effectively and is therefore more causally reliable. Indeed, there is considerable evidence that in the Irish case such a view of nationalism can pay dividends.[27]

On the western seaboard of Europe, the island of Ireland has been situated on a contested fault-line and is the repository of two competing nationalist paradigms; their interaction spawned uneasy co-existence and periodic conflict throughout the twentieth century. The nationalist discourse centred on a rejection of the unionist claim that Northern Ireland has a separate legal constitutional identity outside that of the Irish nation, however loosely defined. This was radically challenged by an emerging peace process in that part of the nation traditionally claimed by the Irish State. An agreement brokered between the Northern Ireland parties by the British and Irish governments under the chairmanship of a former American senator, signed on Good Friday 1998 and ratified by referenda held in both jurisdictions in May 1998, seriously undermined the traditional fabric of Irish nationalism. That fabric was originally designed and stitched together by Fianna Fáil, its largest and most powerful political party. In accepting that sections of the Irish nation can opt out of what was traditionally an unshakeable ideological construct, in both a territorial and spiritual sense has Irish nationalism invalidated its central discourse?

Of crucial importance in analysing nationalism in Ireland is Fianna Fáil's own relationship with its most controversial and most overtly ideological leader since de Valera. Charles J. Haughey's tenure was the subject of unparalleled investigation just as the peace process in Northern Ireland reached a denouement. There is, however, a myopic quality to the tribunals with their narrow focus on his economic policies. It is impossible to analyse Haughey and the internal politics of Fianna Fáil without explicit reference to the ideological theatre in which the key battles for the leadership were fought and won.

Haughey, it will be remembered, viewed Northern Ireland with disdain: 'a failed political entity' was his preferred epithet. Such language would be unthinkable to the current leadership as it repositions itself in the aftermath of allegations of Fianna Fáil's endemic corruption. The leader of the party, Bertie Ahern, is at pains to redefine the nature of the Irish question. Ironically, he has the help of Martin Mansergh, Haughey's most trusted advisor on northern politics.

---

[25] For exposition of this argument, see Anthony D. Smith, *Nationalism and Modernism* (London, 1998).

[26] Anthony D. Smith, *The Nation in History: Historiographical Debates about Ethnicity and Nationalism* (Cambridge, 2000), pp. 59–60.

[27] See Jim Mac Laughlin, *Reimagining the Nation-State: The Contested Terrains of Nation-Building* (London, 2001).

The aim is to ensure the party's centrality as the driving force of identity politics on the island while simultaneously seeking to dissociate it from past, ideologically driven, excesses associated with Haughey. It is an exercise of breathtaking audacity that poses a central question: does Fianna Fáil's apparent willingness to sign up to the Agreement signify that Ireland has become a truly post-national society in which ethnic conflict can be cauterised, or merely that the Republic, still relatively homogeneous, has been redefined as the nation? The answer to this conundrum is to be found in using social science to critically examine the nature of Fianna Fáil, the identity that it created and the consequences of Haughey's tampering with the template.

Fianna Fáil sought to define Irish nationalism in its present form. Its deconstruction offers penetrating insight into the nature of politics in the Republic. Central to its success is its appropriation of nationalism's 'quasi-sacred' nature.[28] The party presented itself as the true defender of the moral imperative to unify the nation, a pursuit that the development of sectional class politics would undermine. It was a doctrine, however, that required stability beyond the border of the Irish State in the contested land claimed by the nation. The revocation of nationalist compliance exposed the emptiness of the rhetoric and the ideological conceit that underpinned Fianna Fáil's pretensions. When Northern Ireland buckled under the weight of its own contradictions in the late 1960s, the paroxysm was clearly felt south of the border. The myth that had nurtured independent Ireland became the greatest single threat to its own stability. The dangers were rendered more acute precisely because the re-emergence of national instability coincided with a transfer of power from the revolutionary generation. At stake, therefore, was not only the leadership of the party but also, in the context of violent disturbances that rekindled ethnic distrust about threatened pogroms, the revolution itself.

How Fianna Fáil handled the disturbances provides a case-study of the dangers inherent in appeals to nationalism. In a telling phrase, Benedict Anderson remarked that the biographies of nations are constructed through the manipulation of indicative deaths, executions and suicides.[29] In the Irish case the lineage of the contemporary nation is traced back to the 1916 Easter Rising. With its heady mix of a proclamation of independence from the General Post Office, messianic blood sacrifice, and the construction of martyrs by the maladroit handling of its aftermath by the British authorities, the Rising has maintained a steely grip on republican orthodoxy ever since.

The trauma associated with the outbreak of the Troubles in Northern Ireland seriously questioned those assumptions. Indeed, they necessitated fundamental revision. This in turn presented problems for those determined to

---

[28] *Ibid.*, p. 31.

[29] Benedict Anderson, *Imagined Communities: Reflections on the Origin and Spread of Nationalism* (London, revised edition 1991), p. 206, with reference to Fernand Braudel, *La Méditerranée et le Monde Méditerranéen à l'Époque de Philippe II* (Paris, 1966).

construct an imagined community. As Anderson astutely pointed out: 'All profound changes in consciousness, by their very nature, bring with them characteristic amnesias.'[30] It is also precisely for this reason that revisionist paradigms positing post-nationalist visions of Irish society are themselves compromised, becoming ideological constructs that buttress the reduction of the Nation to the State.[31] Traditional nationalism with the goal of the revolution remaining at the forefront of policy formulation is not only untruthful and unhistorical but also downright dangerous.[32] Playing politics with cultural nationalism is indeed a dangerous occupation; for stability, it was better then to 'accept constitutional realities and not to play around with the demons of culture'.[33] It is precisely for this reason that Charles J. Haughey was regarded as such a dangerous politician in 1970.

The Arms Crisis, which precipitated Haughey's first humiliation, is representative of that instability. The root cause of the rupture can be found in the way in which ownership of the "national question" provided the feuding factions within Fianna Fáil with a mechanism to assert their position inside the party, the government and the nation. Haughey used the uncertainty surrounding the Irish government's response to the Northern conflict as his opportunity to challenge the leadership.[34] Given tacit authority to intervene in the direction of Northern policy by an indecisive leader, Haughey saw 'the opportunity to change the dynamics of the situation, as well as provide short-term relief to those displaced by the conflagration'.[35] This admission from an authoritative source is important new information about what was really at stake when Haughey was sacked in 1970. He viewed the sacking as 'a politically inspired move to appease the British and itself a ploy in a vicious power struggle'.[36] This, too, helps reposition the debate on the importance of the Arms Trial: it suggests that he regarded the prosecution as a proactive move, rather than a rearguard action to curtail his adventurism. A campaign of that viciousness undoubtedly scarred all the participants and ensured that the northern conflict retained the ability to influence the feuding within Fianna Fáil.

---

[30] *Ibid.*, p. 204.

[31] Conor Cruise O'Brien, *States of Ireland* (London, 1972) could be considered the definitive example.

[32] See Peter Hart, *The I.R.A. and Its Enemies: Violence and Community in Cork 1916–1923* (Oxford, 1998; 1999). The book deconstructed the rationale for killing in Cork during the pivotal years of the Irish revolution and found it totally at variance to the myth.

[33] Patrick O'Mahony and Gerard Delanty, *Rethinking Irish History: Nationalism, Identity and Ideology* (Basingstoke, 1998), p. 11. The authors suggested it is of importance to question the '*responsibility* of Irish nationalism for the subsequent history of the Irish nation-state' (p. 13, emphasis in original).

[34] I seek to demonstrate this using Ball's argument that 'ideologies – or, more precisely, ideological debates and disputes – are the engines of conceptual change': Terence Ball, 'From "core" to "sore" concepts: ideological innovation and conceptual change', *Journal of Political Ideologies* (1999), 4(3), 391–396, p. 394.

[35] Confidential source, interview with the author, Dublin, 24 July 2002.

[36] *Ibid.*

It was ground that Haughey was to return to when he eventually secured the leadership of the party in 1979, although by that stage the revival of the republican ethos was largely limited to rhetoric and the machinations of power had become ends in themselves. It would be a fundamental misconception to believe that this represented the end of ideology within Fianna Fáil. Haughey's success in maintaining his position within the party despite a succession of scandals was directly linked to his ability to manipulate the politics of nationalism, thus providing a distinctive position. This set him apart from his rivals, who agreed fundamentally with the economic and social policies being followed but were challenging the leadership on personal grounds. It was a weak strategic position from which to issue a challenge. As Des O'Malley and George Colley found to their cost, in the absence of any incontrovertible evidence compromising Haughey, the campaign to change the leadership – even if attempted with the support of the media – was destined to failure.

It is by demonstrating how Charles J. Haughey utilised that ideological ambivalence towards violence in his pursuit and maintenance of power that one can assess the power of nationalism to provide the cement to bind disparate groupings together. He built his career on demonstrating that Fianna Fáil's distinctive position could only be maintained by reference to its unique ability to render the disparate needs of various interest groups subservient to an exclusivist reading of the national question. Haughey realised that the national question would provide him with crucial leverage in the wars of position within Fianna Fáil – leverage achieved through the symbiotic linkage of political and economic concerns, which, in turn, had Haughey himself as a reference point. For Haughey, nationalism provided the basis for Fianna Fáil to create a new, quasi-religious construct, with himself in the role of patriarch.[37]

Haughey only became vulnerable to a successful challenge from *within* Fianna Fáil because of the failure to translate the rhetoric of opposition into government policy while in office from 1987–1992. This failure can in part be adduced to the vagaries of minority government and coalition. Largely, however, it was a result of a strategic decision that valued the maintenance of power more highly than a potential breakthrough on the North. It was, in retrospect, a miscalculation. A direct link can be traced between his grip on Fianna Fáil and his ability to advance convincingly a distinctive ideological position over his rivals. By 1992, as the noxious air of scandal permeated Leinster House, he had become an electoral liability, the ideological promise exposed as a sham by his lack of tangible action. The game was up and he knew it.[38]

---

[37] In Gramscian terms, this is a ruse within a war of manoeuvre, designed by political parties to ensure the dominance of the world-view posited. 'The mass following is simply for "manoeuvre" and is kept happy by means of moralising sermons, emotional stimuli, and messianic myths of an awaited golden age, in which all present contradictions and miseries will be automatically resolved and made well.' See Antonio Gramsci, *Selections from the Prison Notebooks* (London, 1998), p. 150.

[38] For a critical analysis of ideological power and how it operates, see the Appendix.

Chapter Two

The Arms Trial Revisited

When you see a minister thinking more of himself than of you, and seeking his own profit in everything he does, such a one will never be a good minister, you will never be able to trust him.

– Machiavelli, *The Prince*, p. 75

The announcement that the Minister for Finance, Charles J. Haughey, had been catapulted from the pinnacle of power came in a terse statement issued in the early hours of 6 May 1970, just in time to catch the city editions of the Dublin newspapers. Haughey, along with the equally influential Minister for Agriculture and Fisheries, Neil Blaney, had been unceremoniously dumped from the government he regarded as his own. The cryptic government statement relayed the belief of the Taoiseach, Jack Lynch, that he was 'satisfied that they [Haughey and Blaney] do not subscribe fully to Government policy in relation to the present situation in the Six Counties as stated by me at the Fianna Fáil Árd Fheis in January last'.[1] It amounted to a charge of treachery.

It is difficult to overestimate the political enormity of the dismissals. Haughey and Blaney were two of the most powerful members of the Fianna Fáil parliamentary party, each with aspirations for the leadership and sufficient control over sections of the party machine to expect to achieve it. The 6 May statement was an open acknowledgment of the implosion of the first post-revolutionary generation Fianna Fáil government, an event that was to see the power struggle for control of the party transfer from the Cabinet table to the High Court.

The Ministers were accused of attempting to illegally import weapons for the use of the nationalist community in Northern Ireland. In reality, the weapons were destined for the Provisional IRA, then emerging from the ghettos of Belfast and Derry. The allegations made a volatile domestic situation positively dangerous.

Conspiracy charges against Neil Blaney were dropped because of a lack of evidence. Haughey was returned for trial along with three other men in September 1970. This first trial collapsed when the judge, who was also the President of the High Court, excused himself following accusations of bias from a barrister representing one of the defendants. The second trial ended with the

---

1 *Irish Times*, 6 May 1970.

acquittal of all of the accused, a verdict that stunned many in the political establishment. The failure to convict set in motion a controversy that has deepened, rather than diminished, with the passage of time. Politically, the outcome was immaterial; by the time of the acquittals, the trials had served their political purpose. Neither Charles J. Haughey nor any other person with designs on power would ever again be able to use the political ideology of the nation to endanger the stability of the State.[2] The demarcation was not, however, drawn so definitively within Fianna Fáil itself, which was not only the largest political party on the island, but one that defined itself as the guardian of the national interest.

The accusation that the former Minister for Finance was involved in political adventurism across the border was the most surprising aspect of the extraordinary affair. Haughey was widely regarded as a pragmatist who focused on attempts to revitalise the Irish economy. Indeed, the leitmotif of his political vision until the sackings was encapsulated in the May 1970 budget. The speech was delivered by the Taoiseach in the midst of the Arms Crisis because his Minister for Finance was indisposed: he had fallen from his horse on the morning of Budget Day. Haughey criticised what he termed the 'futility of excessive increases in money incomes' and accused the trade unions of 'a brutal exercise of their bargaining power' which 'not merely leave little or nothing to spare for anyone else but, by the very size of their inflationary gains, reduce the purchasing power of incomes which are already too small'.[3] It was another echo of a recurring theme.

With a shrewd mix of populism and *laissez faire* capitalism, Haughey sought, throughout his career, to revitalise the economy by playing to the patriotic impulses of the common man while reducing the tax burden on indigenous companies. His problem was that economic prowess alone was not enough to tap into the Fianna Fáil zeitgeist, particularly against as popular a leader as Lynch. Lack of soundness on the national question had bedevilled his earlier aspirations for leadership. Despite marriage into the family of the most influential strategist within Fianna Fáil, former Taoiseach Seán Lemass, some senior party colleagues suspected that he lacked depth, principle, and scruple. Following Haughey's claim in 1962 that his action in offering amnesty to republican prisoners led to the

---

[2] For a detailed examination of the events surrounding the Arms Trial and its significance see Justin O'Brien, *The Arms Trial* (Dublin, 2000).

[3] Charles Haughey, Budget statement, 22 April 1970. Text reprinted in Martin Mansergh, ed., *The Spirit of the Nation: The Speeches and Statements of Charles J. Haughey (1957–1986)* (Cork, 1986), p. 119. The linkage between Haughey and the needs of the entrepreneurial class had been copper-fastened in Haughey's maiden speech to the Dáil in 1957.

> I should like to put forward the proposition that the trouble with this country is that too many people are making insufficient profits. Too many people are actually making losses. The trouble is not that our bloated industrialists make too much profit but that too few of our industrialists are able to carry on at all.

Ibid., p. 1; *Dáil Debates*, vol. 161, col. 1194, 14 May 1957.

ending of the IRA campaign, he had refrained from publicly intervening in the debate on the Six Counties, a situation that was to continue even after the flames spread across the north in August 1969.

Behind the outward veneer of calm, a palace coup had raged with a political ferocity to match the descent into violence across the border. During the Arms Crisis Blaney and Boland were the most ardent public proponents of the republican issue. Haughey's position was at once more sophisticated and, ultimately, more oblique. His rivals' campaign served to undermine, on a daily basis, the policy decisions emanating from the Taoiseach's department, weakening the position of Lynch. But it was Haughey alone who retained the ability to transform the rhetoric into action. As Minister for Finance he was given responsibility for the dispersal of funds to alleviate suffering in the north of the island. The government directive giving him this power, agreed at a Cabinet meeting on 16 August 1969 in the immediate aftermath of the Belfast burnings, was a remarkable document. Not only was the Minister for Finance given latitude concerning what to spend, but he also had complete freedom of manoeuvre regarding how to spend it.

> A sum of money – the amount and channel of the disbursement of which would be determined by the minister for Finance – should be made available from the exchequer to provide aid for the victims of the current unrest in the Six Counties.[4]

Before the crisis reached its denouement the following April over £100,000 (more than one million pounds sterling in today's prices) had been spent, only a fraction of which on what could be termed humanitarian relief. The bulk of the money was used to finance weapons-buying operations on the Continent and in the United States, for the creation of a newspaper that consistently supported the Blaney line in the disputes over northern policy, and, most seriously, for the fomenting of a split within the IRA, already in schism because of its inability to protect Belfast's citizens that fateful August.

Haughey recognised 'the opportunity to transcend the failed politics of partition by changing the dynamics of the situation. Offering guns for protection, if necessary, was central to changing the equation'.[5] His covert backing for Blaney ensured he would not be outflanked on the national question, while his silence ensured that he would be the compromise figure should the destabilisation of Lynch's administration force the leader from office. Thus covert control of the northern issue provided Haughey with the opportunity to wrest control of Fianna Fáil. Recalling the political atmosphere from a distance of thirty years, Des Hanafin, at the time of the Arms Crisis an inexperienced TD, argued the importance of

---

[4] Committee of Public Accounts, 1968–69/70, p. 29, cited in O'Brien, *The Arms Trial* (Dublin, 2000), p. 71.

[5] Confidential source, interview with the author, Dublin, 24 July 2002.

remembering 'how close we were to a civil war at that time. When Boland and Haughey and Blaney walked past you in the corridor you felt like lifting your cap, whether you were wearing one or not.'[6]

Nonetheless, there was a wider strategic purpose than simply the attainment of power. It is undoubtedly true that Haughey used the northern question as a lever to gain control of Fianna Fáil, but there was also a very real sense that a moment of destiny had arrived. In the chaotic circumstances of 1969–1970, Haughey clearly believed that continued pressure on the northern state would force its disintegration and allow for a renegotiation of the Anglo-Irish treaty. Indeed, British diplomatic cables released in 1999 serve to underpin this. As early as October 1969, Haughey had invited the British ambassador to his Kinsealy mansion to discuss the long-term options for unity. Haughey welcomed Andrew Gilchrist into his study for what he termed a 'background briefing'.[7] This briefing offered a fundamental long-term shift in policy.

He proposed a deal in which Britain or NATO could have access to the old treaty ports in exchange for a secret commitment that the border would be the subject of an intergovernmental review. According to Gilchrist, Haughey – whom he described as able, shrewd and ruthless – was insistent that there was 'nothing he would not sacrifice, including the position of the Catholic Church in Ireland, to achieve a united Ireland'.[8] The unprecedented broaching of such diplomatic initiatives to a British ambassador by a Minister for Finance, coupled with the lack of corresponding files from the Department of Foreign Affairs, indicates that Haughey was on a solo run. It raises not only serious questions about Haughey's loyalty to the government he was serving, but, when taken together with the fact that he was actively involved in stoking the flames of division in the North, suggests also a Machiavellian amorality.

Throughout his subsequent political career Haughey openly maintained that the Irish question was one to be determined between London and Dublin, a formulation that minimised any possibility of two separate identities sharing the contested territorial space of Northern Ireland. For Haughey the Irish nation was indivisible and non-negotiable.[9] He self-consciously played the role of vindicated patriot in the aftermath of the 1970 Arms Trial acquittals but it was always incidental to his pursuit of the main prize: control of Fianna Fáil, the Soldiers of Destiny – the Republican Party. For the next thirty years, as Charles Haughey rose to dominate Fianna Fáil, the ideological dispute was to wrench the party asunder. The arena centred – always – on the probity of Haughey, the

---

[6] Quoted in Justine McCarthy, 'In memory of a forgotten leader', *Irish Independent*, 23 October 1999.

[7] Confidential source, interview with the author, Dublin, 24 July 2002.

[8] Sir Andrew Gilchrist to Foreign Office, 10 November 1969, quoted in *Irish Times*, 3 January 2000, p. 6.

[9] Its most open formulation was found in his first leadership Árd Fheis: Charles Haughey, Presidential Address, 16 February 1980, reprinted in Martin Mansergh, ed., *The Spirit of the Nation: The Speeches and Statements of Charles J. Haughey (1957–1986)* (Cork, 1986), pp. 327–338.

support base for the competing factions chosen by reference to positions taken at the Four Courts in October 1970. Lynch's victory then served merely to demarcate the battleground on which the contest for the soul of Fianna Fáil was to be fought in future.

The controversy over the Arms Trial, the most important criminal proceeding in the history of the State, re-ignited on 10 April 2001 with allegations that key witness statements were shorn of their import to strengthen the prosecution case. The claims, made by the RTÉ current affairs flagship programme *Prime Time*, centred on the deletion of critical components of the evidence given by the former Director of Military Intelligence, Colonel Michael Hefferon. The excised material implicated the key prosecution witness, the then Minister for Defence, Jim Gibbons, in the plot to import weapons.[10] *Prime Time* suggested that markings on the file matched the handwriting of Peter Berry, the Secretary of the Department of Justice. It added that the file bore evidence that Berry's political superior, the Minister for Justice Desmond O'Malley, had seen the annotated witness statement within twenty-four hours of it being taken. This was a very contentious, if oblique, connection and, if proved, would have been exceptionally damaging to O'Malley's reputation. However, there is no suggestion that O'Malley, himself a solicitor and therefore an officer of the High Court, had any part in the preparation of the statement or was even aware that any deletions had been made. The former Minister went further in his rejection of the *Prime Time* thesis, arguing that he had not even had sight of the original documents.[11]

The RTÉ programme further alleged that the symptomatic nature of the alterations raised serious questions concerning potential abuse of the rule of law, while being careful to state that no direct evidence existed that either O'Malley or Berry had been responsible for the alterations. The controversy deepened when the *Irish Times* unearthed a document in the National Archives that suggested that the Minister for Justice had ordered that the file allegedly containing the original statement be withheld from the defence teams just after the start of the second Arms trial.[12] The document refers to a claim of privilege which had the effect of precluding the defence from gaining access to the original witness statements. The Minister wrote:

> (1) I have examined and considered the Department of Justice File of Official Papers that bears the identification S/7/70, that is marked "CONFIDENTIAL" and that is entitled "Alleged Plans to Import Arms Illegally". That File of Papers has been signed by me on the cover thereof further to identify it.
>
> (2) I have formed the view and am of opinion that on grounds of public policy

---

[10] 'Evidence of the Colonel', *Prime Time*, RTÉ 1, 10 April 2001.

[11] See below, p. 31.

[12] Claim of Privilege on File of Official Papers S/7/70, dated 7 October 1970. The document, which bears the official stamp of the Department and O'Malley's signature, was published by the *Irish Times*, 13 April 2001. See also O'Malley's rebuttals in the *Irish Times*, 14 April 2001 and 10 May 2001.

> and interest neither Mr Peter Berry nor any other officer of the Department of Justice should in the above proceedings [the Arms Trial] –
>
> (a) produce in evidence the said File or any document contained therein, or
>
> (b) disclose in evidence the contents of any document contained in the said File.[13]

The date of the claim, 7 October 1970, immediately after the opening of the second trial, was crucial. Colonel Hefferon's evidence to the first trial, in which he related all the facts omitted from the Book of Evidence, rendered him a 'hostile witness' against the State for the second trial. Further documents, from Military Intelligence, suggested that there was a concerted effort to discredit the Colonel as a witness and therefore the import of his testimony.[14] The prosecution was not prepared to call him at all until the judge intervened. The privilege issue could therefore be seen as a way to protect the State from precisely the same accusations that did surface thirty-one years later with the release of the documents: was it an attempt to narrow the terms of the prosecution for purely political reasons? For O'Malley, however, no sinister motives could be attributed to the claim of privilege, as:

> the signing of public interest immunity certificates or claims of privilege in the standard form such as this was quite common at the time. The claims of privilege specifically made provision for the judge to see the documents concerned. It is necessary to remind ourselves that where official documents and information were concerned there was a culture of secrecy at that time which was quite different to the atmosphere of freedom of information in which we operate today.[15]

O'Malley then made the further and compelling point that the file in question, S/7/70, 'is now used as the general file or repository for all documents relating to the Arms Trial and arms crisis in 1970... Neither I, nor anyone else for that matter, can at this juncture say for certain what was in File S7/70 in 1970'.[16] In fairness, O'Malley has found it impossible to comprehensively lay this matter to rest because the S/7/70 file could have been contaminated at any time since 1970, thus leaving the matter incapable of definitive resolution.

Thirty years later, reputations made – and destroyed – by the chaotic implosion of Fianna Fáil during the Arms Crisis were suddenly put at risk by allegations that, in the attempt to destroy Charles Haughey, the State had not played by the rules. Haughey felt that vindication might at last occur. According

---

13 *Ibid.*

14 See Mark Brennock, 'Move to discredit Hefferon made after the first trial', *Irish Times*, 14 April 1970.

15 Statement reproduced in the *Irish Times*, 10 May 2001, p. 6.

16 *Ibid.*

to an authoritative source: 'Lynch wanted to control every aspect of the trial. The disclosure that anyone in the Department of Justice had sight of witness statements in a current criminal prosecution serves only to prove the case.'[17]

The glorification of Jack Lynch, which had accelerated after his death in 1999 and which seemed designed by Des O'Malley, was stopped in its tracks. With Lynch and Gibbons dead, the media spotlight was turned relentlessly on the former Minister for Justice. Coincidentally, he was the subject of a four-part political biography to be screened later that month by the same television station that aired the *Prime Time* allegations. Even commentators known for their hostility toward Haughey began to question the Manichean conventional history of the period.[18] Most agreed that Captain James Kelly, the intelligence officer charged along with Haughey, the Belfast republican John Kelly and the Belgian-born businessman, Albert Luykx, had suffered enormously as a result of a political show trial now, apparently incontrovertibly, exposed for what it was. The one exception came from the former Labour Cabinet Minister, Conor Cruise O'Brien, who argued that even if the State had indulged in questionable tactics to ensure that the trial was held, 'if ever there was a case where the end justifies the means, this surely was it'.[19]

O'Malley was clearly discomfited by the public revisiting of the ghosts of 1970. In his initial responses, he oscillated from a denial of any knowledge[20] to rebutting that the complexity of the crisis could not be simplified to the fate of one document.[21] He contented himself by saying: 'It was part of my job to help defend the State and to help the State defend itself... I am proud of what I did.'[22] He then declined to take part in any further discussion of the issue until he had studied the newly-released documents in the National Archives.

A heavily edited interview reiterating the initial statement was clumsily inserted into the first part of the memoir *Des O'Malley: A Public Life*. The programme was breathtaking in its lack of critical balance, juxtaposing pictures of Haughey in formal attire with the carnage associated with the Provisional IRA campaign, notably Bloody Friday 1972, and disregarding the fact that Haughey was at the nadir of political control at the time.[23] It was a misjudgment that prompted further negative comment; re-appraisals of the trial centring on a conspiracy to pervert the course of justice began to take shape and with them a renewed questioning of what the Arms Trial was really all about.

O'Malley then made available a detailed reply to the *Prime Time* allegations. He succeeded in presenting a cogent case that no sinister motive could be linked

---

[17] Confidential source, interview with the author, Dublin, 24 July 2002.

[18] Bruce Arnold, 'Captain James Kelly grievously wronged', *Irish Independent*, 14 April 2001.

[19] Conor Cruise O'Brien, 'How keeping Lynch saved Haughey', *Sunday Independent*, 22 April 2001.

[20] Statement of Desmond O'Malley, *Irish Times*, 12 April 2001.

[21] Second statement of Desmond O'Malley, *Irish Times*, 14 April 2001.

[22] *Ibid.*

[23] *Des O'Malley: A Public Life*, RTÉ 1, broadcast in four parts on 29 April, 6 May, 13 May, and 20 May 2001.

to the deletion from Colonel Hefferon's statement the assessment that the Minister for Defence had given approval to the project.[24] He dissected the available evidence while rebuking those who claimed he had been less than comprehensive about his role, if any, in the case. Still, he wanted to place it on record that the task facing anyone trying to vindicate such a position would be 'tedious, laborious and time consuming... thirty-one years after the event with very limited and incomplete papers available and with virtually all his colleagues who might have been able to render assistance or advice either dead or otherwise unavailable'.[25]

His rebutting argument was centred on three main grounds. First, the markings on the original file did not correspond fully to the deletions. Secondly, not all the deletions benefited the prosecution; these were excised simply because they were not statements of fact, but opinion, and therefore inadmissible in court. Thirdly, he pointed out that the Book of Evidence had not been compiled within the Department of Justice, so there could be no suggestion that as Minister he had been in any way involved. He also stoutly defended Jim Gibbons.

> I cannot imagine anyone less likely to commit perjury than the late Jim Gibbons. He was a man of considerable religious scruples, obsessed with the truth, and possessed of a deep and genuine private morality, often expressed to me and indeed expressed publicly and visibly from his voting record in Dáil Éireann on other matters.[26]

He concluded somewhat baldly: 'The facts of the Arms Crisis of 1969 and 1970 speak for themselves and history will get it right when we are all dead and gone.' Three weeks later in the Dáil, following the release of three detailed reports commissioned by the government and apparently designed to offer definitive judgments, O'Malley reverted to the unfinished business.

> I am glad to note that my reputation and that of the late Peter Berry have been vindicated. Now that these issues have been determined, I want answers as to the arms crisis itself. Who conspired to import arms? Which politicians conspired to defeat the democratic process through this illegal importation? Which politicians conspired with members of illegal organisations? Which politicians encouraged the establishment of the Provisional IRA? What happened to the bulk of the money voted for the relief of distress in Northern Ireland? These, and many other questions about the events of 1969 and 1970, merit answers.[27]

---

24 *The Irish Times* published the full transcript of the statement on 10 May 2001. The online version is available at http://www.ireland.com/newspaper/special/2001/omalley.htm

25 Statement of Desmond O'Malley, TD, 9 May 2001, p. 1, released by the Progressive Democrats headquarters and reproduced in *Report of the Attorney General on Questions Concerning the Prosecution of the Arms Trial in 1970* (July 2001), available from the Department of Justice, Equality and Law Reform.

26 *Ibid.*, p. 18.

27 *Dáil Reports*, vol. 540, col. 1058, 6 July 2001.

Despite the potential this rich vein of Irish history offered to explore, the media frenzy that accompanied the initial *Prime Time* disclosures abated just as dramatically. O'Malley's response had provided a reasonable rationale for the deletions from the witness statement. The *Irish Times*, which had covered the developments in considerable detail, made the editorial decision to print the full text of O'Malley's explanation. It seemed an attempt to bring closure to an increasingly acrimonious discussion that had degenerated from debate about the fundamentals of the Arms Crisis into an arcane analysis of documents few commentators had actually bothered to read. RTÉ stood charged of a naïve, unhistorical reading of the Archive – but was this really the case, or did the controversy provide more confirming evidence of the zero-sum orthodoxy that has defined the power struggle for control of Fianna Fáil since the Arms Crisis? Could criticism of the actions of the State in 1970 be construed as an attempt to exculpate Haughey's conduct not just in terms of the Arms Crisis but during his subsequent tenure as Taoiseach?

This certainly was the inference adduced by the Ulster Unionist leader, David Trimble. Speaking in the House of Commons during a debate on the responsibility of Fianna Fáil in setting up the Provisional IRA, he accused sections of the Dublin media of attempting to undermine the legacy of Jack Lynch, James Gibbons and Des O'Malley. The damage was allegedly caused by the asking of awkward questions about the actions of the State that Trimble had himself previously wanted to investigate. Resurrecting the ideological disputes of 1970 was clearly becoming exceptionally problematic. Fianna Fáil was preparing for celebrations to mark its seventy-fifth anniversary and Northern Ireland itself was in the midst of a polarised general election campaign.

Scrutiny of the origins of the unity by consent formula, conceived by Lynch in the aftermath of the Arms Trial and ratified in referenda to endorse the Good Friday Agreement over thirty years later, raised uncomfortable questions. An interview given by the Sinn Féin President, Gerry Adams, in which he outlined his party's intention of using the devolved structures at Stormont to become the most powerful political party on the island, served only to raise the stakes. In a clear reference to the desire of Sinn Féin to utilise the structures of the Good Friday Agreement to dismantle the northern state, he posited the possibility that the unity by consent principle could be undermined if Fianna Fáil was to countenance in future a coalition with the political wing of the Provisional IRA. Adams proclaimed that Sinn Féin was 'not in the Irish government, yet!'[28]

Within the Republic, too, it was increasingly clear that past events had the potential to rocket out of control, poisoning the relationship between Fianna Fáil and its current coalition partner, the Progressive Democrats. The actions of

[28] *Hearts and Minds*, BBC Northern Ireland, 10 May 2001. That concern was heightened when the votes counted on 8 June showed that Sinn Féin now represented the dominant voice in northern nationalist politics and had correctly interpreted the mood in the Republic with its campaign against the Nice Treaty.

the State during the Arms Crisis continue to resonate to this day, particularly the acute difficulties surrounding the diametrically opposed political legacies bestowed on the nation by Charles Haughey, and Jack Lynch and Des O'Malley. The sometimes uneasy coalition between Fianna Fáil and the Progressive Democrats – already shaken by Taoiseach Bertie Ahern's penchant for pursing policies without keeping his junior partners informed (from grandiose visions of a national sports stadium to the plans for the timing of another abortion referendum) – was in danger of fracturing from the unwelcome intrusion of the past.

The Arms Trial controversy was, it turned out, merely a prelude to a gargantuan battle over intellectual ownership of the contemporary history of Fianna Fáil. O'Malley set out his position, unchallenged, on four successive Sunday evenings on prime-time television.[29] According to the portrayal in *A Public Life*, if Haughey was a threat to the State in 1970 by pursuing adventurist policies, his tenure as Taoiseach represented an actual attempt to destroy democracy. In O'Malley's estimation, only the establishment of the Progressive Democrats after his expulsion from Fianna Fáil in 1986 avoided dictatorship. As the series continued, the analysis became increasingly shrill, bordering on hysterical fantasy. The Coalition government in 1989 between Fianna Fáil and the Progressive Democrats was deemed necessary to defend the State from fascism. The clear inference was that those who remained faithful to Fianna Fáil under Haughey instead of defecting to the Progressive Democrats were unbecoming of the ideals of the Republic that Jack Lynch had defended against sinister manoeuvrings within his Cabinet in 1970. These ideals were apparently defended by only Des O'Malley and his new party of patriots.

Throughout the controversy one person held his counsel: Charles J. Haughey. In part this reticence can be attributed to the divergence in the defences used at the initial Arms Trial. Both his co-accused had argued that the arms importation was sanctioned at the highest levels of the government. Haughey claimed that he was merely trying to facilitate military intelligence; he did not know that the consignment bound for Dublin Airport on 20 April 1970 contained weapons. Other, more recent, reasons for Haughey's silence can also be adduced. He had been exceptionally reticent in evidence to the Tribunals of Inquiry set up to investigate his tenure as Taoiseach. His counsel had claimed repeatedly that his memory was frail. They had provided medical evidence to back up the assertion, but this was discounted heavily by both Justice Moriarty and the wider media. The embattled former Taoiseach might have viewed the discomfiture of Des O'Malley with wry amusement, but engaging in public debate on political minutiae risked an unwelcome reappearance before Moriarty. He contented himself by suggesting to friends that RTÉ would be better served by reinstating

---

[29] For withering criticism of the biographical series, see: 'Pillars of society: Des O'Malley', *The Phoenix*, 11 May 2001; Vincent Browne, 'O'Malley series is a disgrace', *Irish Times*, 16 May 2001. For a more sympathetic reading of O'Malley's career, but not of the series, see Fintan O'Toole, 'O'Malley blessed in his enemies', *Irish Times*, 22 May 2001.

the recently axed popular soap *Glenroe* than by a four-hour series on his greatest adversary.[30] Haughey found it impossible to remain dispassionate about O'Malley, whom he privately regarded as 'motivated by overweening ambition and personal vendettas which he pursued to the end'.[31]

Although reluctant to place further pressure on the relationship with his coalition partners, Taoiseach Bertie Ahern was compelled to join the public debate. Given the depth of the bitterness between the factions within Fianna Fáil and their erstwhile colleagues who left to join the Progressive Democrats, now once again partners in government, and the friction exposed by the O'Malley memoir, Ahern had little option but to question the assumptions that lay behind *A Public Life*. His telling responses in an interview with the *Irish Times* in May 2001 indicated the personality conflicts that had dogged Fianna Fáil since the decision by Seán Lemass to step down in 1966. Far from viewing Haughey as a dictator, Ahern felt that his predecessor had done 'great things and he served well and he worked hard'. History, said the Taoiseach, would be more balanced in its assessment of 'The Boss'.

> There is no doubt about it, wrongdoing of whatever type is always damaging and the things that happened that are now the source of the tribunals did create damage [to the party]. It did, I think, shake peoples' stability in that they do not believe that people in office could get involved in these, as they see them, unacceptable things and that was wrong... A lifetime in politics and a lifetime in the public service for the party. I think the vast majority of that was done as a genuine person who came from a working-class background. He worked hard to become a chartered accountant and a barrister. The mistake in my view is that public service is public service, and there is a sacrifice about public service and that is that you have to forgo other things... I think he has taken a bad hit for that, his family has, and by extension Fianna Fáil has, and by extension I have because I have had to defend all of that... But he did an enormous amount of good through all his years for the Irish people.[32]

For O'Malley, however, no amount of public good could compensate for what he viewed as Haughey's betrayal of the State in the struggle for control of Fianna Fáil in 1970. It was a view stridently expressed in his eulogy to Jack Lynch on the twenty-ninth anniversary of the Arms Trial acquittal.

> Thirty years ago as a nation we were confronted with a stark choice. We could have caved in to sinister elements and put our country at mortal risk. But Jack Lynch chose not to. Confronted with some of the most difficult decisions to face any Taoiseach of the modern era, he took determined and resolute action to defend democracy and uphold the law.[33]

[30] *Sunday Independent*, 29 April 2001.
[31] Confidential source, interview with the author, Dublin, 24 July 2002.
[32] Bertie Ahern quoted by Alison O'Connor, 'Bertie: From the Inside Out', *Irish Times Magazine*, 19 May 2001, pp. 19–20.
[33] Ralph Riegel, 'Haughey booed at funeral of Lynch', *Sunday Independent*, 24 October 1999.

This view permeated O'Malley's detailed response to the *Prime Time* allegations. It is one that was also tacitly accepted by the Attorney General, Michael McDowell, coincidentally a senior member of the Progressive Democrats. The Attorney General's report was one of three government analyses of the Arms Trial released simultaneously and quietly by the Department of Justice, Equality and Law Reform at the end of the Dáil session for summer 2001.[34] He rejected any suggestion of a conspiracy to pervert the course of justice but accepted in his concluding remarks that the original statement was embarrassing politically.

> Col. Hefferon's original statement was potentially embarrassing to Minister Gibbons and, probably, to the Government of which he was a member. By excising most (but not all) of the material in the Statement which suggested knowledge, if not explicit approval, of the importation attempts, Col. Hefferon's statement could be said to have been made look much more compatible with the line taken by Minister Gibbons in his series of statements to the Gardaí.[35]

McDowell rejected the suggestion that the initial Hefferon statement was of such importance that had it been available the trial would have been aborted. He noted approvingly the submission of the trial judge, Seamus Henchy, that there had been a case to answer in any event, by virtue of the fact that the arms were demonstrably not for the use of the Defence Forces of the State.[36] Given this point, 'the question of whether the Minister for Defence authorised the importation of the arms was not material to the charge to be put before the jury'.[37] The excision of Gibbons's evidence, therefore, could be legally justified. For McDowell, this might 'have been an unduly narrow view of the case but this is very different from saying that the editing was done for improper reasons'.[38] In a crucial conclusion, the Attorney General argued that 'it may well be that the drafters deliberately decided in good faith to confine their proposed testimony to the narrow issue and that they deliberately chose not to include matter which, however interesting or relevant to political responsibility, was not relevant to their case'.[39]

---

[34] For a trenchant analysis see Emily O'Reilly, 'Arms Trial report slipped in quietly', *Sunday Business Post*, 8 July 2001; see also Emily O'Reilly, 'The gaps in O'Malley explanation', *Sunday Business Post*, 13 May 2001. The full texts were not published by the newspapers but are available from the Department of Justice, Equality and Law Reform: 'The Arms Trial: Changes made to Colonel Hefferon's Statement', *Report by the Minister for Justice, Equality and Law Reform*; 'Release of Documents on Arms Trial, 1970', *Patrick Byrne, Commissioner of An Garda Síochána* (15 May 2001); and *Report of the Attorney General on Questions Concerning the Prosecution of the Arms Trial in 1970* (July 2001).

[35] *Report of the Attorney General on Questions Concerning the Prosecution of the Arms Trial in 1970* (July 2001), p. 42.

[36] Tom Mac Intyre, *Through the Bridewell Gate, A Diary of the Dublin Arms Trial* (London, 1971), p. 105.

[37] *Report of the Attorney General on Questions Concerning the Prosecution of the Arms Trial in 1970* (July 2001), p. 26.

[38] *Ibid.*, p. 27.

[39] *Ibid.*, p. 40.

He further noted:

> Mr Justice Henchy made it clear in his summing up, that is at the conclusion of the second trial and after Colonel Hefferon's evidence as to the Minister for Defence's knowledge in relation to the importation had been fully aired, that he rejected the contention of the Defence that the prosecution was not properly brought by the Attorney General. He did this whilst expressing no view on whether the prosecution should succeed or as to whether the jury should accept or reject Mr. Gibbons['s] evidence.[40]

McDowell contended that 'there is no reason to believe that the original statements of all witnesses were not available in court to be called for by the defence in cross-examination as to credibility, by the prosecution in order to have a witness declared hostile, or by the Court itself in ruling whether a witness should be called'.[41] However, this was simply conjecture. There was no attempt to question Justice Henchy's recollection that the original document was not available to the court,[42] a development that clearly could have affected the nature of the summing up. Despite the apparent gaps in the historical record, the Attorney General came to definitive conclusions.

> I have come to a clear personal conclusion that the establishment of some form of official public inquiry – either into the narrow issue of the conduct of the prosecution or the broader issue of the attempted importation of arms – would serve no useful purpose at this stage. There is simply no prospect of an official, authoritative, objective and generally accepted history of those events being written now.[43]

The report issued by the current Fianna Fáil Minister for Justice, John O'Donoghue, was grounded less on technicalities of legal procedure than political realism.

> If it were established, as a reasonable possibility, that the Minister for Defence [Jim Gibbons] was in effect also a conspirator, then it is difficult to imagine that this would not have been seen as a sensational development or that it would have had no bearing at all on the trial. While it cannot be said that it would, in itself, have had the effect of undermining the specific charges against the accused, it seems reasonable to recognise that the impact of such a development in itself could have led to that result.[44]

---

40 *Ibid.*, p. 42.

41 *Ibid.*, p. 14.

42 See discussion of this in Alison O'Connor, 'Arms Trial judge unaware statement withheld', *Irish Times*, 16 April 2001.

43 *Report of the Attorney General on Questions Concerning the Prosecution of the Arms Trial in 1970* (July 2001), p. 4.

44 'The Arms Trial: Changes made to Colonel Hefferon's Statement', *Report by the Minister for Justice, Equality and Law Reform*, para. 19.

He observed that 'material tending to suggest that Mr. Gibbons had knowledge of what was taking place is omitted'.[45] That being said, on the basis of the available evidence, '[as] the possibility that an attempt to suppress evidence cannot be ruled out definitively, it seems reasonable to infer... that the likelihood is remote'.[46]

Definitive judgments from the Irish sources alone are rendered almost impossible given the failure of the National Archives or the Attorney General to locate key government files. These included the entire prosecution strategy, the Garda file, any working papers relating to the preparation of the case, transcripts of the trial itself and the audio record of the proceedings – including legal argument – used by the prosecution to review proceedings and prepare for the next day's sitting. The Attorney General also declined to interview surviving Garda officers involved in the case, the defendants or, indeed, the trial judge to adjudicate on the purpose of the trial, and had only 'brief informal conversations with some of the lawyers involved'.[47] As Alan Shatter of Fine Gael pointed out to the Dáil following the release of the 2001 reports: 'It is little short of scandalous that crucial and essential documentation relating to one of the major historical and political events of the early 1970s cannot be located.'[48]

So, despite the seriousness of the allegations, the attempts to deduce the truth about the Arms Trial and, consequentially, the nature of the 1970 administration, the reports issued by the government were deficient in one remarkable respect: they took scrupulous care to avoid the political context of the trial, which, of course, was central to the argument about the nature of the prosecution.

There is certainly enough evidence, however, when material from the Irish files is triangulated with contemporaneous reporting and the British files, to suggest that the trial should be viewed as a political rather than a purely legal or criminal affair.[49] On this reading, the unanswered question surrounding the trial and its aftermath is not whether a single document was shorn of its import, tampered with, or doctored. Rather, it concerns whether remarkable efforts were made to limit the terms of the conspiracy, to insulate the chief prosecution witness (the former Minister for Defence, Jim Gibbons) from the self-destruction of the Fianna Fáil government, and on what subsequent manoeuvrings occurred to protect the State following the failure to convict.

A deconstruction of the recently released documents, when read in tandem with the 1970 files from London and Dublin, reveals the true extent to which the Arms Trial centred on a vicious power struggle for the leadership of Fianna

---

[45] *Ibid.*, para. 23.

[46] *Ibid.*, para. 26.

[47] *Report of the Attorney General on Questions Concerning the Prosecution of the Arms Trial in 1970* (July 2001), p. 5.

[48] *Dáil Debates*, vol. 540, col. 1050, 6 July 2001.

[49] The central Irish file is S/7/70 in the National Archives. Its British counterpart is FCO 33/1207 in the Public Records Office.

Fáil, the Soldiers of Destiny, and just how far the Lynch government went to protect its legacy from the threat posed by the hawks in the Cabinet and the undeclared opposition of Haughey. It also demonstrates the failure of contemporary Ireland to come to terms with the machinations of power, its pursuit, and its maintenance. In an acute observation, British Ambassador John Peck noted as much in a despatch to the Foreign Office on 16 December 1970.

> The acquittal of all the defendants, and in particular of Mr. Haughey, precipitated a fresh crisis inside the ruling party... It was not, strictly speaking, a new crisis, but another phase of the battle for the leadership of Fianna Fáil, and this in its turn is the practical manifestation of the conflict about the nature of Republicanism and attitudes towards partition.[50]

It is difficult to exaggerate the impact the Northern Ireland civil rights movement had on the politics of both jurisdictions on the island. By August 1969 the situation had become uncontrollable. Sectarian forces lurking just below the surface of Northern Irish society erupted in a rage of fury. In short, for some factions battling for control of Fianna Fáil, the cataclysmic events in Northern Ireland provided an opportunity to complete the unfinished business of the Irish revolution. A cable from Peck's predecessor as British ambassador, Sir Andrew Gilchrist, caught the volatile mood when he told the Foreign Office: 'All in all we are in for a fairly difficult time from the Irish... if I were a fire insurance company I would not like to have the British embassy on my books. (Fortunately, though highly flammable, it isn't ours.)'[51]

The rhetoric of nationalism had the potential to suck the Republic into the vortex. The chances of involvement were maximised because the violence in the North coincided with a vicious power struggle for control of Fianna Fáil: the opposing sides used the disturbances to further their own competing agendas by proffering differing strategies. Chaos was a valuable political commodity in the battle for control of the party. The threatened destabilisation of the Republic was possible precisely because important figures in Fianna Fáil were prepared to use ownership of the national question to assert their position within the State, the party and, ultimately, the nation. It was a defining moment in Irish political history. Responsibility for this state of affairs rested squarely with Jack Lynch. He delegated control over Northern policy to Charles Haughey and Neil Blaney in the confused days of August 1969 and only really took matters into his own hands with the sacking of those Ministers in 1970.

From the first burnings in Belfast, the priority in Dublin was to ensure that, if confrontation was inevitable, the government would have some control

---

[50] John Peck to Alec Douglas-Home, MP, Secretary of State for Foreign & Commonwealth Affairs, 16 December 1970, FCO 33/1207, paras 2 and 3.

[51] Sir Andrew Gilchrist to Foreign & Commonwealth Office, 14 August 1969, quoted in O'Brien, *The Arms Trial* (Dublin, 2000), p. 50.

of the situation, at all costs preventing the contagion from spreading South. If that meant supplying arms and expertise, then Military Intelligence was quite prepared to do so. The pivotal figure in the crisis was Neil Blaney, whose power and influence within the political machine have since been largely overshadowed. Blaney's motivation throughout the period was to weaken the Official IRA, to destroy the Northern state and, most importantly, to assume the leadership of Fianna Fáil from a leader he openly despised. Throughout late 1969 and 1970 his public denunciations of Lynch's stated policy – that unity could only be achieved by peaceful means and with the consent of the Northern majority – were the only outward signs of the deep divisions within the Cabinet over the way forward.

Giving a speech in Letterkenny on 8 December 1969, to mark his twenty-first anniversary as a TD, Blaney was in a belligerent mood.

> [N]o-one has the right to assert that force is irrevocably out. No political party or group at any time is entitled to pre-determine the right of the Irish people to decide what course of action on this question may be justified in given circumstances. The Fianna Fáil Party has never taken a decision to rule out the use of force if the circumstances in the Six Counties so demand.[52]

Lynch put the speech down to a bout of 'intemperate impetuosity', despite the fact that it had been widely circulated in advance to the media. Blaney followed up this challenge with a bid for the leadership in an RTÉ interview. He buttressed his case by using the power delegated to a Cabinet sub-committee on Northern policy, run by himself and Haughey, to organise arms expeditions to New York and Europe. He also encouraged Northern delegations to keep the pressure on the Cabinet by lobbying for arms. Lynch's policy was under intense scrutiny when he addressed the 1970 Árd Fheis and it was by no means certain that his calls for restraint would prevail. He concluded with a direct challenge to those determined to question his leadership: 'If anybody wants to change the policy that I have set out, this is the place to do it, now is the time.'

The Blaney challenge evaporated without Lynch taking the opportunity to remove his recalcitrant Minister from a position that would allow him to continue operating a covert Northern policy. The fact that the most pressing issue facing the State was no longer decided solely in the office of the Taoiseach gave considerable decision-making latitude or, as John Peck would later refer to it, 'perfect cover' to the hawks. Despite the commitment at the Árd Fheis to the pursuit of unity by consent, those directing Northern policy retained, in private, the option of military engagement as a matter of policy. This was copper-fastened by a directive from the Minister for Defence, Jim Gibbons, on 6 February 1970, instructing the Army to prepare for invasion and to provide weapons, if appropriate.

---

[52] *Irish Times*, 9 December 1969, p. 13.

It is certainly arguable that this contingency plan was evidence that the weapons-buying expeditions were compatible with the terms of the directive.[53] When Lynch finally moved to sack Haughey and Blaney in May 1970 for contravening government policy, it was therefore imperative that Gibbons be insulated from the crisis. This was necessary not only to justify the sackings but also to proceed with a prosecution. According to the Firearms Act, under which the defendants were charged, weapons could be imported only with the authorisation of the Minister for Defence; this was the key plank of the defence case and that this permission had been given formed the central import of Colonel Hefferon's testimony.

Jack Lynch had made the decision to rid himself of his most powerful opponents for the leadership of Fianna Fáil. Lynch claimed *prima facie* evidence of an attempt to import weapons in which the two ministers, along with Captain James Kelly, were involved. The sackings were deemed necessary because of Lynch's conviction 'that not even the slightest suspicion should attach to any member of the Government in a matter of such urgency'.[54] It quickly became apparent that the forced resignation of the Minister for Justice, Micheal O Morain, was inextricably linked to high-level Cabinet feuding. Lynch admitted that the decision to replace O Morain was made 'to dissociate him from the action I was subsequently going to take'. In other words, Lynch was admitting taking over the political functions of the Department of Justice for a particular reason. His surprise choice for the sensitive post, at a difficult time, was a young Limerick TD from a family with a political pedigree, Desmond O'Malley.

It quickly became apparent that Jim Gibbons had been involved in the affair after all. His exposure was orchestrated by Paddy Kennedy, the Belfast MP for the Stormont parliament. Kennedy was a key link between the emerging Belfast Provisional IRA and Charles Haughey. He told a Dublin news conference in May 1970 that the involvement of Captain Kelly would be very surprising 'without the full knowledge of his superior officers and the Minister for Defence'. Further evidence was produced by Billy Kelly, a leading figure in the Provisional IRA in Belfast and a brother of John Kelly. He spoke of a secret meeting with Lynch in March 1970 at which the demand for guns was raised and claimed Gibbons had told them that 'if the worst came to the worst there was no need to fear'.[55]

The exposure of Gibbons was part of a concerted and calculated strategy in large part designed to further undermine the credibility of Lynch. The interests of the Provisional IRA conjoined with those of the accused ministers. In the

---

[53] Interestingly, this appears to have been the view of the British ambassador in his 16 December 1970 summation of the case: John Peck to Alec Douglas-Home, MP, Secretary of State for Foreign & Commonwealth Affairs, 16 December 1970, FCO 33/1207.

[54] *Dáil Debates*, vol. 246, cols 642–643, 7 May 1970.

[55] *Irish Times*, 9 May 1970. The importance of the intervention is analysed in Justin O'Brien, *The Arms Trial* (Dublin, 2000), pp. 138–139.

volatile atmosphere Lynch could only justify the ministerial sackings and retain power if the 'slightest suspicion of ministerial wrongdoing' could be hardened into criminal charges. For this to happen, the high-risk extrication of Gibbons became the key imperative.

In an attempt to solidify his position, Lynch provided the opposition with a promise and his own party with an explicit threat. He announced that he had turned over the details of the importation attempts to the Attorney General to ascertain whether criminal charges should, or could, be brought. However, he continued: 'If [the Attorney General] takes no action, that will not be the end of the matter. I am not afraid to give to the country what evidence I have and the information I have about this whole transaction, but this is not the time.'[56] The Attorney General did decide that sufficient evidence was available to justify a prosecution and charges were laid.

It was at this stage in the controversy that Colonel Hefferon was interviewed. The results caused further problems for the credibility of the Lynch administration and raised questions about his judgment in protecting Gibbons. Colonel Hefferon indicated clearly to investigating gardaí his belief that the Minister for Defence had detailed knowledge of the attempts to import weapons.

> It is my opinion that Mr. Gibbons knew that Captain Kelly was involved in assisting the Defence committees in the North to procure arms.[57]

This sentence was one of the key deletions from Hefferon's statement, which O'Malley and McDowell later suggested could be explained by the legal requirement to obviate hearsay. Yet the cumulative effect to the Book of Evidence of the deletions from both Colonel Hefferon and Jim Gibbons's statements was to minimise the extent of the Minister for Defence's knowledge; McDowell accepted that this served to make the statements more compatible.[58] There is no way of knowing at this stage who authorised the deletions or who decided to limit the nature of the conspiracy charges. Throughout the summer the preparations for the Arms Trial were made at the Special Detective Unit (Special Branch), to which, unusually, was given the task of not only collecting the evidence but also assembling the statements to be used in court, under the direction of the legal team detailed by the Attorney General's Office to prosecute the case.[59]

The notation on the files demonstrates that the witness statements were

---

[56] *Irish Times*, 15 May 1970, p. 9.

[57] 'Comparative Text of Copy of Col. Hefferon's Statement on Department of Justice File with Statement of Proposed Evidence in Book of Evidence', *Report of the Attorney General on Questions Concerning the Prosecution of the Arms Trial in 1970* (July 2001), p. 36, deletion no. 20. In his analysis of deletion no. 20, the Attorney General judged 'that part where the witness gave his opinion as to the Minister's knowledge was undoubtedly properly excluded' (p. 39).

[58] *Report of the Attorney General on Questions Concerning the Prosecution of the Arms Trial in 1970* (July 2001), p. 42.

[59] 'Release of Documents on Arms Trial, 1970', *Patrick Byrne, Commissioner of An Garda Síochána* (15 May 2001).

passed directly to the Department of Justice and its influential Secretary Peter Berry at a very early stage in the process, at best blurring the line of independence between the prosecution and the executive. Notations on the witness statements in Berry's handwriting suggest that these documents were perused by his political superior. At no stage in his recent, spirited defence of his actions did O'Malley accept that he saw Colonel Hefferon's original witness statement but referred to the timescale making such an occurrence 'unlikely': because the statement was taken at a weekend, it was not possible that he saw it in the timescale suggested by the annotations.

It is, however, undoubtedly the case that the policy to provide Gibbons with protection from even suspicion was determined by Lynch from the moment the crisis emerged in April 1970. It was a policy that was facilitated by the manner in which the leader of the opposition, Liam Cosgrave, responded to the budding controversy. Before the crisis broke, he received, anonymously, the names of those involved. The message, on An Garda Síochána notepaper, was presumably from the senior source within the security establishment who had previously leaked the information to the *Sunday Independent*; the newspaper had declined to publish the information.[60] Speaking in the Dáil, Cosgrave intoned that:

> this is a situation without parallel in this country, that not merely involved here is the security of this State but that those who were drawing public money to serve the nation were, in fact, attempting to undermine it, and that there was a failure to deal with this situation by the Taoiseach.[61]

But Cosgrave was circumspect when it came to publicising the full list. He referred only to 'a Captain Kelly, the former Minister for Finance, the former Minister for Agriculture and two associates of the Ministers',[62] yet he had been explicitly told that both Gibbons and the Director of Military Intelligence, Colonel Hefferon, were also implicated.[63] The question of why Cosgrave did not denounce Hefferon and Gibbons now assumes central significance. He never spoke openly again about those events, but it is understood that he accepted the private assurances of Jack Lynch in advance of the sackings that neither Gibbons nor Hefferon was involved.[64]

As the judicial process began with the arrests of Blaney, Haughey, Captain James Kelly, and the Belfast republican John Kelly, another hawk within Fianna

---

[60] A week later, somewhat melodramatically, the newspaper revealed that possession of the note had presented the paper's editor with an exquisite dilemma: 'Where did his duty lie as a newspaperman, to his country or his profession? The Editor decided not to print the story, holding that the proper place to have the matter raised was in the Dáil.' See the *Sunday Independent*, 10 May 1970. For an assessment of the origins of the note see O'Brien, *The Arms Trial* (Dublin, 2000), p. 251, n. 101.

[61] *Dáil Debates*, vol. 246, col. 645, 6 May 1970.

[62] *Ibid.*

[63] See Justin O'Brien, *The Arms Trial* (Dublin, 2000), p. 130.

[64] Interview with Garret FitzGerald, February 1999. See also Justin O'Brien, *ibid.*, pp. 129–130.

Fáil launched an attack on what he regarded as the duplicity of the Lynch government towards northern nationalists and southern sensibility. Kevin Boland, the combative former Minister for Local Government, had resigned in protest against the ministerial sackings. Now, with the decision to charge John Kelly, he accused Lynch of treason and treachery. By using the most extreme language in the Irish political lexicon, namely the accusation of treason, Boland raised the political temperature to dangerous levels. He called for a special Árd Fheis to unseat Lynch, an incitement that challenged the party's rule of law. In this he was headed off by O'Malley, who issued a statement saying that he was precluded from further comment, as the matters surrounding the arrests were now before the court. It was a move that secured the tacit approval of the British ambassador in Dublin, John Peck:

> This means that the trial evidence which is bound to have strong political implications will not be made public until the autumn. This will suit Lynch and his government, since it will enable him to tackle his three critical problems, viz., situation in North, pressure for a debate in the Dáil, and possible involvement in the trial of members of present government, in succession and not simultaneously.[65]

Lynch's government was now safe until the court case and the summer was spent attempting to stabilise the politics of nationalist and republican Ireland. This was to be achieved by gaining a renewed consensus on unity by consent inside the State and through the development of the Social Democratic and Labour Party (SDLP), formed in the summer of 1970 with considerable input from key officials inside the Department of Foreign Affairs to reinforce the constitutional route in the north. Each policy was designed to buttress and reinforce the other. The aim was to retract the aspirations of the nation to the territorial confines of the State and reposition opinion prior to the impact of the impending trial.

Further disturbing questions about the actions of the executive in the run up and during the trial itself surround O'Malley's refusal to provide his predecessor, Micheal O Morain, with access to confidential papers commissioned by the latter. Peter Berry, the legendary Secretary of the Department of Justice, kept detailed phone records. One memo details a remarkable exchange with O Morain the day before the Arms Trial was due to begin. Berry began the conversation by telling his former Minister:

> [K]nowing that you wanted to see the papers this evening I immediately consulted the Attorney General's Office who said to me that you had no legal entitlement to see the papers and that I myself would be in breach of the Official Secrets Act if I were to communicate them to you without the [current] Minister's direction. The Minister has authority, of course, under the Act to

[65] John Peck to Foreign & Commonwealth Office, 17 July 1970, FCO 33/1207.

direct, you see, but I would be in breach if I did. So there is the position until I see the Minister tomorrow morning.

O Morain: In the first place, just for the record, I want to say here and now I don't accept this at all. If necessary I'll brief counsel and go in and make application to this bloody Judge about this.

Berry: Yes.

O Morain: If I am forced to do this it's an extraordinary bloody attitude for them to take.

Berry: Yes.

O Morain: The documents that were in fact, of course, made to [*sic*] me as Minister for Justice at the time. So I had better... Is this thing starting tomorrow morning ... Mr Berry in view that I will have to do something about this – the attitude. I will want, pretty soon, I will want to know if this is your Minister's attitude as well.[66]

O Morain rang again that afternoon at 4.50. According to Berry's transcript:

Berry: [The Minister] said to me that the request was refused.

O Morain: He said?

Berry: That is right, [y]es. I told him of your request, I told him of the Attorney General's advice that you hadn't a legal entitlement... He did say to me that he intended to say to you that the request was refused.[67]

In testimony to the first trial, O Morain confirmed that Lynch had been told about the weapons importation and that contingency plans included arming northern nationalists. He stated, however, that he could not provide details because of the obstruction of the Minister for Justice. The claim of privilege was based on legal advice and on what O'Malley termed the 'culture of secrecy' at the time. Nevertheless, it is certainly arguable that the net effect of claiming privilege on the contents of the file, whether intended or not, was to limit any collateral damage to the overall administration emanating from the documents held by the Department of Justice.

Moreover, key statements that showed that the Taoiseach was centrally involved in building the case were excised from the Book of Evidence. The Secretary of the Department of Finance, Anthony Fagan, for example, confirmed to Special Branch on 27 May 1970 that he was acting on his Minister's specific instructions when he asked for a shipment to pass through Dublin Airport, but:

[66] 'Transcript of telephone conversation between Deputy Ó Moráin and the Secretary, Department of Justice, on 21st September', Department of Justice S/7/70.

[67] 'Record of telephone conversation of 21st September 1970 between Mr. Ó Moráin, TD and the Secretary, Department of Justice': Department of Justice, S/7/70.

> I definitely did not know at that time that arms or ammunition were involved, and the first time I heard the word arms mentioned was by An Taoiseach when he spoke to me on or about 28th April, 1970. This was the first time arms were mentioned in my presence, but I had suspected that arms were in fact involved, particularly because of the involvement of Army Intelligence.[68]

Deleting this hearsay served to distance the Taoiseach from the planned prosecution, obviating any possibility that he would be called to give evidence. Further evidence of attempts to limit the exposure of the government surround the almost feverish drafts of various claims of privilege to prevent the disclosure of documents which would reveal Berry's stated doubts about the position of the Taoiseach and Berry's subsequent decision to go to President de Valera for advice. It is clear from the differing drafts involved, and the signature of the Minister on the 7 October 1970 version, whatever other documents he did or did not see, O'Malley must have had sight of the details of Berry's concerns.

Furthermore, in the context of the overall trial itself, and the extent to which it was a theatre of operations in the power struggle for control of Fianna Fáil, it is surprising that Michael McDowell relegated the importance of the documents. He argued that 'that the major preoccupation of Mr. Berry in claiming privilege was to keep confidential his dealings with President De Valera'[69] and did not even appear to countenance the fact that the withholding of the papers from the trial primarily buttressed the interests of the government.

The briefing papers provided by Berry to prosecuting counsel were intended to be detailed evidence of his earlier attempts to persuade the government to act on information questioning the loyalty of Haughey. More damaging for the government of the day was how the Secretary of the Department of Justice began to view the activities of army intelligence as something that had official sanction.

> On 20th August the Gardaí reported that, from confidential sources that had proved reliable in the past, they had become aware that a Member of Government had had a meeting with Goulding, Chief of Staff of [the] IRA and that "a deal" had been arranged by the Minister that if the IRA should cease their physical force activities in the South in relation to the destruction of foreigners' property etc., in turn, they could have a free hand in moving weapons into the Six Counties. They also said that the Taoiseach's statement of 19th August had bewildered the IRA in view of "the deal" with the Member of Government... I made a general note on 20/8/69 to the Minister, Mr Ó Móráin, and we conjectured as to what Member of Government might be involved. Later, the Minister told me that he had mentioned the matter informally at a Government meeting and that Mr. Haughey had said that he had had a *casual*

[68] Statement of Anthony Fagan to Special Branch, 27 May 1970, Department of Justice, S/7/70.

[69] *Report of the Attorney General on Questions Concerning the Prosecution of the Arms Trial in 1970* (July 2001), pp. 19–20.

> meeting with some member of the IRA organisation who had asked to meet him. The Special Branch learned from their own sources, the identity of the Minister and they did not view the meeting between Mr. Haughey and Goulding as a casual one, to be treated lightly.[70]

Special Branch officers had also discovered that:

> small consignments of arms were being imported by the IRA without customs checks at Dublin Airport and at Dun Laoghaire sea-port... [I]t was freely said in Special Branch circles that Mr. Charles J. Haughey was aware of what was going on.[71]

Berry again told his Minister of the involvement of Blaney and Haughey and of the dangerously high levels of discontent within the security forces: 'I had been warned that within the Special Branch and in Garda Headquarters criticism of Government was becoming caustic and was mounting.'[72] This, then, was the context for Berry's concern when the attempt was made to import the weapons at Dublin airport in April 1970.

> I viewed the matter in the light of my earlier knowledge of his meeting with Goulding, the Chief of Staff of the IRA, of [text blocked out] IRA associations and payments to Goulding for the purchase of arms and Captain Kelly's direct negotiations with the Northern Ireland IRA Command. At no time did it enter into my mind that the arms were being imported, not for the IRA but for the purpose of giving means of self-defence to ordinary people in Northern Ireland and I never heard of the notion until after the public disclosures in relation to the Ministers' participation in the attempted importation of arms. Ordinary men have no wish to handle firearms.[73]

The Secretary felt alone. He:

> could not reconcile the Taoiseach's repeated public statements as to the Government's peaceful intentions towards the North with the action of one of the Ministers, Mr. Haughey, who, it appeared to me, was acting treacherously towards him... I was in a frightful dilemma. It occurred to me that if the Taoiseach had been, for diplomatic reasons, speaking with two voices, I would put him in a most embarrassing position if I were to go direct to him with the information as to Mr. Haughey's action... I decided to consult the one person whom I felt I could trust to give me good advice as to whether I would be behaving with propriety in going over my Minister's head direct to the Taoiseach.

---

[70] Emphasis in original. Peter Berry, 'Attempted Importation of Arms at Dublin – March/April 1970, Part II, Explanatory note of events leading up to the attempted importation of Arms at Dublin', Department of Justice, S/7/70, para. 4.

[71] *Ibid.*, para. 5.

[72] *Ibid.*, para. 7.

[73] *Ibid.*, para. 9.

> I 'phoned the President and told him that information of a very serious character of perhaps, immediate[,] national significance had come into my possession and that it might not reach the Government in the normal course of events. I asked him would he advise me as to whether my loyalty ended with informing my Minister or whether I would be justified in speaking direct to the Taoiseach. The President asked if I were sure of my facts and I said yes. He again questioned me saying was I *absolutely sure* of my facts and I said that I was absolutely sure. The President then said that my loyalty was to Government and that I should communicate with the Taoiseach.
>
> I did not inform the President of the nature of my information and he did not ask me any question in relation to its nature.[74]

The result of claiming privilege on these documents was to limit not only the knowledge of Minister O Morain but also the doubts expressed by Berry on the stated government position. This was of even more importance than in the case of Hefferon's statement. It stopped the calling of Lynch and de Valera to the stand. This reading of the matter was reinforced by the blunt observations of the British ambassador, John Peck, who, in a briefing document sent to London in the aftermath of the trial, noted how it had offered 'a revealing glimpse of the nature of Cabinet government in Ireland, the chaos of the administration and the folly of a number of individuals who, to put it no higher, should have known better'. Peck further complained about the 'many political red-herrings and dubious claims to privilege by Ministers and officials'.[75]

Although all sides accepted that the trial was politically explosive, none could have foreseen the calamitous performance of Jim Gibbons under pressure. He was a disaster to his cause. Journalist Bruce Arnold suggested that he was merely confused, torn between the deviousness of Haughey and Blaney, and lacking the intellectual acumen to do his job properly.[76] Actually, the confusion long predated the poor performance at the trial and was attributable to the difficulty of maintaining the innocence of someone who was clearly aware of the intricacies of the operation.

An analysis of the various statements given by James Gibbons to investigating officers from Special Branch and deleted from the official Book of Evidence demonstrates not only an awareness of the conspiracy long predating the shipments arriving at Dublin airport but also brings into focus inconsistencies with other people's testimony. As early as 8 June 1970 Gibbons had admitted knowledge of an attempt to import weapons.

---

74 Emphasis in original. Explanatory note of Peter Berry in relation to the events of 18th to 22nd April 1970, Department of Justice, S/7/70. Interestingly, this is the document for which the Minister for Justice Desmond O'Malley claimed privilege.

75 John Peck to Alec Douglas-Home, MP, Secretary of State for Foreign & Commonwealth Affairs, 10 November 1970, FCO 33/1207, paras 1 and 3.

76 Bruce Arnold, *Jack Lynch: Hero in Crisis* (Dublin, 2001), p. 149.

> It was becoming apparent that such a project was under way. Capt. Kelly told me (early April) of an abortive attempt to send in arms by sea. This consignment was to be met at Dublin docks when those who were to meet it arrived there, they found Irish Army Troops taking delivery of Army materials. I understood from Capt Kelly that this illegal consignment never left Europe (Belgium). N. Blaney also mentioned this incident to me about the same time. It was about this time too that Mr. Blaney sounded me on my willingness to permit the importation of arms by use of my office of Minister for Defence.[77]

Gibbons went on to admit that the first indication of a gun-running plot long predated this meeting.

> The first intimation of gun running that I recall was Col. Hefferon's suggestion that an application for leave by Capt Kelly to visit his sister in Frankfurt might be used as an opportunity to 'vet' guns… I think the time of this interview with Co. Hefferon was after the visit of the N.I. deputation (March 5[, 1970]) (which met the Taoiseach, Dr. Hillery, Mr. Blaney & myself) but I am not sure.[78]

Yet in an earlier statement on 22 May Gibbons had acknowledged that he was aware that Captain Kelly was under surveillance for *something*. Gibbons told Special Branch that 'the Minister for Justice, Mr O Morain, had mentioned to me that Kelly was under surveillance. This would be sometime in March'. This is interesting for three reasons. Gibbons was aware that one of his intelligence officers was being investigated by Special Branch but did not move to close the operation down or report to the Taoiseach that two arms of government were apparently working at cross-purposes. More surprisingly, alongside this section of the statement, in Peter Berry's handwriting, is the following annotation: 'But Mr O Morain had known for several months and only acted after I jogged his memory.'

According to John Peck, who observed the trial, Gibbons was the 'anti-star' of the proceedings. 'From his evidence it is hard to avoid drawing a number of inferences, all unflattering.'

> Gibbons was given a rough time in the witness-box and he performed miserably. He was self-important and pompous. By refusing to admit error or bad judgement in the smallest details he destroyed his credibility in the more important matters.[79]

---

[77] 'Answers given by Mr. James Gibbons, Minister for Agriculture' to Special Branch questioning on 8 June 1970, Department of Justice, S/7/70.

[78] *Ibid.*

[79] John Peck to Alec Douglas-Home, MP, Secretary of State for Foreign & Commonwealth Affairs, 10 November 1970, FCO 33/1207, para. 6 and accompanying confidential memorandum, 'The Dublin Arms Conspiracy Trial', para. 9. Peck was even more forthright in the immediate aftermath of the acquittals, describing Gibbons as 'either a fool or a liar, and a considerable embarrassment to Lynch': John Peck to Foreign & Commonwealth Office, 24 October 1970, FCO 33/1207, para. 5.

Peck could not hide his incredulity at the poisonous atmosphere in Dublin. He provided important evidence of the mood within the Lynch camp as the trials proceeded.

> Mr Lynch, before he went to New York [in October 1970], and while the trial was still in progress, told me privately that he was furious with Mr. Gibbons for his performance as a witness, and that he seemed to be getting into an impossible position. I thought it very likely that his resignation would be ready to put in the Taoiseach's hands when he returned.
>
> But it has not worked out that way. Mr. Lynch has retained Mr. Gibbons in his Government and given him his full backing. He is a severe political embarrassment... The judicial process is ended, and the affair passes back into the arena of politics impure and unsimple.[80]

Peck was clearly intrigued by the complex manoeuvrings in Dublin. In a telegram to the Foreign Office in the immediate aftermath of the trial, he remarked that the:

> [l]eadership crisis is now back in full force. Haughey, Blaney and Boland, each in his own way, are in full cry after Lynch. Both opposition parties are calling for an election, mainly on economic issues but in fact of course to exploit the fissures in Fianna Fáil and the evidence of ineptitude and worse revealed by the Arms Trial.
>
> But the only serious challenge to Mr Lynch comes from inside his own party. Mr Haughey has lost no time in making plain his bid for leadership. As was the case before the trial, the crucial factor in the struggle will be whether Mr Haughey can obtain overwhelming support inside the party to force Mr Lynch to resign, without bringing about a split and the consequent fall of the Fianna Fáil government. To Fianna Fáil, almost anything is acceptable except opposition: and the cardinal sin is to risk the party...[81]

In a further despatch to the Foreign Secretary he cautioned that more was likely to emerge about the machinations of the Fianna Fáil government. He described that administration as guilty of 'an almost unbelievable degree of administrative sloppiness in the Cabinet, the civil service, and the army which the would be gun runners have exploited to the full both in planning the operation and in defending themselves when charged'.[82]

Peck also made clear that Lynch was seeking to solidify his leadership. Even though Lynch regarded Gibbons as a disaster, he felt that he had to keep him in government in order to stabilise his hold over it. He was prepared to go

---

[80] John Peck to Alec Douglas-Home, MP, Secretary of State for Foreign & Commonwealth Affairs, 10 November 1970, FCO 33/1207, paras 6 and 7.

[81] John Peck to Foreign & Commonwealth Office, 24 October 1970, FCO 33/1207, paras 2 and 3.

[82] John Peck to Foreign & Commonwealth Office, 27 October 1970, FCO 33/1207, para. 2.

further, however, using the Northern situation to justify his stewardship in a way that a generation of his opponents within Fianna Fáil have since been castigated for. According to Peck, when Haughey launched his short-lived push for the leadership:

> [Lynch,] isolated in Washington... asked the Prime Minister whether he could find an opportunity to say how much he (Mr. Lynch) had contributed to trying to keep the temperature down between the two sides of the border, as he was in for a very difficult time.[83]

The Taoiseach clearly had a close relationship with the British Ambassador in the crisis months of October and November 1970. Lynch's biographer, the critic Bruce Arnold, has presented the Peck correspondence as confirming evidence of the essential truth of the Lynch interpretation of events. Certainly, even after the conspiracy trial had sown doubt, Peck was convinced that 'once Lynch discovered what was going on he quickly put a stop both to irregular practices and also to activities which, though officially sanctioned, were clearly inappropriate'.[84] However, other extracts from the documents present a different picture.[85]

> So Mr. Lynch wins again. But though the dust has settled once more, there is still a lot of pollution in the Dublin air... [T]he principal casualty of the power struggle of the last six months is parliamentary government itself. The disclosures in the arms conspiracy trial, whatever the verdict, were discreditable to Ministers, administration and government agencies alike. The judiciary did not cover themselves with glory. Fianna Fáil, with the misguided but honourable exception of Mr. Boland, put party and power above principles; and the possibility of a general election called attention to the sterility of the opposition parties and the lack of a convincing alternative to a Fianna Fáil government.[86]

The contention that Lynch was a leader in control of events from the beginning of the Arms Crisis was palpably not true. There was a failure to control Blaney throughout the autumn and winter of 1969–1970; a lack of action in response to Berry's claims that he had presented evidence of a conspiracy involving ministers in advance of April 20, the day after the attempted importation at Dublin airport; vacillation that allowed such latitude to the hawks in the first place; and, crucially, the performance of Gibbons in the witness box. In the telling phrase penned by Ambassador Peck, the power play surrounding the Arms Trial was 'politics impure and unsimple'. Despite the resolve that Lynch undoubtedly displayed during the

---

[83] John Peck to Alec Douglas-Home, MP, Secretary of State for Foreign & Commonwealth Affairs, 16 December 1970, FCO 33/1207, para. 4.

[84] John Peck to Foreign & Commonwealth Office, 27 October 1970, FCO 33/1207, para. 2.

[85] Bruce Arnold, *Jack Lynch: Hero in Crisis* (Dublin, 2001), p. 148.

[86] John Peck to Alec Douglas-Home, MP, Secretary of State for Foreign & Commonwealth Affairs, 16 December 1970, FCO 33/1207, para. 8.

Arms Crisis and the undoubted skill with which he out-manoeuvred his political opponents, it was only in the aftermath of the crisis that he achieved absolute control over Fianna Fáil, a full four years after he acceded to the leadership – and even then it was only temporary. As Bruce Arnold observed:

> By the end of 1970 Lynch, whose whole attitude had hardened, and whose public statements could now express his position in terms of absolute control of the Fianna Fáil organisation, surveyed as Hercules might the desolation left after his own victories.[87]

There is no doubt that the stability of the State was threatened in 1970 by the lengths to which factions within Fianna Fáil were prepared to go to further base ambition and that the most powerful weapon in the leadership dispute became the ideology of the State itself. It is also beyond question that if Haughey or Blaney, now known to have been active supporters of republicanism, had gained control in the chaotic circumstances of the time, the alienation of the Catholic minority within Northern Ireland would have intensified, with unknown consequences. These, however, were questions to be resolved not in the Four Courts but around the Cabinet table; ultimately, Lynch failed to control his government.

Boland fell on his sword and resigned from the party in an electrifying speech to the Dáil on 3 November 1970. Concluding that there was nothing left to retain except his honour, he opted to leave Fianna Fáil.

> All of my energy since I left the Army after the Emergency – and both before and since my election to the Dáil – has been spent in an effort to maintain the efficiency of the party organisation and the strength of the party here in this House. But, since last May, I have had an opportunity of surveying the end product of all that effort by myself and by others – notably by Deputy Blaney and Deputy Haughey. I have had an opportunity of seeing the end product of all that effort since last May. As I look around me, I can see quite clearly that there is nothing left to me but my own personal honour, such as it is – and I propose to retain that.[88]

According to British Ambassador Peck, it was the only honourable thing to come out of the sordid proceedings. Blaney, in many ways the true instigator of the plot to arm the Provisionals, was expelled and retreated to the political wilderness of the Inishowen peninsula. Haughey, by contrast, still desired power, but over the entire organisation rather than just a rump. It was for this reason that he abased himself when Lynch demanded full loyalty to his government in the Dáil confidence motion following the acquittals at the Four Courts in

---

87 Bruce Arnold, *Jack Lynch: Hero in Crisis* (Dublin, 2001), p. 160.
88 *Dáil Debates*, vol. 249, col. 464, 3 November 1970.

November 1970 – even though that meant supporting Jim Gibbons, who, it appeared from the verdict of the jury, had committed perjury in the Arms Trial. Haughey voted with the government in every subsequent division, toured the country to drum up support, and always, always, looked for an opportunity to swoop on the mandarins who had denied his ambition.

From 1970, as Haughey began the long climb back to power, he was deemed by the leadership of both Fianna Fáil and Fine Gael to be the biggest threat to the entire political establishment. This perception underpinned the rationale for establishing the Public Accounts Committee hearings into the Arms Crisis. Convened on 11 December 1970, the veracity of the evidence was not the task at hand, as Garret FitzGerald, a senior member of that Committee, has confirmed.

> Certainly when someone [Haughey] who had set out to betray the state while in government and got away with it and was seeking to undermine the law and demanding that the Taoiseach resign – we couldn't take that. There was a great sense of solidarity against the undermining of the state. In a crisis like that party politics are not that significant.[89]

Despite ninety-two meetings the Public Accounts Committee failed to establish any definitive conclusions about the Arms Crisis debacle. By its own admission 'the evidence contained much that was irrelevant, hearsay or personal opinion. The Arms Trial and its consequences seemed to have coloured and polarised the attitudes of some witnesses'.[90] Crucial evidence was either destroyed or rendered unavailable to the Committee and a constitutional challenge by Haughey's brother, Paraic, upheld by the Supreme Court on 24 June 1971, deprived the Committee of the power to compel witnesses to attend.

As with the trial itself, considerable efforts were made within the administration to insulate Lynch from any responsibility and the Department of Justice moved to curtail any disclosure from its Secretary, Peter Berry, that questioned the timing of events laid down by the Taoiseach.[91] It was symptomatic of the volatile mood at the time that Berry, in giving evidence to the Committee, brandished his gun on the witness table and claimed that he was under physical threat because of his action in exposing Haughey's involvement.[92] The Committee's main conclusion deserves close attention.

> Arising from evidence given to the committee of a lack of clarity in the chain of responsibility, and of confusion with respect to the question of authority, in

89 Garret FitzGerald, interview with the author, February 1999. See Justin O'Brien, *The Arms Trial* (Dublin, 2000), p. 220.

90 Dáil Committee of Public Accounts 1969/70, p. 25.

91 See Vincent Browne, 'The Peter Berry Papers', *Magill*, May, June, and July 1980.

92 Garret FitzGerald, interview with the author, September 1999. See Justin O'Brien, *The Arms Trial* (Dublin, 2000), p. 220.

> the Public Services, including the Defence Forces, the Committee recommends that the Government examine the position in these respects, and take whatever remedial measures that may be called for.[93]

Although accepting that the Arms Crisis centred on a breakdown in the chain of command, there was to be no censure of the commander-in-chief. Contradictory evidence from Jim Gibbons, which cast further doubt on the official version of events, was ignored. As the historian T. Ryle Dwyer has perceptively observed recently, in criticising what he termed its 'monumental ineptitude', the Public Accounts Committee 'never questioned the Taoiseach, and it meekly accepted Gibbons' insistence that his discussions with the Taoiseach were confidential'.[94] But by that stage the damage had been done. Haughey was now damaged goods.

Lynch was indisputably in control of the party. Official displays of republicanism were frowned upon as the State sought to protect itself from the contagion of violence now unleashed north of the border in the wake of the introduction of internment by the British Government. His Minister for Justice, Des O'Malley, re-introduced the non-jury Special Criminal Courts to hear cases impinging on national security and anti-terrorist legislation. The rhetoric of republicanism, the keenest weapon used to control Fianna Fáil, had undermined national security and would never be allowed to subvert either party or State again.

But in the absence of a political settlement or stability across the border this decision to rein in republican expression was fundamentally flawed. Such orthodoxy was and is a key component of the Fianna Fáil make-up. It may be cosmetically hidden but it provides the very basis for the party's remarkable ability to withstand the ferocious electoral storms occasioned by both political and financial scandal, disturbances that undoubtedly would have destroyed any other political party. By harnessing that power Haughey demonstrated that even those at the nadir of political control can stage a remarkable return to the centre.

Lynch may now be revered as the hero of the Arms Crisis, the man who saved Ireland from itself, but the electorate denied Fianna Fáil in 1973. When he returned to power with an enhanced mandate in 1977, he sought to spend his way out of a financial crisis that deepened inexorably; at the same time he remained reticent about expressing any support for the republicanism that had hitherto defined the party and cushioned it during times of economic depression. When fiscal instability threatened the only rationale underpinning Lynch's leadership in 1979, Haughey managed to steal the leadership from the ground carefully prepared by the favoured candidate – and architect for the disastrous programme for government – the Minister for Finance, George Colley, precisely because he

---

93 Dáil Committee of Public Accounts 1969/70, p. 65.

94 T. Ryle Dwyer, 'Lynch's biggest mistake was not ousting Jim Gibbons', *Irish Examiner*, 25 April 2001.

On the set of RTÉ's *Today Tonight* programme, 8 June 1981. *(Derek Speirs/Report)*

Right: During the Arms Crisis of 1970, with his broken arm still in a sling from a riding accident, Haughey staunchly faced the music. (*Irish Independent*)

Above left: Brian Lenihan, Jack Lynch and George Colley confer at the Fianna Fáil Cairde Fail, Burlington Hotel, Dublin, 13 October 1979. *(Derek Speirs/Report)*. *Above right:* Jack Lynch. *(Derek Speirs/Report)*.

Above: At Fianna Fáil headquarters following the election of Charles Haughey to the leadership of the party, 7 December 1979. Seated, *from left*, Ray MacSharry, Ben Briscoe, Charles Haughey, Michael Woods. *(Derek Speirs/Report)*

Below: Ministers Ray MacSharry and Albert Reynolds congratulate their leader's mother, Sarah Haughey. *(Derek Speirs/Report)*

Left: With the new junior Minister for Justice, Sean Doherty, 27 March 1980. *(Derek Speirs/Report)*

Below: Campaigning in Wexford for the 1981 general election. *(Derek Speirs/Report)*

Top: Neil Blaney and Síle de Valera at a press conference after the visit of European MPs to the Maze Prison, 20 April 1981. *(Derek Speirs/Report)*

Centre: Supporters of the H-Block prisoners protest during Haughey's visit, Drogheda, 29 May 1981. *(Derek Speirs/Report)*

Left: Rathmines, Dublin, 30 May 1981. *(Derek Speirs/Report)*

Above: Garret FitzGerald and Charles Haughey in relaxed mood at RTÉ for the general election programme, June 1981. (*Derek Speirs/Report*).

Right: Haughey was characterised in *Magill* magazine as 'an ageing vulture'. This caricature was drawn by Littleman. (*'Littleman' for Magill*).

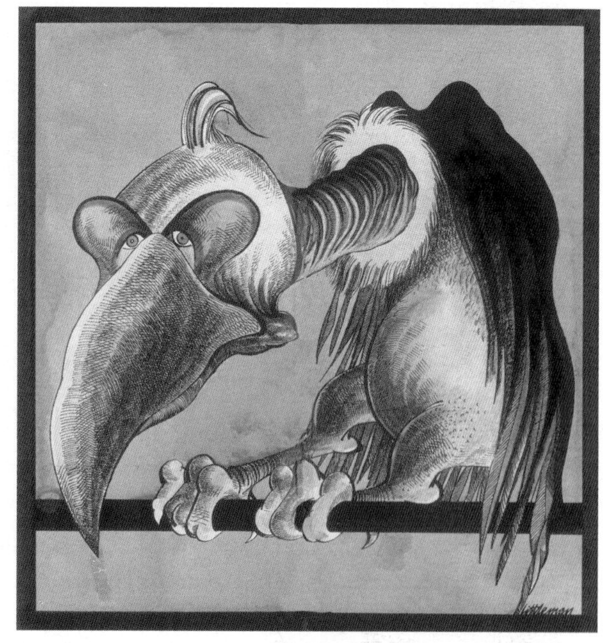

Top: With his wife Maureen and daughter Eimear on a general election walkabout in North Dublin, 7 February 1982. *(Derek Speirs/Report). Centre:* The grounds of Abbeville . . . *(Eamonn Farrell/Photocall Ireland). Bottom:* . . . and inside, 1981. *(Derek Speirs/Report)*

Above: Haughey controls the microphone at a tense election press conference, 2 February 1982. *(Derek Speirs/Report)*

Below: After his successful election to the office of Taoiseach, 9 March 1982. To Haughey's left (*front*, by the car door) is John Kelly. *(Eamonn O'Dwyer/Report)*

offered to reconnect Fianna Fáil with its ideological inheritance.[95] By 1979, as the chaotic events surrounding the Arms Crisis faded into history, Lynch's greatest contribution to providing stability for the Republic had sown the seeds for his downfall. It was Haughey's perceived, rather than stated, hawkishness regarding the Northern question, coupled with a very real fear within Fianna Fáil that economic policy alone would not save the party from electoral meltdown, that eventually provided the vehicle for the most stunning political comeback in Irish history.

95 See, for example, Haughey's speech to the Pádraig Pearse Commemoration Dinner, Dublin, 10 November 1979: reproduced in Martin Mansergh, ed., *The Spirit of the Nation: The Speeches and Statements of Charles J. Haughey (1957–1986)* (Cork, 1986), pp. 309–312.

Chapter Three

The Ascent to Power: National Priorities and the Creation of Hegemony

In all his doings a prince must endeavour to win the reputation of being a great man of outstanding ability.

– Machiavelli, *The Prince*, p. 72

The chamber of Dáil Éireann was packed to capacity on 11 December 1979 as Charles J. Haughey sought the Irish parliament's backing for his elevation to the highest office in government. He was to be the seventh Taoiseach and the fourth leader of Fianna Fáil to hold that position, following de Valera, Lemass and Haughey's personal nemesis, the Cork hurler Jack Lynch. Lynch had thwarted his ambition in 1966 and nearly destroyed his career irreparably during the chaotic implosion of Fianna Fáil in 1970. From the beginning of the debate it was clear that this was not going to be an ordinary nomination. It was clear, too, that Colley's 1967 jibe of 'low standards in high places'[1] would form the centrepiece of opposition taunts about the suitability of the Modern Prince to lead the Irish government.

It was the most remarkable comeback ever witnessed in Irish politics. Haughey was viewed with distrust by as many within his own party as outside it. His overwhelming ambition was almost unstoppable. The question was: what he would do with power if given the opportunity to wield it? it was the articulation of this potential risk that dominated the debate. Even from the distance of more than two decades, when reading the records of Dáil Éireann one is struck by the poisonous atmosphere within the chamber. It is therefore instructive to examine the depth of opposition to Haughey before deconstructing the oblique mechanism through which he achieved his ambition.

---

[1] Cited in T. Ryle Dwyer, *Short Fellow: A Biography of Charles J. Haughey* (Dublin, 1999), p. 88. The remark was made at a Fianna Fáil youth conference in 1967. Colley encouraged his audience not to become cynical or 'dispirited if some people in high places appear to have low standards'. Although he was widely thought to be referring to Haughey, as Dwyer pointed out, Colley claimed he had been referring to the opposition leaders.

Opening proceedings, the Fine Gael leader, Garret FitzGerald, who had known Haughey since student days in University College Dublin forty years previously, referred to the Fianna Fáil leader's 'flawed pedigree'. It was to set the tone for all that followed. He cited a widely shared belief by those both inside and outside the party that ascribed to Haughey 'an overweening ambition which they do not see as a simple emanation of a desire to serve but rather as a wish to dominate, even to own the state'.[2] FitzGerald neatly dissected the open feuding within Fianna Fáil that had allowed Haughey to accede to the leadership despite having the declared support of only three out of ten members of the Dáil and without that of any of his cabinet colleagues. Haughey's supporters were disparagingly described as the personally driven coupled in a marriage of convenience with those expressing 'a narrow and dangerous nationalism'. Such sentiments were, in FitzGerald's august opinion, 'not merely misguided but dangerously misguided'.[3] Haughey's imminent triumph, watched from the public gallery by his seventy-nine-year-old mother, was proclaimed to be the malign manifestation of the 'totally irrelevant' dark shadow of Civil War politics cast over the contemporary State.

> That long shadow which many of us had led ourselves to believe had long since lifted, darkens our understanding here today and inhibits this house from dividing along the lines of conviction, along the lines that divide those who honestly seek Irish unity to agreement, and by agreement only, from those who, while they talk of peaceful means, still think at least subconsciously of constraint. It also divides true patriots from political opportunists.[4]

Haughey was deemed dangerous for four specific reasons, each largely unsubstantiated.[5] These were: an 'indecent ambiguity' over the use of violence; his (unspecified mis)use of public relations; his action in 're-institutionalising denominationalism' by a contorted liberalisation of contraception; and, crucially, 'his failure to articulate any idealism that might inspire the younger generation and because of his own lifestyle'.[6] It was an audacious and, ultimately, futile attempt to prevent the inevitable. The Manichean arithmetic of party politics, with Fianna Fáil commanding an overall majority, preordained the outcome. Haughey would become Taoiseach despite the infliction of an even greater character assassination than that experienced during the heated debates of May

---

2 *Dáil Debates*, vol. 317, col. 1327, 11 December 1979.

3 *Dáil Debates*, vol. 317, col. 1330, 11 December 1979.

4 *Dáil Debates*, vol. 317, col. 1331, 11 December 1979.

5 For a searing indictment of FitzGerald's approach see Vincent Browne, 'Going Cool on Garret,' *Magill*, February 1980. Browne described the speech opposing Haughey's nomination as being permeated with unsubstantiated, righteous vehemence. The article echoed an earlier editorial in *Hibernia* which decried the 'sanctimonious invective' deployed by the opposition: Editorial, 'Judgement Reserved', *Hibernia*, 13 December 1979.

6 *Dáil Debates*, vol. 317, col. 1335, 11 December 1979.

and November 1970. Typical of the venom was the coruscating attack by the Labour leader Frank Cluskey. He described Haughey as the epitome of the Mohair generation, 'a group of young well educated, very clever, highly articulate young men, who also had one other quality, they were totally ruthless and they had a clear indication of what their personal ambition was.'[7] Cluskey continued in sociological mode.

> The term Mohair Suit was not used to describe a mode of suit. It was a term that described a philosophy of life that meant there should be unbridled opportunity for the economically strong, the clever, the sharp; a philosophy of life that totally exploited the basic needs of the majority of our people. Apart from the normal intelligence which most of us have, only one thing was needed, that was a total lack of scruples, a total lack of principle and a total lack of either personal or business integrity. [8]

Continuous references were made by the opposition to concern that the Lynch policy of unity by consent would be irretrievably damaged by the accession of Haughey. Much was made of his ambition and the myopic nationalism he was believed to be guilty of harbouring. The most devastating assault came from Dr Noël Browne of the Labour Party. He regarded the failure of the overwhelming majority of the outgoing Cabinet to support Haughey as 'extraordinary'.

> Anyone who overlooks this reality without dwelling on its implications for all of us and for the country is either totally ignorant of the dynamics of power in politics, in the workings of parliamentary democracy, or else has some ulterior motive in furthering the career of the individual concerned. [9]

Browne identified Haughey's success as resting on his 'total cynicism', a character trait that rendered him too powerful and too dangerous; it was a combination that brought comparison to the politically contaminated capitals of Washington and Lisbon. 'He has done everything to get power and I think he will do anything to hold power. Does anybody think there are any limits to what he will do?... My awful nightmare is that this man is a dreadful cross between Richard Milhous Nixon and Dr Salazar.'[10] Browne reserved his greatest derision for those he

---

[7] *Dáil Debates*, vol. 317, col. 1337, 11 December 1979.

[8] *Dáil Debates*, vol. 317, col. 1339, 11 December 1979.

[9] *Dáil Debates*, vol. 317, col. 1370, 11 December 1979.

[10] *Dáil Debates*, vol. 317, cols 1375–1376, 11 December 1979. Browne was never one to moderate his language when it came to Haughey. He was later to review Haughey's collection of speeches for a music magazine. He regarded the 1,216-page tome, published while in opposition in 1986 and quoted throughout this book, as a reflection of 'the egomaniacal self-image of a profoundly insecure, troubled personality, desperately needing public reassurance': quoted in John Waters, *Jiving at the Crossroads* (Belfast, 1991), p. 134. Waters himself provided a superior profile of the Haughey enigma: 'Haughey seemed to have conducted a detailed study of the dynamics of power... He possessed an acute understanding of the necessary schizophrenia of politics: the need to have a

referred to as 'sectarian nationalists, crypto-Provos',[11] a diverse collection of TDs and commentators from the media who had been responsible for nurturing the myth of Charles J. Haughey that now had the potential to destroy the fabric of society.

> It used to be Ciano in Mussolini's Italy or Stricher in Hitler's Germany. It was the journalists who helped to make these dictators. The journalists have a great responsibility and it is my belief that they have betrayed that responsibility on this occasion in respect of this man. Most of them failed to tell us of the total failure of this man in their continuous eulogies of him on the run up to this day. The mind-forming process, which is their privilege, helps to put us where we are and to put us out. They helped to put out the man [Lynch] who has gone.[12]

The vehemence of Browne's intervention was perhaps surprising, given that he was talking about the son-in-law of Seán Lemass, a Fianna Fáil leader for whom he had the utmost respect.[13] Some of the language employed by Browne verged on the hysterical, including his assertion that Haughey would not voluntarily hand over power in the event of failing to win a vote of confidence in the Dáil, but his commentary on the open feuding within Fianna Fáil did ring true.

Throughout the debate Haughey sat alone on the front bench. Precluded from taking part in the nomination process and employing a tactic that did not allow any minister or backbencher to speak on his behalf, he sought to bind the party to himself from the very beginning. The proposed Taoiseach was determined to compel loyalty to his leadership by ensuring that the fortunes of Fianna Fáil and Charles J. Haughey became inter-dependent: an attack on the party was an attack on its leader and vice versa. Loyalty had been the defining characteristic in 1970 when Haughey subjugated himself in the Lynch confidence motion. Now, in what must have been the sweetest moment in his political career, he forced a similar loyalty of Lynch, Colley, O'Malley and Gibbons. Following the vote, Haughey contented himself with a brief statement: 'I am deeply conscious of the great honour just conferred upon me, and I extend my most sincere gratitude to Dáil Éireann.'[14]

All the scheming and subterfuge to achieve his ambition had succeeded. Charlie had power and the ability to prove his worth to a sceptical nation, state, parliament and party.

---

number of different personae – some for commanding respect, others for cultivating popularity' (p. 142).

[11] *Dáil Debates*, vol. 317, col. 1371, 11 December 1979.

[12] *Dáil Debates*, vol. 317, col. 1374, 11 December 1979. By way of contrast see the highly readable account of life in journalistic circles during Haughey's tenure by John Waters, *Jiving at the Crossroads* (Belfast, 1991).

[13] See John Horgan, *Noël Browne: Passionate Outsider* (Dublin, 2000), p. 183. Horgan refers to the relationship between Lemass and Browne as almost paternal.

[14] *Dáil Debates*, vol. 317, col. 1425, 11 December 1979.

The transfer was, as Jim Mitchell of Fine Gael pointed out, 'the most traumatic since the hand over by W.T. Cosgrave to Eamon de Valera' in 1932.[15] Given the controversy attached to Haughey then, the enigma to be resolved was why the trust of so many within the Fianna Fáil parliamentary party reposed with him? Was it the whiff of cordite, a demonstration of the abiding power of political charisma, or merely the naked self-interest of backbench Fianna Fáil TDs whose loyalty depended on a pragmatic decision about who was more likely to preserve their seats? It is by dissecting the mechanism through which Haughey achieved his ambition that the full truth behind the enigma can be revealed.[16]

Lynch had retreated further and further into a private world in the aftermath of the Arms Trial, distrustful of the parliamentary party and relying instead on a small coterie of ministers. As the veteran political correspondent Michael Mills reported nearly thirty years later, the experiences of 1970 haunted the Taoiseach. 'Lynch told me shortly afterwards that he lost all trust in people after the event. I suggested to him that there were many people around whom he could trust, to which he replied: "How can you expect me to trust anybody after what had happened?"'[17] Paradoxically, as Lynch himself noted in the aftermath of the 1977 victory, the scale of the Fianna Fáil majority rendered once again possible the political luxury of factional disputes.

The new establishment retreated still further as an economic crisis gathered pace. Power rested primarily with Lynch's economics advisor, Martin O'Donoghue, the Minister for Industry Commerce and Energy Desmond O'Malley, and the Minister for Finance George Colley. None of the three had any real contact with the backbenches. O'Donoghue had been catapulted to the Cabinet following his first election to the Dáil in 1977. Colley had failed to build a significant power-base within the parliamentary party despite his stated intention to become the next leader of Fianna Fáil. To compound matters, the party's poor showing in the first direct European elections in June 1979 showed the potential scale of electoral loss. The senior minister appointed to the task of reassuring the restive backbenches in Colley's subsequent leadership campaign

---

[15] *Dáil Debates*, vol. 317, col. 1474, 11 December 1979.

[16] The best contemporaneous accounts are to be found in the news magazines *Hibernia* and *Magill*. See John Mulcahy, 'The Making of a Leader', *Hibernia*, 13 December 1979. The most detailed account of the manoeuvrings can be found in Vincent Browne, 'The Making of a Taoiseach', *Magill*, January 1980. Browne suggested that Haughey had little to do with the plotting, positing instead the power of the backbenches against the establishment on solely economic grounds. For more Machiavellian readings that place Haughey at the centre from the start, see Stephen Collins, *The Haughey File: The Unprecedented Career and Last Years of The Boss* (Dublin, 1992), pp. 24–33, and Bruce Arnold, *Jack Lynch: Hero in Crisis* (Dublin, 2001), pp. 216–217.

[17] Michael Mills, 'Kelly believed Government authorised action', *Irish Times*, 30 April 1998. The quotation is included in the final article of a three-day series reassessing the Arms Trial. It was printed in the wake of a *Spotlight* programme on the crisis produced by the author and presented by BBC Dublin Correspondent Shane Harrison: 'Patriot Games', *Spotlight*, BBC Northern Ireland, 10 March 1998.

was the abrasive Des O'Malley, supported by Martin O'Donoghue.[18] By O'Malley's own admission:

> I have not concerned myself unduly with the public relations side of being a politician and that given my personality I have often gratuitously insulted and been rude to people. . . But I do find the self-projection aspect of politics somewhat repellant and I find myself quite incapable of dealing with [it]. I must live with the political consequences of this deficiency. . .[19]

O'Malley used a 1979 interview to posit the view that Jack Lynch deserved the support of the party and the country. He argued that the country needed to focus on 'concrete economic realities [rather] than on vague theoretical generalities' – and this was indeed the problem. Fianna Fáil's retraction under the Lynch government to patriotism based on economic performance alone rendered the philosophy O'Malley posited vulnerable to the vagaries of voters in the political marketplace. There were, at this stage, those in a position to offer a potentially better trade. Careful not to overtly blame Haughey for hawking such wares in 'the recent past', O'Malley decried 'several people who have made public statements from time to time which have had the intention of undermining his [Lynch's] leadership. But not only those. I also had in mind members who gossip behind his back in a manner deeply damaging not just to Jack Lynch's position but to the interests of the party and the Government'.[20]

In stark contrast to the imperious framework of government under Lynch, Haughey had acute political antennae, honed during the long years in the political wilderness when, in a major effort to rehabilitate himself, he repeatedly canvassed every constituency in the country. Given the paucity of ministerial talent and the fact that Haughey had given the Taoiseach no rational ground for staying his return to the front bench, it was inevitable that he would be recalled. Haughey retained the health portfolio gained in opposition in 1975 when Fianna Fáil returned to government two years later, an appointment that considerably enhanced his public profile but which would provide fundamental distance from the economic policies that were to hurtle the country towards bankruptcy. Nevertheless, Haughey's accession to the leadership, made without the active support of a single serving Cabinet minister, was a momentous achievement.[21] When the Fianna Fáil party voted between Haughey and Colley, he won 39 backbench votes. As one backbench TD quoted in the *Irish Press* noted: 'They

---

[18] Stephen Collins, *The Haughey File: The Unprecedented Career and Last Years of The Boss* (Dublin, 1992), p. 31. See also interview with Vincent Browne, 'O'Malley's prospectives', *Magill*, December 1979.

[19] Desmond O'Malley, quoted in Vincent Browne, *ibid.*, p. 53.

[20] *Ibid.*, p. 51.

[21] Although Brian Lenihan refused to propose him in the leadership race, Haughey did have his support in a contest Lenihan described as being 'between a fool and a knave': see James Downey, *Lenihan: His Life and Loyalties* (Dublin, 1998), p. 107.

[the Colley faction] were voting for their jobs, we were voting for our seats.'[22] The question was: why?

Vincent Browne's seminal article for *Magill* in January 1980, 'The Making of a Taoiseach', gave a number of interesting pointers. He argued that the reasons for the revolt centred primarily on the government's handling of the economy, but also that Haughey played little demonstrable role. In contrast to Noël Browne's assertion when Haughey bid for the leadership that parliamentary democracy was turned on its head, this was an example, according to Browne, of that democracy really functioning. '[E]lected representatives exercised their constitutional right to influence and change policy, instead of providing mere lobby fodder for a party oligarchy.'[23] Yet, what is also clear – indeed, explicitly stated by the *Magill* editor – is that the method chosen to destabilise the government was in fact the northern question and it was the northern question alone that provided the locus for discontent. The primary beneficiary, of course, was Haughey, whose 'indecent ambiguity', in FitzGerald's memorable phrase, differentiated him from the rest of the political establishment.

The North impinged upon the consciousness with a vengeance on 27 August 1979. The former Viceroy of India and the Queen's uncle, Earl Louis Mountbatten, had just left the harbour at Mullaghmore in County Sligo when a powerful bomb detonated on board his boat, the *Shadow V*. Four people were killed: Earl Mountbatten, his grandson Nicholas Knatchbull, the dowager Lady Brabourne, and deckhand Paul Maxwell, a fifteen-year-old schoolboy from Enniskillen.[24] The same afternoon eighteen British soldiers were killed in a devastating attack at Narrow Water, just outside Warrenpoint. As a military convoy passed by, the IRA detonated a powerful booby-trap bomb. A second bomb exploded as reinforcements arrived, hampering the rescue operation and adding to the death toll.[25] The bombs were detonated via remote control by an IRA active service unit watching the carnage unfold from across Carlingford Lough in the Irish Republic.[26]

The murders on both sides of the border claimed the biggest military loss of life in a single day in the course of the Troubles, the impact rendered more powerful by the horrendous nature of the deaths, as body parts despoiled offshore

---

22 Anonymous backbencher quoted in John Mulcahy, 'The Making of a Leader', *Hibernia*, 13 December 1979.

23 Vincent Browne, 'The Making of a Taoiseach', *Magill*, January 1980, p. 24.

24 Lady Brabourne died from her injuries the following day. The IRA had targeted Mountbatten from as early as 1970 and plans to kill him had reached an advanced stage the year before. See J. Bowyer Bell, *The Irish Troubles: A Generation of Violence 1967–1992* (Dublin, 1993), p. 571. The IRA operator convicted of the killing, Tommy McMahon, was released in August 1998 under the terms of the Good Friday Agreement.

25 For full details of the attacks at Narrow Water and Mullaghmore see Toby Harnden, *'Bandit Country': The IRA and South Armagh* (London, 2000), pp. 197–237. See also David McKittrick *et al.*, *Lost Lives* (Edinburgh, 1999), pp. 793–799.

26 Toby Harnden, *'Bandit Country': The IRA and South Armagh* (London, 2000), pp. 198–199.

waters on the east and west coasts. Lynch, on holiday in Portugal, made the fateful decision to stay abroad, leaving George Colley in charge. Haughey was on his holiday island off the coast of Kerry and also declined the opportunity to return to an emergency Cabinet meeting. His decision prompted the current affairs weekly *Hibernia* to comment sardonically on 'yet another indication of the extraordinary remove from any affairs of state not directly connected with his own ministry. Obviously he wants no part in the collective responsibility of the Cabinet for the overall political and economic conduct of this administration. With Jack Lynch's popularity on the decline, Haughey is now playing for the highest stakes.'[27] Characteristically, Haughey maintained an enigmatic silence that only further increased the speculation that Lynch was losing control.

With the British tabloid press demanding an urgent security crackdown, British Prime Minister Margaret Thatcher arrived in Northern Ireland. Promptly travelling to the heavily fortified village of Crossmaglen in South Armagh, she was photographed in combat fatigues. In a gruesome incident which no doubt steeled the Prime Minister's resolve, the local brigade commander tossed the epaulets of an officer who died at Narrow Water, Lieutenant Colonel David Blair, onto the table before her, saying: 'This is all that's left of one of my bravest officers.'[28] The IRA was unmoved by the outrage. An editorial in the republican newspaper *An Phoblacht* gave an indication of its contempt when it described Mountbatten's murder as 'a discriminate operation to bring to the attention of the English people the continuing occupation of our country. We will tear out their sentimental imperialist heart. The execution was a way of bringing emotionally home to the English ruling class and its working-class slaves that their government's war on us is going to cost them as well.'[29]

In public, the British had seized the propaganda initiative and set an agenda in which the Irish Cabinet was out-manoeuvred at every step. Lynch's return to Ireland did not improve matters. Significantly, when a welcome party was convened to greet the returning Taoiseach now facing a political crisis – in a repeat of the highly impressive show that had been made in October 1970 in the aftermath of the Arms Trial acquittals – Haughey stayed away. In 1970, the party had calculated that Lynch represented electoral salvation; a decade later the winds of change were blowing and Haughey, with his acute ability to read the political barometer, sensed it. Conditional loyalty had been replaced with open derision.

The dissent gathered pace in response to media interviews with RTÉ and the BBC in which Lynch appeared to unilaterally resile from the 1975 Fianna

[27] Darach McDonald, 'Cabinet in Crisis', *Hibernia*, 6 September 1979. Colley is quoted in the same issue saying: 'in some cases the criticism is understandable, but in others it is purely malicious.' Either way it was undeniable that Colley, given the opportunity to provide decisive leadership, had balked.

[28] J. Bowyer Bell, *The Irish Troubles: A Generation of Violence 1967–1992* (Dublin, 1993), p. 574.

[29] *An Phoblacht/Republican News*, 1 September 1979.

Fáil policy formulation that called for a 'British commitment to implement an ordered withdrawal of their involvement in the six-counties of Northern Ireland'.[30] On the BBC's *Panorama* programme, Lynch suggested the goal of his government was to create 'an administration in the North to which the minority could give their consent'.[31] Perhaps even more damaging domestically was his *volte-face* on RTÉ's *This Week* programme the day before. Then he had argued that, given the prevailing circumstances, the government would be satisfied 'at this stage' with an internal solution *without* the external dimension of a Council of Ireland ceded by the British to a Fine Gael-Labour coalition at Sunningdale in 1973.[32] Such a move, even for short-term political expediency, represented a rupture from traditional policy and prompted serious questions about the rationale for Fianna Fáil's very existence. Without providing leadership on the national question, the party ceased to have a definable, distinct purpose.[33]

The centrepiece in this battle was the manoeuvring surrounding Síle de Valera's speech at Fermoy in County Cork, in which she openly called for an unequivocal declaration of British intent to withdraw in advance of a political settlement in the North. The timing of the speech, coming after intense criticism of the Taoiseach's handling of the diplomatic fallout associated with the August violence, could not have been worse. Its import strengthened by the fact that this could not be ascribed to an outburst of 'intemperate impetuosity', rather a carefully calculated snub designed to maximise Lynch's discomfiture. There were remarkable parallels with the assault launched by Blaney in Letterkenny exactly ten years before, in both cause and effect. On both occasions the text was distributed to newsrooms in advance of vetting by the Taoiseach's department; both provided surface manifestations of the level of dispute inside Fianna Fáil. They differed in the extent of the open contempt expressed, a symptom only of the relative standing of each challenger. While Blaney, one of the most powerful mandarins in Fianna Fáil, refused to even send Lynch a copy of his speech, de Valera, at this stage a relatively lowly backbencher, did accede to a request to meet with the Taoiseach. What happened next is a matter of some dispute but both available interpretations cast Lynch's ability to control his party in a weakened light.

De Valera claimed on 28 September that Lynch had told her he did not want to censor her, but would have liked to add to the speech if it had not been already in the public domain.[34] But Lynch contradicted this version of events to the Dáil on 17 October. He explained that confusion had arisen when his press secretary had said to reporters:

---

[30] It was to this formulation that Haughey pledged loyalty when he returned to the front bench in 1975.

[31] *Panorama*, BBC Television, 3 September 1979; *Irish Times*, 4 September 1979.

[32] Quoted in *Irish Times*, 3 September 1979.

[33] See Editorial, 'The Ripples from Fermoy,' *Hibernia*, 13 September 1979.

[34] De Valera recounted this to a parliamentary meeting: see Vincent Browne, 'The Making of a Taoiseach', *Magill*, January 1980, p. 35.

> it was indicated to Deputy de Valera from a very high source in the party that the speech should not be delivered, that it was not in conformity in all aspects with Government policy. It was only when the Government Press Secretary came back to me again… I said then that he could say to the press that such a meeting took place.[35]

The Trojan horse, Síle de Valera, shook her head in disbelief.[36] She had not technically deviated from party policy, but had merely switched the primary emphasis from an internal power-sharing solution towards a commitment from Britain that it should withdraw. De Valera maintained that Provisional IRA violence was the result of a political vacuum occasioned by the failure of politicians and warned against the introduction of 'half measures', which 'can only serve to exacerbate and fester the problem'. It was a calculated swipe at the apparent repositioning of Fianna Fáil in the aftermath of the August violence and one that de Valera maintained would lead only to further deaths. 'If our political leaders are not seen to be furthering our republican aspirations through Constitutional means the idealistic young members of our community will become disillusioned with the politicians and, far more importantly, they will be lost to the political and Constitutional process and turn to violence to achieve the aims which the politicians in their eyes have ceased to further'.[37]

Lynch was now being portrayed not only as a traitor to republican goals but also as the unwitting harbinger of death. The importance of de Valera's intervention cannot be underestimated. She had been recruited at an early stage into a caucus of discontented backbench TDs. Known as the Gang of Five, the group met regularly in the coffee restaurant at Jury's Hotel in Ballsbridge. Representing a disparate mix of constituencies and motives, they were determined to force a change of leadership; they agreed that Haughey alone could provide it,[38] but openly canvassing on the basis of economic policies risked the impression of incoherence at the heart of the party. As with the battle to undermine Lynch in 1969, raising the national question provided a useful cloak for the power games now being conducted at the heart of the Fianna Fáil parliamentary party.[39]

---

[35] *Dáil Debates*, vol. 316, col. 16, 17 October 1979.

[36] *Ibid.*

[37] Síle de Valera, speech at Liam Lynch commemoration, 9 September 1979; 'Ms de Valera urges militant line on Lynch at ceremony', *Irish Times*, 10 September 1979.

[38] For an early indication of the backbench dissent see *Hibernia*, 5 July 1979 and 12 July 1979.

[39] Here a distinction must be drawn between inter and intra-party considerations, particularly in reference to Fianna Fáil politics from the beginning of the Troubles in 1969 until Haughey's resignation in 1992. It is undoubtedly true that, with the exception of the 1981 snap general election that was conducted in the midst of the IRA hunger strikes, Northern Ireland has failed to feature as a locus of general election campaigning. For a penetrating analysis of inter-party competition see Peter Mair, *The Changing Irish Party System* (London, 1987), pp. 142–147. But within Fianna Fáil the national question remained the key ideological battleground. For a theoretical framework see Ian Lustick, *Unsettled States, Disputed Lands: Britain and Ireland, France and Algeria, Israel and the West Bank-Gaza* (Ithaca, 1993).

According to Vincent Browne, de Valera was regarded as so important to the dissidents within Fianna Fáil precisely because her family name guaranteed widespread media coverage.[40] In this it was exceptionally successful. The speech prompted a major debate in the Irish media, rendered more acute because Lynch had released a statement on the same day chastising the backbencher. Nevertheless, Fianna Fáil TDs felt sufficiently emboldened by de Valera's imprimatur to register support, including Mark Kililea and Charlie McCreevy, whose criticism of the leadership to date had centred only on economic concerns.[41] The fact that de Valera departed for the United States in the immediate aftermath of the speech meant that the debate would continue in her absence. Lynch would be forced on the defensive and the issue could not be satisfactorily resolved until her return, prompting a further possible deterioration of his leadership standing. The timing of this renewed debate on the nature of republicanism also meant the autumn session of the Dáil would be dominated from the very beginning by the question mark over Lynch's ability to control his party.[42]

A classic war of position had begun in which the chief weapon was the underlying ideology of the State. Just as in the Arms Trial controversy a decade earlier, those challenging for the leadership saw the destabilisation occasioned by a descent into violence as a mechanism to assert their position. They were helped considerably because the deteriorating public finances had weakened Lynch's once unassailable standing. The ideological challenge was coupled with an expectation that economic policy could also be changed. The confluence significantly enhanced the influence of the dissidents within Fianna Fáil, demonstrably no longer under the control of the party leader.

Two further developments relating to the North provided the final

---

40 Vincent Browne, 'The Making of a Taoiseach', *Magill*, January 1980, p. 34.

41 See the contrasting positions taken by editorial writers in *Irish Times*, *Cork Examiner*, and the *Irish Independent*, all 10 September 1979, cited in 'Soldier of Destiny haunts Jack Lynch', *Hibernia*, 13 September 1979. The *Irish Times* spoke of 'general bewilderment and anxiety' at the contradictory approaches adopted by the Taoiseach and his turbulent backbencher. The *Cork Examiner* put the speech down to an 'emotional outburst from Fianna Fáil's Iron lady'. Emotional it may have been but, as *Hibernia* pointed out in its editorial entitled 'The Ripples From Fermoy': 'her sentiments go right to the heart of the rank and file.'

42 See Bruce Arnold, *Haughey: His Life and Unlucky Deeds* (London, 1993), p. 149: Arnold noted sardonically that 'the burden of its content was more suited to a party in opposition and its hidden purpose was really to voice the frustration of a "party in opposition" – the one within Fianna Fáil, trying to hasten the departure of Jack Lynch and to replace him with Haughey'. See also Ian Lustick, *Unsettled States, Disputed Lands: Britain and Ireland, France and Algeria, Israel and the West Bank-Gaza* (Ithaca, 1993). A sophisticated mechanism for testing the application of Lustick's arguments to the politics of Fianna Fáil can be found in the work of the political scientist Terence Ball. He argued that ideologies are action-orientated and centre on two specific areas: 'core' and 'sore' concepts. A core concept is 'both central to, and constitutive of, a particular ideology and therefore of the ideological community to which it gives inspiration and identity'. By contrast, a 'sore' concept can be defined as 'a core concept whose meaning is unstable, undecided, in short, contested.' See Terence Ball, 'From "core" to "sore" concepts: Ideological innovation and conceptual change', *Journal of Political Ideologies*, 1999, 4 (3), pp. 391–392.

measurements for Lynch's political coffin. As noted above, in the wake of the Mountbatten deaths Lynch had discussed greater security with Margaret Thatcher's government. The measures introduced included the provision of an air corridor to enable British forces to pursue suspects five miles into Irish airspace. The agreement was highly confidential but was leaked to the *Irish Press.* It provided the opportunity for Tom McEllistrim, one of the Gang of Five, to table a motion on the grounds that national sovereignty was being infringed. Lynch, commenting during his tour of the United States, denied that this was the case but acknowledged that some concession had been made.[43] This prompted another of the caucus, Bill Loughnane, to brand the Taoiseach a liar in an interview with the *Irish Independent*. Lynch was furious and demanded Loughnane's expulsion. The task was given to George Colley, who proved unable to force the issue through a deeply divided and restive party that Colley and Lynch were shown unable to control.[44] Every issue of late had become reducible to a question of leadership and the autocratic style of government instituted by Lynch served only to exacerbate the situation. His maladroit handling of the de Valera controversy served only to heighten the perception of a leadership in retreat. Prestige and authority were gradually ebbing away. As Michael O'Leary of Labour had astutely pointed out a month beforehand, 'the Taoiseach's policy should have the full support of his party and that is lacking'.[45]

Haughey was characteristically calculated. In September his silence over the de Valera controversy signalled tacit support, yet when Colley advocated Loughnane's expulsion, he received backing from the semi-detached Minister for Health. The most likely explanation for this apparent paradox lay in Haughey's response to the confidence motion Lynch forced through the parliamentary party on the day he was sacked from government in May 1970. Then Lynch had demanded the unquestioned right – as Taoiseach – to appoint or fire, a point acceded to by Haughey. There were obvious tactical and strategic reasons for supporting such a motion in both instances, as such control is a necessary component of political power. In both instances Haughey played for control of the entire organisation, rather than settling for a rump. Behind the scenes in late 1979, the preparations for a palace coup were now in place and this time the inspiration predated the formation of Fianna Fáil. Haughey was about to claim the revolution for himself.

Using a speech at the Burlington Hotel in Dublin organised to celebrate the hundredth anniversary of Pádraig Pearse's birth, Haughey laid down his claim to the revolutionary tradition, rejecting partition as a 'British inspired' mechanism to artificially divide the Irish nation.

> It was perfectly natural for Pearse to consider the north-eastern minority as people who would take their place with full rights of political expression and

[43] Eunan O'Halpin, *Defending Ireland: The Irish State and its Enemies since 1922* (Oxford, 1999), p. 331.
[44] Dermot Keogh, *Twentieth-Century Ireland: Nation and State* (Dublin, 1994), p. 343.
[45] *Dáil Debates*, vol. 316, col. 8, 17 October 1979.

> participation within the context of the country as a whole... He believed that Ireland's history, the common past which all her men and women share, makes her spiritually, emotionally, intellectually and politically one indissoluble nation... The history of the people of every part of this island is one of unfulfilled aspirations, exploitation, disappointments and set-backs. We share the heritage in common. Pearse wanted a nation in which that long and troubled story could be brought to an end and in which all the divergent strands could be pulled together in the achievement of greatness.[46]

The threat posed by the invasion of the national question was underscored by a survey conducted by the Economic Social Research Institute, which detected an underlying republican ethos among the public. Seventy-eight per cent of those questioned were in agreement with the need for a British withdrawal, the cornerstone of Fianna Fáil policy which now appeared to be resting on very shaky foundations. More worrying for Lynch was that no less than forty-two per cent of people in the Republic supported IRA motives and a staggering twenty-one per cent supported IRA activities.[47]

It was against this background that the media reports became much more virulent, with the political correspondents openly displaying their colours.[48] Sensing that the denouement was approaching, journalist Bruce Arnold warned the party against choosing Haughey as a potential leader.

> There are too many question marks over Charles Haughey. He stalks the corridors of Leinster House, the silken predictions of control and power emanating from his person. Yet nobody knows the nature of his republicanism and how it would manifest itself in terms of policy on Northern Ireland or a new attitude towards Britain. It would be more hard-line that Jack Lynch's. But how? And to what purpose? And with what results? Nobody knows what the economic recipes would be. Nor whether they would work... He has created an illusion and it is this: that once the mantle of power falls upon his shoulders, he will then get it all together. But at what price?[49]

---

[46] Charles Haughey, speech at the Pádraig Pearse Commemoration Dinner, Dublin, 10 November 1979, reprinted in Martin Mansergh, ed., *The Spirit of the Nation: The Speeches and Statements of Charles J. Haughey (1957–1986)* (Cork, 1986), pp. 311–312.

[47] For full details of ESRI report see *Hibernia*, 18 October 1970.

[48] By way of contrast, see John Waters, *Jiving at the Crossroads* (Belfast, 1991). Waters remarked: 'It was almost an article of faith among journalists and other citizens of Dublin 4 that Haughey was the anti-Christ' (p. 132).

[49] Bruce Arnold, 'Politics and Politicians: Jack Lynch's Dilemma', *Irish Independent*, 17 November 1979, cited in his 1993 biography of Haughey, p. 152. Arnold tells of visiting Lynch to implore him to stay on because of his (Arnolds's) misgivings about possible contenders for the leadership: see Bruce Arnold, *Haughey: His Life and Unlucky Deeds*, pp. 153–154. In Arnold's latest book he rejects any suggestion that his political reporting at the time should have been balanced. Recounting the vote for the Fianna Fáil leadership on 7 December he recalled that Vincent Browne had admonished him to 'be more impartial. I told him that judgements had to be made. How could I write otherwise?': Bruce Arnold, *Jack Lynch: Hero in Crisis* (Dublin, 2001), p. 222. For a critique of Independent Newspapers' handling of the leadership challenge, see 'Why I Picked Charlie George', *Hibernia*, 13 December 1979.

Such judgments prevail to this day. Stephen Collins has referred to the Haughey faction's campaign as:

> intense and unscrupulous... There were rumours of bribery and intimidation and claims that uncommitted backbenchers were subjected to a great deal of pressure. Haughey was said to have offered considerable sums to wavering TDs to cover their "election expenses" and there was talk of votes being traded for promises of office.[50]

Yet firm evidence of such an 'unscrupulous' campaign emanating from Haughey is absent. Indeed, one could argue that the placement of such rumours suggests the source lay in the Colley camp, a position that Haughey's critics seem unwilling or unable to contemplate.[51]

Apprised of the difficulties within the party and the circulation of a secret petition advocating a change of leadership, Lynch determined to go. Not only had he recognised the loss of power within the party, but the parallel loss of Gerry Fitt as leader of the SDLP because of his party's internal opposition to a solely Northern Irish settlement meant that Lynch lacked constitutional nationalism backing in the northern arena also. The IRA kept up the pressure, too, with a renewed bombing campaign, including the detonation of twenty-four firebombs in Belfast on 26 November.

Two days after Arnold's appeal, Lynch informed Colley that he would be resigning after the European Summit on 29 November. Colley assured him he had secured the numbers to win but without, it appears, having done as much as a cursory check on backbench sentiment. It was a classic example of ministerial arrogance that comes from viewing the backbench with derision. On Wednesday, 5 December, the Taoiseach announced his decision to resign at a parliamentary meeting, a decision described as 'one of the worst miscalculations in recent Irish political history'.[52] The backbenches had revolted and took control of the establishment. In Stephen Collins's telling words: 'the outcasts took over power to the chagrin of those who believed themselves to be the natural ruling élite.'[53]

It was indicative of Colley's inability to read the mood of the party that Ray MacSharry, the Minister of State at the Department of Finance, actually proposed Haughey rather than his boss. It was wishful thinking for Lynch to confide in his press spokesman the night before the vote that 'George [Colley]

---

[50] Stephen Collins, *The Power Game: Fianna Fáil since Lemass* (Dublin, 2000), pp. 112–113.

[51] Similar credence is given to the view that Haughey was involved in the attempt to stymie Patrick Hillery's entry into the contest by suggesting that he may have had an affair. The charge that the attempt was linked to the leadership issue was made explicitly in Stephen Collins, *ibid.*, p. 111, citing hints Hillery gave in an *Irish Times* interview. A more plausible version appears in T. Ryle Dwyer, *Short Fellow: A Biography of Charles J. Haughey* (Dublin, 1999), pp. 156–160.

[52] Dermot Keogh, *Twentieth-Century Ireland: Nation and State* (Dublin, 1994), p. 343.

[53] Stephen Collins, *The Power Game: Fianna Fáil since Lemass* (Dublin, 2000), p. 111.

and Martin [O'Donoghue] tell me that they will pull it off'.[54] His use of O'Donoghue, with no experience of backbench life, to handle his campaign was an even greater blunder. By way of contrast, Haughey's campaign managers had at least ten years of experience. Not only did they know their men; they knew the value of their promises.

Two key sets of defections on the morning of the vote cast the die. The Cork TD Gerry Cronin, promoted by Lynch to the ministry of Defence in 1970, had been jettisoned when the party returned to power in 1977. He knew no loyalty or reason for advancement under Colley, a rationale that also greatly influenced the decisions of fellow Cork TDs Sean French and Tom Meany. Just as the electorate had forsaken Lynch in early December, now the Fianna Fáil parliamentary representatives from the Lee were rejecting his clearly preferred successor. Any residual thought of the survival of the establishment was disabused when the Minister for Foreign Affairs, Michael O'Kennedy, declared his support for Haughey. He had been regarded as a firm supporter of the status quo because of his approval of the decision to withdraw the whip from Bill Loughnane.

It was indicative of Haughey's political style that his sole public intervention in advance of the Lynch resignation was confined to the speech at the Burlington commemorating the progenitor of the Easter Rising, Pádraig Pearse. Following the years in the political wilderness after his sacking in 1970, Haughey had long realised the importance of the outward appearance of loyalty to a regime for which he clearly felt contempt. A commanding source suggests that Haughey regarded Lynch as an essentially decent man who was badly served by his lieutenants.

> Lynch was never really a true Fianna Fáil person adhering to the core values of social compassion. He stood for the respectable business elite, pandering to their whims. He never believed in the ideology underpinning Fianna Fáil. It was therefore relatively easy to advance an internal settlement even if that meant jettisoning principle.[55]

In some respects Haughey's approach was redolent of the post-1962 interregnum in China. Then Mao ZeDong and his acolytes had sought to criticise the technocratic elite through a debate on the classics, a development that was to lead in time to the Cultural Revolution.[56] Reclaiming the spirit of Pearse was

---

[54] Quoted in Stephen Collins, *The Haughey File: The Unprecedented Career and Last Years of The Boss* (Dublin, 1992), p. 32.

[55] Confidential source, interview with the author, Dublin, 24 July 2002.

[56] The use of historical allusion is a classic weapon in the ideological armoury. The factional disputes within the Chinese communist party are perhaps the most sustained example. Mao used the media in Shanghai to criticise the Beijing leadership in 1965. His criticism of a play set in the seventeenth century but written by the Deputy Mayor of Beijing could be read as a critique of the cult of personality. See James Miles, *The Legacy of Tiananmen: China in Disarray* (Ann Arbor, 1996), pp. 78–79.

sufficiently distant from the controversies of the present to be regarded as an open declaration of disloyalty to the current leadership.

The strategy worked. The importance of the speech and its hidden message remained undetected by many in the press corps, who were covering the events from the United States, where Lynch was on an official visit. The speech was telexed to the Taoiseach, who read it while travelling from Boston to New Orleans. Lynch knew immediately that Haughey's intervention signalled the breaking of cover. The government press secretary, Frank Dunlop, provided copies to reporters. According to Dick Walsh of the *Irish Times*, none of the reporters thought it amounted to much; his own first opinion was that it was just another rhetorical foray into the past. Only one journalist in the party accompanying Lynch to New Orleans could see its potential. Sean Duignan, an RTÉ journalist who was later to become Albert Reynolds's press spokesman, told Walsh: 'You have to know the code... They're sending semaphore messages to each other across the Atlantic. The people in the back know what it means and they don't like it.'[57]

That code was well understood within the Fianna Fáil party. Haughey was signalling his tacit approval of the destabilisation of Lynch's government, a process which had begun with de Valera's assault at Fermoy the previous September. Taking advantage of the Taoiseach's absence, Haughey's speech lauding Pearse was carefully designed to offer the party an alternative leader. It promised not only a tangible means of reconnecting the party with its lost ideological inheritance, it also signalled contempt for the current leader of the party. Haughey implied Lynch's actions on the national question were antithetical to what Pearse had stood for.

> Pearse was a separatist, not because he wished to separate the north-eastern minority from any of their traditional allegiances, but because he saw the British presence in Ireland as a source of conflict and a barrier to progress, and because he believed their withdrawal was a pre-requisite to the creation of a harmonious, civilised society in which all Irish men and women could develop their full potential.[58]

It was a theme picked up by the *Irish Press* immediately after Haughey secured the leadership, when it opined in a gushing editorial: 'A new Ireland has dawned... A post-British-withdrawal Ireland is a sane, respectable vision.'[59] Certainly, the Ireland he inherited was awash with economic problems that ideology alone was incapable of dealing with. An exultant Síle de Valera neatly caught the mood of excitement and apprehension when she exclaimed after his election: 'We've

---

[57] Dick Walsh, *The Party: Inside Fianna Fáil* (Dublin, 1986), pp. 140–141.

[58] Charles Haughey, speech at the Pádraig Pearse Commemoration Dinner, Dublin, 10 November 1979, published in Martin Mansergh, ed., *The Spirit of the Nation: The Speeches and Statements of Charles J. Haughey (1957–1986)* (Cork, 1986), p. 311.

[59] 'HMS Cruiser Fatuity', *Irish Press*, 10 December 1979.

got what we needed, a strong man, able to handle the political and economic challenges now facing the country.'[60] What the public did not know was that Haughey's own financial predicament mirrored that of the nation and his personal survival depended not only on securing but maintaining power over a deeply divided party. The dichotomy was reflected in Haughey's own public persona.[61]

The key supporters in the overt leadership campaign were awarded ministerial rank. Albert Reynolds was made Minister for Posts and Telegraphs and Ray MacSharry was promoted to Agriculture. Sean Doherty, the former policeman who had been such a pivotal figure in the original 'Gang of Five', was later promoted to junior ministerial rank, as were Tom McEllistrim and Jackie Fahey. Maire Geoghegan Quinn became the first woman to hold Cabinet rank since Countess Markievicz in 1920. Charlie McCreevy, who had enthusiastically backed Haughey, was passed over. The Colley faction, although humiliated, retained the semblance of power. Only O'Donoghue, Bobby Molloy at Defence, and Jim Gibbons, the chief prosecution witness at the Arms Trial, were demoted. The functioning of the separate Department of Economic Planning and Development was subsumed into a greatly expanded Department of the Taoiseach. Molloy had been jettisoned to make way for Reynolds, but with Gibbons the matter was clearly personal. Taken in the round, however, the changes were relatively minor. Far from heralding a political bloodbath, the first Cabinet changes reflected accurately the depths of divisions within the party. Put simply, given the open questioning of Haughey's very fitness for office, he could not afford the carelessness of allowing former Cabinet colleagues to build new alliances from the backbenches. He reasoned that tighter control could be exerted by binding them to collective responsibility.

Yet the presence at Cabinet level of such powerful forces meant Haughey's hold on power without achieving a mandate in his own right was never assured. Given the fact that he had secured power in what amounted to a palace coup, until he achieved the popular support of the electorate the Modern Prince would be susceptible to further challenges from within the parliamentary party. Electoral success, while not providing a cure, certainly could have helped manage the illness. The battle for Fianna Fáil, defined by reference to positions taken at the Arms Trial ten years previously, continued unabated as Haughey sought to preserve his tentative grip on power.[62]

All eyes were on the Dáil chamber to establish whether Haughey in

---

[60] Quoted in Bruce Arnold, *What Kind of Country* (London, 1984), p. 141.

[61] The most detailed exposition of Haughey's money woes and his travails with his bankers, Allied Irish Banks, can be found in Colm Keena, *Haughey's Millions: Charlie's Money Trail* (Dublin, 2001), pp. 42–77. The book is essentially an account of the evidence provided to the Moriarty Tribunal, which Keena covered for the *Irish Times*. Written before the Moriarty Tribunal published its findings, its only drawback is that it lacks sourcing; those seeking detailed information are advised to access the *Irish Times* website at http://www.ireland.com for Keena's scrupulous daily reporting.

[62] For a relatively sympathetic reading of Haughey's predicament see J.J. Lee, *Ireland 1912–1985: Politics and Society* (Cambridge, 1989), pp. 499–506.

government would demonstrate a hawkish approach to Northern Ireland. Haughey returned to the first principles underscoring the 1975 policy statement that he had endorsed following his return to the Fianna Fáil front bench that year.[63] The language deployed was unmistakably more hard-line than that of the Lynch government, but he did allow himself latitude.

> I want to emphasise that it will be the constant endeavour of this Government, as it has been of their predecessor, to achieve the unity of the people of Ireland by peaceful means, by agreement, in independence and in a harmonious relationship with our neighbour, Britain. We totally reject the use of force as a means of achieving that end... The principles of the policies we will pursue to that end will be those which have guided Fianna Fáil since it was founded. These were as stated in our policy statement of October 1975. There may be changes of emphasis.[64]

Haughey himself regarded the policy as a positive approach. In another speech he maintained that

> [t]he responsibility of ensuring that the achievement of Irish unity is kept firmly at the centre of democratic Irish politics seems clearly to devolve on Fianna Fáil... The British presence in the North and a constant reiteration of British determination to maintain the presence has not brought, nor can it ever hope to bring peace.[65]

The questioning of Haughey's policy towards Northern Ireland continued throughout January 1980, as he declined to give interviews. His silence added to the mystique but it also raised again the Fine Gael charge that he displayed 'indecent ambiguity' towards the IRA. Such perceptions were heightened by the way in which the IRA commandeered the funeral in Tralee of Kerry football legend John Joe Sheehy. An armed colour party fired a gun salute over the corpse in full view of a junior minister, Tom McEllistrim, whose protestations that he did not witness it were greeted with derision by some back in Dublin. The lack of censure from the new Taoiseach served only to add to the perception that Haughey was prepared to countenance IRA displays of defiance.[66]

---

[63] The full text of the 1975 statement, quoted in Martin Mansergh, ed., *The Spirit of the Nation: The Speeches and Statements of Charles J. Haughey (1957–1986)* (Cork, 1986), pp. 207–208, read:

> Encourage the unity of Ireland by agreement in independence and in a harmonious relationship between the two islands and to this end to declare Britain's commitment to implement an ordered withdrawal from her involvement in the Six Counties of Northern Ireland.
>
> Enter into an agreement guaranteeing appropriate financial support for a specified period to enable the transition to take place smoothly in stable, economic conditions.

[64] *Ibid.*, p. 321.

[65] Speech at the Annual Dinner of the Dublin Artane Fianna Fáil Constituency Organisation, 19 November 1975, *ibid.*, p. 209.

[66] For full details of John Joe Sheehy's funeral see 'Why Haughey stays silent on Sheehy funeral', *Hibernia*, 31 January 1980.

But Haughey was playing a different game, presenting an image of a man in control of the wider geo-political situation and carefully pacing performance. It would be a further twenty years before the opening of the 1969 archives revealed that the first diplomatic initiative broached by Haughey to the British ambassador, Sir Anthony Gilchrist, had taken place at his home in Kinsealy while he was Minister for Finance.[67] By February 1980, Haughey had outlined in detail the political thinking implicit throughout his career.

Thousands of rapt supporters crammed the party's Árd Fheis in Dublin to witness a volatile mix of crazed idolatry and mass hysteria. Now in power, as Taoiseach, Haughey proclaimed that Northern Ireland was the 'major national issue and its peaceful solution is our first political priority'; its resolution was necessary to lift the long, dark shadow cast across the island that distorted Anglo-Irish relations.[68] Not since Lynch's speech, delivered under pressure in the confused days of August 1969, had such overt language been deployed by a leader of Fianna Fáil.

> For over sixty years now, the situation in Northern Ireland has been a source of instability, real or potential, in these islands. It has been so because the very entity itself is artificial and has been artificially sustained. In these conditions, violence and repression were inevitable... We must face the reality that Northern Ireland, as a political entity, has failed and that a new beginning is needed. The time has surely come for the two sovereign Governments to work together to find a formula and lift the situation on to a new plane, that will bring permanent peace and stability to the people of these islands. No settlement can be contemplated now which merely sows the seeds of future discord.
>
> There are massive financial, security and constitutional questions to be solved, guarantees to be worked out. But a start must be made. In my view, a declaration by the British Government of their interest in encouraging the unity of Ireland, by agreement and in peace, would open the way towards an entirely new situation in which peace, real lasting peace, would become an attainable reality.
>
> For our part, we gladly declare that we have no wish to dominate or coerce. The evils of domination and coercion at the hands of others are too deeply embedded in our folk memory for us ever to start down along that reprehensible road.[69]

Haughey offered a special priority to the northern Protestants to safeguard their interests, a suggestion he was later to offer in the Dáil. Despite noting 'dovish details' in the official lexicon, such as the use of 'Northern Ireland' rather than the more loaded 'six counties' to describe the failed entity, *Hibernia* noted Haughey

---

[67] See above, p. 28.

[68] Charles Haughey, Presidential Address, 49th Fianna Fáil Ard-Fheis, 16 February 1980. Text reprinted in Martin Mansergh, ed., *The Spirit of the Nation: The Speeches and Statements of Charles J. Haughey (1957–1986)* (Cork, 1986), pp. 327–338.

[69] *Ibid.*, pp. 334–335.

had succeeded in steering Fianna Fáil to an 'essentially and fundamentally more hard-line than the latter-day Lynch position'.[70] The question was: could Haughey deliver on his promises to reach an historic understanding with a Prime Minister who associated herself with the politics of English nationalism?[71]

The man charged with finding out was the newly appointed Minister for Foreign Affairs, Brian Lenihan. Lenihan's biographer traced the origins of the diplomatic initiative to a cultural festival in London at which the Minister for Foreign Affairs was guest speaker. The organiser, John Stephenson, recalled being struck by the charm and intelligence of Lenihan in convincing London mandarins that change must be made.

> I watched him charm the British with his bonhomie and clever wit, then begin to manifest his knowledge and intelligence. He began to challenge them. They had to play. It was like watching tennis. Back and forth. I sat spellbound.... Then: What are we going to do about this situation, lads? How do we deal with these recalcitrant Northerners? I could see them thinking, these are civilised people, we can do business with them, the problem is sorting out all those Northerners.[72]

Once in power Haughey had to be seen to be delivering to an expectant constituency, a need rendered more acute by the dire economic situation now facing the country. He played the republican card with some skill 'through a nubile display of political body language that once again underlined his sheer political artistry on his home ground'.[73] The tactic was to deal directly with London alone, referring continuously to Northern Ireland as a 'failed political entity' which had no right to opt out of the Irish nation. Haughey attended a summit in London on 21 May 1980 in which he put his theories to Margaret Thatcher. Somewhat surprisingly, from the narrow nationalistic impulses of both came a desire to provide a breakthrough. One possible explanation was advanced by a critical biographer, Hugo Young, who commented on the 'mutually roguish admiration' the leaders held for each other.[74]

The communiqué from the summit referred to the wish 'to develop new and closer political cooperation between their Governments' and, with this purpose in mind, to hold regular meetings.[75] Haughey returned to Ireland

---

[70] Editorial, 'The First Political Priority', *Hibernia*, 21 February 1980.

[71] For an assessment of the strategic considerations facing the British government which suggests that an international dimension had to be attempted, see Brendan O'Leary and John McGarry, *The Politics of Antagonism: Understanding Northern Ireland* (London, 2nd edition, 1996), pp. 214–216.

[72] John Stephenson, quoted in James Downey, *Lenihan: His Life and Loyalties* (Dublin, 1998), p. 111.

[73] J.J. Lee, *Ireland 1912–1985: Politics and Society* (Cambridge, 1989), p. 504.

[74] Hugo Young, *One of Us* (London, 1989), p. 466.

[75] The full text of the communiqué is published in Martin Mansergh, ed., *The Spirit of the Nation: The Speeches and Statements of Charles J. Haughey (1957–1986)* (Cork, 1986), p. 362. For an even-handed assessment of the importance of the summit in paving the way to the Anglo-Irish Agreement see Feargal Cochrane, *Unionist Politics and the Politics of Unionism since the Anglo-Irish Agreement* (Cork, 1997),

convinced that a new beginning was indeed possible – on Irish terms. Although the communiqué accepted that there could be no change in the constitutional position of Northern Ireland without the consent of the northern population, Haughey was preparing the ground for fundamental change. His speech to Dáil Éireann on 29 May 1980 outlined the template and can now be seen as the architectural framework for the current peace process.

> We seek an arrangement whereby all Irishmen, no matter what their traditions, would manage the affairs of this island without British participation but with active British interest and goodwill. This aspiration for unity is a fact of history, of geography, of politics, of the deepest feelings and sentiments of the vast majority of Irishmen everywhere. That aspiration will not go away, nor can it be put away as long as Irishmen inhabit this island. To propose or suggest a solution which takes no account of it is to fail to understand the very nature of the problem and the situation.[76]

Haughey maintained that the only way to find the solution to an intractable problem that was causing instability was to reformulate it by seeking 'to bring about some fundamental change so that slowly but surely we alter the terms of the problem as a whole'.[77] Haughey traced the three dimensions to the problem, which in turn required a three-dimensional solution: the internal affairs of Northern Ireland; the relationship between Northern Ireland and the rest of the country, and the relationship between London and Dublin that provided the key to unlocking the other aspects. 'I believe that it is in this context of closer political co-operation that a permanent and lasting solution to the problem of Northern Ireland can be found.'[78]

The diplomatic initiative gathered pace in early June. In an interview with BBC television's *Panorama* programme he detailed the rationale underpinning his policy in a manner designed to appeal directly to the British people.

> The real root of the problem is the guarantee, the flat-footed unremitting guarantee which the British Government extends to the Unionist section of the population of Northern Ireland. I want to, if I can, to the British Government and to the British public, identify that, isolate that, as the stumbling block, the great big, immovable object. Until such time that something is done about that, some modification, some way round it is found, there will be no movement.[79]

---

pp. 1–34. See also Paul Arthur, 'Anglo-Irish Relations' in Arthur Aughey and Duncan Morrow, eds, *Northern Ireland Politics* (Harlow, 1996), pp. 113–120.

[76] Quoted in Martin Mansergh, ed., *The Spirit of the Nation: The Speeches and Statements of Charles J. Haughey (1957–1986)* (Cork, 1986), p. 366.

[77] *Ibid.*, p. 367.

[78] *Ibid.*, p. 368.

[79] Charles Haughey, interview with *Panorama*, BBC Television, June 1980, quoted in Martin Mansergh, ed., *The Spirit of the Nation: The Speeches and Statements of Charles J. Haughey (1957–1986)* (Cork, 1986), p.

Haughey also recognised that significant pressure would need to be exerted in the United States. This was a key element in the internationalisation of the conflict. The problem for Haughey was that he was forced to make it on the defensive, following a furore over attempts to remove the Irish ambassador to Washington, Sean Donlon, who had been openly accused by Blaney of curtailing the activities of legitimate republican groups.[80] Following the intervention of the U.S. Senators Tip O'Neill and Ted Kennedy, Haughey was forced to back down and keep Donlon in the post. It was no coincidence that the dispute followed disclosures on Haughey's role in the Arms Crisis in *Magill*, which centred on diaries prepared by the late Secretary of the Department of Justice, Peter Berry. Although the series concluded that Haughey was more sinned against than sinner, it did provide ammunition for Haughey's critics in both the Dáil and the media. The Donlon affair demonstrated that Haughey did not have total control; a speech designed to cover the cracks displayed the sense of harassment the Taoiseach felt just as he was developing a new initiative.

> On 13 December last, in the debate on the nomination of the Government, I said: "We totally reject the use of force as a means of achieving that end."
>
> Later in that speech, I said: "We are determined that that principle of the rejection of force will be clearly translated into practice."
>
> In the course of my speech to the Fianna Fáil Ard-Fheis on 16 February last, I said: "All but a tiny minority understand that violence can never bring a solution and that it serves only to perpetuate divisions and hatred."
>
> Again in the course of my speech in the Dáil on 29 May, I said: "We totally reject force as a means of obtaining our aim. We seek our objective only by peaceful means."
>
> I cannot, therefore, accept that there can be any genuine doubt in any quarter as to our attitude to violence, whether it is politically motivated or sectarian in origin...

---

363. See also Haughey's speech to Dáil Éireann, 25 June 1980, when he again stated the position:

> I believe it is important that I should state, again, our view that a proposal which is not acceptable to all the community in Northern Ireland and which does not recognise the reality of the physical, political, social and economic relationship between Northern Ireland and the rest of the country will not succeed and it is only in the context of new and closer political co-operation between the Irish and British Governments that a permanent and lasting solution will be found...

See Martin Mansergh, ed., *ibid.*, p. 374.

[80] See Andrew J. Wilson, *Irish America and the Ulster Conflict 1968–1995* (Belfast, 1995), pp. 165–167. Jack Holland, one of the most respected Irish-American journalists, took a more neutral view of the difficulties facing Haughey and quoted unnamed sources suggesting that Donlon's behaviour bordered on obsessive: see Jack Holland, *The American Connection: U.S. Guns, Money, and Influence in Northern Ireland* (Boulder, 1999), p. 136. A more sympathetic reading of the spat can be found in T. Ryle Dwyer, *Short Fellow: A Biography of Charles J. Haughey* (Dublin, 1999), pp. 182–183, and Tim Pat Coogan, *The Troubles, Ireland's Ordeal 1966–1995 and the Search for Peace* (London, 1995), p. 348. It is important to note, however, that the proposed move of Donlon to the United Nations was not a demotion. Ireland was scheduled to take up the chairmanship of the Security Council and Donlon's experience would have been invaluable.

> What is required is not mere condemnation as such but effective action to provide those who are in sympathy with the objectives of Irish unity with an alternative – a clearly defined Irish Government policy to which they can dedicate themselves. This is a need also stressed by our friends among the major political leaders in the United States; a clear objective and a policy which Irish-Americans can support and evidence that progress is being made towards that objective, through the implementation of that policy.[81]

Shortly after this, the entire enterprise collapsed as a consequence of the Maze Prison disputes. The unrest would result in the deaths of ten republicans, some of whom attained membership of the British or Irish parliaments as well as entry into the pantheon of Irish martyrs. The Maze Prison, ten miles outside Belfast, gave tangible expression to the British determination to criminalise the republican movement. Ten men were to starve themselves to death inside the H Blocks, named after the cellular structures, rather than wear prison uniforms or do prison work. They strove to be treated as political prisoners, instead of criminals. From the moment the Maze prison opened in 1976, Republicans refused prison clothing. Blankets protected their dignity. Two years later they refused to slop out in what Britain regarded as the most modern and secure prison in Europe. They began 'the dirty protest' by smearing excrement on the walls of their cells. The Maze prison had become an unmanageable battleground. According to one of those who took part in the 1980 hunger strike, it was only a matter of time after the introduction of the policy of criminalisation before the prison dispute reached a denouement.

> We decided at that stage that our options were running out to come to a settlement, to reach a settlement. Moreover we did detect at that time that morale was flagging among Republican prisoners. Not disappearing, but somewhat flagging and the decision was taken that we had to make a serious effort to break the impasse and therefore we opted for what was effectively the weapon of last resort of any prisoner, the hunger strike.[82]

The 1980–1981 hunger strikes were indeed the weapon of last resort for Republicans and proved to be defining historical acts. At stake was the legitimacy of the State, pitted against the ideology of armed struggle against that administration. If the Arms Trial represented a hinge moment in the politics of the Republic, the hunger strikes in 1980 and 1981 can now be seen as equally pivotal in the North. They were also events that would destroy the carefully laid plans of the Taoiseach.

---

[81] Charles Haughey, Address to Members of the Fianna Fáil Organisation, Cork, 27 July 1980, reprinted in Martin Mansergh, ed., *The Spirit of the Nation: The Speeches and Statements of Charles J. Haughey (1957–1986)* (Cork, 1986), pp. 385–387.

[82] Tommy McKearney, interview with author, February 2001.

By 1980 conditions within the prison had deteriorated to almost unimaginable levels. Rotten food in corners bred maggots and entire walls were smeared with excrement. With neither side prepared to compromise, mediation was sought. The Catholic Primate Cardinal Tomas O Fiaich engaged the then Secretary of State Humphrey Atkins in dialogue and visited the jail on 3 March. He emerged describing the conditions as akin to the Black Hole of Calcutta, with gaunt bearded men living in total squalor.[83] Attempts by the Cardinal to intercede on the prisoners' behalf met baleful silence from the British government, now intent on asserting the primacy of a security response to deal with what was essentially a political issue. The criminalisation of the republican movement, which had begun with the previous Labour administration, was now accompanied by a massive increase in the military apparatus at the Army's disposal. In the absence of an overarching framework, Dublin was powerless to intervene beyond issuing ad hoc statements of concern. Haughey would require a bilateral relationship based on equality to make a difference in British attitudes. The prison dispute, simply another theatre of operations, forced an escalation imperative that served only to emphasise the powerlessness of Dublin in the current circumstances.

Although the hunger strike has a long tradition in Irish politics, the Provisional IRA could not afford a further setback to its cause and was exceptionally reluctant to risk a propaganda disaster if it failed. The final decision was made despite opposition from the republican leadership, according to the Officer Commanding of the IRA prisoners inside the jail.

> I got a visit from Danny Morrison and I went down to see Danny and Danny told me that, and I knew this as soon as I seen Danny's face, that nothing was coming off Cardinal O Fiaich's meeting with Margaret Thatcher and he told me Thatcher just shut the door on his face. And Danny said to me: "What are you going to do now?" And I said: "Well, we have no option but to go onto hunger strike." I informed Danny to start planning for hunger strike – that we were going on hunger strike.[84]

Seven prisoners went on hunger strike on 27 October 1980 to demand specific improvements to the conditions of their incarceration. There were five key demands: the refusal of prison issue clothes or work; permission to organise; weekly visits from family; free association with other prisoners; and full entitlement to remission lost as a result of the dirty protest. The issue of political status was inferred but not rendered explicit.[85] As a strategy it proved remarkably effective and suddenly the H-Block Committees found their supporters' parades larger than any produced in the Catholic community since the early seventies. But

---

[83] For full text see David Beresford, *Ten Men Dead* (London, 1994), pp. 183–185.

[84] Brendan Hughes, interview with author, February 2001.

[85] See Liam Clarke, *Broadening the Battlefield: The H Blocks and the Rise of Sinn Féin* (Dublin, 1987), p. 123.

with Republican and Loyalist violence continuing on the streets outside, little sympathy was forthcoming from Unionist quarters or Margaret Thatcher's government. Sinn Féin's publicity director, Danny Morrison, who had been visiting IRA leaders Brendan Hughes and Bobby Sands for over a year, sensed a hidden British agenda.

> Bobby was just convinced that the battle lines had been drawn. The British Government had put so much significance into this battle within the prisons because you have to understand the significance of it. The British Government was attempting to defeat in prison IRA volunteers and other republicans who it couldn't defeat outside the prison and it was hoping to inflict a humiliating defeat and force the prisoners to accept criminal status with untold repercussions for the morale and of the struggle on the outside and the perception of the struggle on the outside so Bobby could see that it was a life and death situation.[86]

Haughey's attempt to broker a new understanding with Britain was placed at risk by the actions of the IRA, which was no longer under any restraint. The republican movement was horrified at Haughey's surprising lack of overt sympathy for their cause. They expected better. Crucially for Haughey, so did some of his own TDs. The harbinger of doom was, unexpectedly, Síle de Valera, whose speech at Fermoy a year earlier had paved the way for Lynch's downfall. Now de Valera accused Haughey, by inference, of standing idly by while a British government was about to let young men die on hunger strike in the Maze Prison.

At a by-election rally in Letterkenny in November, de Valera condemned what she termed Mrs Thatcher's lack of compassion and her 'callous, unfeeling and self-righteous statements' in relation to her handling of the prison dispute. Haughey was aghast and within hours a statement was issued to the press 'emphasising that neither the Taoiseach nor any member of the government had seen her script in advance and that her remarks had not reflected the views of the government'.[87] The row was immaterial to the result: a Fianna Fáil by-election victory for its candidate, Clem Coughlan, and a victory, too, for Haughey, his hand now strengthened within the parliamentary party – but the gap between rhetoric and the ability to influence British policy had been ruthlessly exposed and with it the powerlessness of any Taoiseach, even one as ideologically driven as Charles J. Haughey. His continued preoccupation with finding an overall breakthrough that transcended the specific issue of prison dispute spelt the end of his first administration.

Haughey's response to the hunger strikes was predicated on a much bigger prize than resolving the prison issue, although he was prepared to take credit for

---

[86] Danny Morrison, interview with the author.

[87] T. Ryle Dwyer, *Short Fellow: A Biography of Charles J. Haughey* (Dublin, 1999), p. 183. Dwyer reports de Valera as perplexed because Haughey had lifted the ban on her speaking about the North soon after he had become Taoiseach (p. 184).

it as a welcome side effect, should it come to pass. Following Síle de Valera's public comments, he outlined his position to the Dáil. Warning that the hunger strikes could lead to an even greater level of violence, he maintained that 'some adjustment could be made in the prison rules themselves or in their interpretation or their application' in order to resolve what he termed 'the present dangerous situation'. Haughey sidestepped the central issue of political status by suggesting merely that it should not be an issue, presumably because the prisoners had not asked for it explicitly. Haughey argued there was a 'political and moral obligation on all leaders in this country as well as myself to endeavour to take any action open to them to procure and bring forward a solution'. But, given the sensitivity of the issue, he maintained that open debate was counter-productive. 'It behoves us all to be especially careful in anything we wish to say in this House or elsewhere lest in any way we contribute to increasing the dangers or hardening of attitudes.' After spending years utilising the national question for his political advantage, Haughey was now closing down debate, as the North threatened to implode. The difficulties were compounded by the strident approach adopted by Margaret Thatcher at Westminster:

> May I make one point about the hunger strike in the Maze Prison. And I want this to be utterly clear. There can be no political justification for murder or any other crime. The Government will never concede political status to the hunger-strikers or to any others convicted of criminal offences in the province.[88]

Martin Mansergh, the Fianna Fáil advisor on the North, asserted at a workshop held in June 2001 to commemorate the twentieth anniversary of the hunger strikes that Haughey had worked 'very hard to defuse the hunger strike' but was constrained not only by:

> Fianna Fáil's wafer thin parliamentary majority of the time and Thatcher's obduracy... an open standoff (between Haughey and Thatcher) would probably have wiped away whatever potential progress that was achieved in 1980.[89]

Mansergh was correct, however, in highlighting the significance of the Anglo-Irish summit in December 1980. It produced a determination to examine the

---

[88] Quoted in 'The Hunger Strike: Dying for Ireland', *Insight*, UTV, 27 February 2001. Transcript available at http://www.utv.co.uk/insight

[89] Quoted in Criostóir de Rálaigh, 'Dublin debates the hunger strike', *An Phoblacht/Republican News*, 28 June 2001. It is indicative of the attempt to demonise Haughey that *An Phoblacht* carried a statement from Cionnaith Ó Súilleabháin, the PRO of Clonakilty Hunger Strike Commemoration Committee, citing Haughey's culpability. 'Let's not forget that Garrett FitzGerald let the first five men die while he was Taoiseach, and Charles Haughey as Taoiseach allowed Thatcher to leave the second five men die': *An Phoblacht/Republican News*, 15 February 2001. Although Haughey was in power when Sands died, his loss of office was owing to the election of two hunger strikers that denied him a majority in the June 1981 election. That being said, prior to the election Haughey had inherited a majority. The reticence in pushing the British government, because of the potentiality of a settlement, meant that the rhetoric was necessarily subdued.

'totality of relationships between these two islands'; the template for what eventually became a solution. Yet, the price, in terms of the Good Friday Agreement with its de facto acceptance of a two-nation settlement, was one that Haughey himself would not have paid.

In 1980, however, Haughey was determined to make his mark on Anglo-Irish relations in a way that had not been seriously attempted before by an Irish government. He spared no expense in wooing the British Prime Minister. The gift of a Georgian teapot at the May summit in London was augmented with a banquet at which the British delegation included the British Foreign Secretary and the Chancellor of the Exchequer. Mrs Thatcher is quoted as having regarded Haughey as a 'a romantic idealist', a claim that prompted some to speculate on her deficiencies as a judge of character.[90] It is certainly the case, however, that both were undoubtedly the finest politicians of their generation, with a capacity and determination to further a revolution rather than merely govern. In historian Bowyer Bell's exquisite phrasing: 'they seemed more of a pair: ambition triumphant, power achieved, the future open, and both at the height of power deployed.'[91] The extent to which the inter-governmental approach could be institutionalised, however, and in so doing offer fundamental change, can be gauged from the joint studies set up. The communiqué read:

> The Taoiseach and the Prime Minister agreed that the economic, social and political interests of the peoples of the United Kingdom of Great Britain and Northern Ireland and the Republic are inextricably linked, but that the full development of these links has been put under strain by division and dissent in Northern Ireland. In that context, they accepted the need to bring forward policies and proposals to achieve peace, reconciliation and stability; and to improve relations between the peoples of the two countries.
>
> They considered that the best prospect of attaining these objectives was the further development of the unique relationship between the two countries.
>
> They accordingly decided to devote their next meeting in London during the coming year to special consideration of the totality of relationships within these islands. For this purpose they have commissioned joint studies, covering a range of issues including possible new institutional structures, citizenship rights, security matters, economic co-operation and measures to encourage mutual understanding.[92]

---

[90] See, for example, James Downey, *Lenihan: His Life and Loyalties* (Dublin, 1998), p. 112. Downey concluded that the failure of Haughey to consolidate the gains from his discussions with Thatcher came from at least three interlinked reasons: the hunger strikes, the dispute over the Falklands, and deep suspicions of Haughey in the British establishment generally (p. 114). Senior British Security Service sources refuse to be drawn on Haughey. One confidential London source told the author in December 2001 that the scale of the surveillance on Haughey could not be divulged: 'The issue is still regarded as much too sensitive.'

[91] J. Bowyer Bell, *The Irish Troubles: A Generation of Violence 1967–1992* (Dublin, 1993), p. 601.

[92] Anglo-Irish Summit Communiqué, 8 December 1980, reprinted in Martin Mansergh, ed., *The Spirit of the Nation: The Speeches and Statements of Charles J. Haughey (1957–1986)* (Cork, 1986), p. 406.

Opposition politicians, including some in Fine Gael, regarded the initiative with suspicion, almost as though the prioritising of northern would infect the southern political establishment. The fact that the hunger strike was a reaching critical point served only to heighten perceptions that Haughey was playing a dangerous and volatile game. By contrast, Haughey saw in the communiqué the possibility of actualising a dynamic 'to transform the situation' which centred on London and Dublin acting in concert and which he had put to the British Ambassador in 1969. An authoritative source suggests that the communiqué represented, for the Modern Prince, 'a towering achievement that redefined the problem and pointed the only way to a solution. History is only now beginning to give it its due importance'.[93] The potential for a diplomatic breakthrough, however, was dependent on the stabilisation of the environment within Northern Ireland: that potential stability was being undermined by unionist suspicions of a sell-out by Perfidious Albion and republican prisoners' use of the weapon of last resort, the hunger strike.

Having advocated the hunger strike option, Brendan Hughes felt it right to go forward himself, leaving Bobby Sands to take over as IRA leader in the prison. The hunger strike might have been a weapon of last resort but for those taking part it was a process fraught with danger.

> [E]veryday the medics would come in and check your blood pressure and check everything. Then the weight started to come off, you lose the fat first, the fat goes and whatever excess fat you have it starts to go. Then your muscles start to go and your mind eats off the muscles, the glucose in the muscles and you can feel yourself going, you can actually smell yourself rotting away or dying away. That was one of the most memorable things for me, the smell, the smell of almost death... From my own body, yes. Remember this we had long beards and long hair, we hadn't shaved in years, we hadn't cut our hair in years, we hadn't washed in years. Then your body starts to deteriorate, your body starts to eat itself. I mean that's basically what happens during hunger strike until the point when there's no fat left, there's no muscles left, your body starts to eat off your brain. And that's when your sense starts to go, your eyesight goes, your hearing goes, all your senses starts to go when the body starts to eat off the brain.[94]

The physical symptoms were becoming deadly apparent when Haughey met Margaret Thatcher and her entourage in Dublin with thousands of people demonstrating on the streets outside. To have secured the commitment to examine 'the totality of relationships' in such inauspicious circumstances was no mean achievement.

Unknown to Haughey, the British government was already undermining any joint governmental approach. Secret negotiations involving the Foreign Office,

---

93 Confidential source, interview with the author, Dublin, 24 July 2002.

94 Brendan Hughes, interview with the author, February 2001.

the international security service, MI6, and the IRA leadership appeared to have found a solution to satisfy both sides. As the document was being flown from London by an MI6 officer, Brendan Hughes was facing a dilemma. Denied access to the leadership outside, he was on his own. It was December 18, day 53 of the hunger strike, and Sean McKenna was nearing death. The new deal offered appeared to concede the right of the prisoners to wear their own clothes but the devil was in the detail.

In the following days, the prisoners discovered that the British were offering no more than had been on the table before the hunger strike. They felt cheated and, as the deal unravelled, so did any modicum of trust, as Monsignor Denis Faul explained in a recent television reassessment. "Now they were given some conditions or letters it never was clarified exactly what they were offered but the British double-crossed them so the result was they got nothing." Driven by the failure of the first fast, Bobby Sands went on hunger strike on 1 March 1981 – determined that the prisoners would now set the agenda for a showdown with Britain. In this struggle the Anglo-Irish dimension became a mere sideshow whose importance diminished in inverse proportion to the protestations of Haughey that it could provide an ultimate solution.

Likewise, Haughey's problem with the Anglo-Irish summit was political perception, particularly in the loyalist heartlands. The first meeting of diplomats to the joint studies proposals agreed at the Dublin summit on 2 February was followed four days later by the appearance of the third force, a Paisleyite show of defiance against what the DUP leader termed the process of all-Ireland integration. While for domestic purposes Haughey suggested that the development heralded a new beginning, the reality was it offered merely the *potential* for significant movement: the initiative was oversold as historic but it only held out the opportunity to be so.[95]

There was no let-up in the violence on the streets outside as the second hunger strike moved inexorably towards its deadly conclusion. A radio discussion programme on BBC Northern Ireland three weeks after the start of the second hunger strike made matters worse when Lenihan argued that the 'totality of relationships' concept would open the way for Irish unity within a decade. When Lenihan repeated the assertion in a further interview, Mrs Thatcher was

---

[95] For a robust defence of the importance of the summit see Martin Mansergh's commentary on the communiqué. He classed it as:

> a radically different approach... It was an ambitious attempt to create an institutional framework between Britain and Ireland, which could form a key part of an overall settlement involving the reunification of Ireland at some future stage. While the joint studies were to concentrate on a number of practical subjects, the phrase "the totality of relationships", notwithstanding British denials, could not logically exclude constitutional questions, even if these were not on the immediate agenda.

See Martin Mansergh, ed., *The Spirit of the Nation: The Speeches and Statements of Charles J. Haughey (1957–1986)* (Cork, 1986), p. 407.

horrified.[96] Despite attempts by Britain to cool the atmosphere, Ian Paisley launched a series of meetings to protest against the dagger pointing to Ulster's breast and late night rallies in Newry, Armagh and Gortin in early April in which clashes took place with the RUC. Thatcher did not want another front opening with the loyalists as the threat of death once more permeated the prison complex outside Belfast.

The unexpected death of nationalist MP Frank Maguire raised the stakes across the British Isles. The political temperature soared when Sinn Féin announced that Sands would stand for the vacant seat. It provided an acid test of public opinion and, as such, was a very risky strategy for the Provisional IRA, a movement deeply sceptical of constitutional politics. Its atavistic belief that conventional politics could not work was conceptualised as the Stormont government buckled under the weight of its own contradictions in August 1969. It was forged by the behaviour of Fianna Fáil during the Arms Crisis and copper-fastened with a bombastic response to the Sunningdale power-sharing initiative in 1973. As the Troubles intensified, the IRA moved effortlessly into the self-appointed role as the vanguard of the revolution, contemptuous of democratic accountability. As Danny Morrison recalled, considerable debate took place before the risk of political contagion was deemed acceptable.

> People only see it in terms of its successes, people only see it in terms of its legacy of the electoral rise of Sinn Féin and the peace process but nobody realises the gamble that was involved in it because Bobby could have lose and had he lost even by a small margin then Mrs Thatcher would have crowed victory. She would have said that even the nationalist people reject you and your prisoners and it would have been a body blow to the political development of the republican movement.[97]

It was against this background of a deteriorating situation in Northern Ireland that Haughey used a rescheduled Fianna Fáil Árd Fheis – the day after Sands was elected – to reach even higher rhetorical flights, invoking in his leadership the spirit of the nation. He implored unionists to look at the talks between the British and Irish governments as an opportunity for a new beginning.

> The present state of affairs is the end-product of a succession of failed political experiments stretching back over a wearisome sixty years. To the spectres of violence and tragedy, political collapse and confusion in Northern Ireland, has now been added an economic collapse far worse than is being experienced anywhere else in Europe.
>
> What we have to offer ultimately is an opportunity for the people of both traditions in Northern Ireland and their leaders to move out of their present

[96] Tim Pat Coogan, *The Troubles: Ireland's Ordeal 1966–1995 and the Search for Peace* (London, 1995), p. 187.
[97] Danny Morrison, interview with author, February 2001.

> confines into a constructive partnership with us which would of course acknowledge the special relationship that exists between Ireland and Britain.[98]

Haughey acknowledged the serious economic difficulties facing his administration but asked to be judged on his handling of the national question alone.

> [L]et me say that it is my conviction that a nation which recoils from one of its major problems and makes no real effort to resolve it will find its capacity to solve any of its problems seriously impaired.
>
> There were those also who in the recent past, clearly intimidated by the intractable nature of the problem, committed themselves to a policy of doing nothing. That sort of defeatism we could never accept... [W]e work today for an Ireland that is, first of all, unified and free, an Ireland, which respecting all its diverse historical traditions, will have finally liberated itself from the last remaining distortion of history.[99]

Partition was, according to Haughey, an intolerable situation and Fianna Fáil 'the only party with a truly national vision and a historical tradition which gives us the will and the precedent for the endeavours on which we are now engaged'.[100] It alone had the capacity to deliver precisely

> because it represents, not this pressure group or that sectional interest, this class or that creed, but because, in the broad sweep of its membership and their faith and devotion to their country, there resides what one can well call 'the Spirit of the Nation'.[101]

The moral rectitude of that spirit was being tested as never before by the deterioration of Bobby Sands, MP, former OC of the IRA in the Maze and now close to death. Less than a week after the Árd Fheis, Haughey authorised a delegation comprising Síle de Valera, Dr John O'Connell, and Neil Blaney to visit the prison and report its findings to Downing Street. The message back to Britain from both prisoners and the Irish government was implacable. Haughey was again rebuffed by Margaret Thatcher in the strongest terms possible, during her visit to Saudi Arabia: "It is not my habit or custom to meet MPs of a foreign country about a citizen of the United Kingdom. We are not prepared to consider special category status for certain groups of people serving sentences for crime. Crime is crime, it is not political."[102]

---

[98] Charles Haughey, Presidential Address, Fianna Fáil 50th Ard-Fheis, 11 April 1981, reprinted in Martin Mansergh, ed., *The Spirit of the Nation: The Speeches and Statements of Charles J. Haughey (1957–1986)* (Cork, 1986), p. 476.

[99] *Ibid.*, pp. 479–480.

[100] *Ibid.*, p. 481.

[101] *Ibid.*, p. 480.

[102] Part of the press conference was aired in 'The Hunger Strike: Dying for Ireland', *Insight*, UTV, 27 February 2001, produced by the author. Transcript available from http://www.utv.co.uk/insight

Bobby Sands's election to Westminster brought international attention to what had been largely a local issue. It was the impetus for renewed attempts to find a solution but again the British government found itself caught on a hook of its own making. After sixty-six days Bobby Sands died in the Maze Prison hospital and another patriot was added to the republican lexicon. Francis Hughes followed him into the grave. Both deaths attracted international opprobrium but the British government refused to budge.[103] Haughey released a statement declaring that events had proved once again that 'Northern Ireland, as at present constituted, is no longer a viable political entity'.[104] Raymond McCreesh and Patsy O'Hara were the next sacrificial offerings from the Maze on the day Haughey called a snap general election, after receiving private polling suggesting that his party was likely to achieve an overall majority.[105] It was a dirty, nasty campaign in which he was frequently jostled in ugly confrontations orchestrated by H Block campaigners across the country from Navan to Donegal, who were convinced that the party was not doing enough to end the torment in Northern Ireland. They determined to force the issue to the top of the agenda and in so doing undermine Haughey's claim that only a Fianna Fáil initiative could provide both short term stability and a long term solution to the problem.

Haughey's anger at being jostled in Ballyshannon erupted at a rally in neighbouring Bundoran when he criticised the protestors for sullying the independence of Ireland. '[Do not] let yourselves be bullied or intimidated or downtrodden,' he told the crowd. 'When my father went out to fight for the freedom of this country he did not do so to have that freedom impaired or besmudged by anyone.'[106] Throughout the campaign Haughey maintained that a humanitarian solution should be sought. He tried to persuade the families to intercede with the European Court but refused to raise the stakes by threatening to withdraw the Ambassador to Britain or in any way publicly admonish the British handling of the dispute.

Haughey attempted once again to broker a compromise by endorsing the work of the Commission for Justice and Peace in the dying hours of his administration. The involvement of the Commission raised hopes that a solution could be found. Its members spent an intense week in Belfast during the summer of 1981. One of these, Father Oliver Crilly, suffered added anguish during attempts at mediation. Two of his cousins were taking part in the hunger strike. He didn't get to see Francis Hughes before he died, a week after Bobby Sands, but he did have a chance to talk to Thomas McElwee. Father Crilly found himself negotiating

---

[103] For international press coverage on Sands see David Beresford, *Ten Men Dead* (London, 1994), pp. 131–132.

[104] Statement made on 12 May 1981, reproduced in Martin Mansergh, ed., *The Spirit of the Nation: The Speeches and Statements of Charles J. Haughey (1957–1986)* (Cork, 1986), pp. 490–491.

[105] T. Ryle Dwyer, *Short Fellow: A Biography of Charles J. Haughey* (Dublin, 1999), p. 191.

[106] *Irish Times*, 29 May 1981, p. 1.

with Northern Ireland Prisons Minister Michael Allison and meeting his cousin Tom across a prison hospital table.

> It's not easy to stay in the abstract mode of moral judgement when you sit opposite people who are at that stage of weakness. There was a strange paradox if you like, a strange distance between the physical weakness and the mental strength and determination that was there. But I'm still convinced after that meeting that, if the Northern Ireland Office had sent the senior person in, as in more recent times Mo Mowlam was prepared to go into the prison to talk to loyalist prisoners – if something like that had happened I still believe that our initiative could have brought an end to the hunger strike at that point. But in fact that was not to be.[107]

At this stage it was too late for Haughey, who, with opposition looming, declared for the first time that 'primary responsibility rests on the British Government to make an immediate effort to find a solution'.[108] Garret FitzGerald, his old adversary, managed to win power in a hotly contested general election in which the victories of two hunger strikers denied Haughey power.

Now it was FitzGerald's turn to see duplicity. Britain had opened a secret channel with the IRA, bypassing the Commission, and apparently offering better terms.[109]

> Somebody in London got on to the IRA and brought them into the process and wrecked the whole thing as it happens so frequently at other times the British failure to understand how you deal with the position with the IRA precipitated the problem and led to many more deaths than had taken place because once that happened the Commission for Justice and Peace went to the Minister and said are you talking to the IRA and then alarm bells started to ring and the British pulled back and the resolution that could have happened didn't happen because of the intervention of the British with the IRA the situation should have been handled without the IRA in it so it was very badly mishandled from the British side yes by talking to the IRA at that time.[110]

This assessment was shared by Father Crilly, who remembered being spirited

---

[107] Father Oliver Crilly, interview with the author, February 2001.

[108] Statement made on 29 June 1981, reproduced in Martin Mansergh, ed., *The Spirit of the Nation: The Speeches and Statements of Charles J. Haughey (1957–1986)* (Cork, 1986), p. 491. Haughey went further in a press conference after meeting Owen Carron, who had succeeded Sands as MP for Fermanagh/West Tyrone because the British government changed electoral rules to prevent another hunger striker taking his place. He maintained that a solution had to be found on the basis of the prisoners' five demands. 'The British government must now, above all else, be made to see that the prison situation is causing serious disruption in the friendship between our two countries and having an effect on long term Anglo-Irish relations.': *ibid.*, p. 488.

[109] See David Beresford, *Ten Men Dead* (London, 1994), pp. 293–311.

[110] Garrett FitzGerald, interview with the author, Dublin, February 2001.

out of his hotel to meet Gerry Adams in a west Belfast safe-house.

> He made it clear to us that while we were carrying on our negotiations that the British Government were carrying on indirect negotiations. Well when I say indirect, direct negotiations between the British Government and Sinn Féin. Though by an indirect route, I think through phone calls from the Foreign Office or somewhere else. But while we were discussing the different details of the five demands and so on with the British Ministers, the British Government from London were carrying on a parallel negotiation. And the strange thing was, they seemed to be offering more to Gerry Adams at that time than they were offering through our particular process. But it was clearly a very confused situation and I don't know what the British Government was doing. Whether they were trying to play one off against the other to see which method would yield the most satisfactory result from their point of view – I really don't know what they were doing but I know whatever it was, it was quite mad and it blew up in everybody's face eventually.[111]

The national question had backfired on the man who had self-consciously portrayed himself as the Spirit of the Nation. Haughey's attempt to create a new dynamic failed to energise the electorate in spite of its deep concern at the mayhem in Northern Ireland. The IRA were impervious to his appeals to concede leadership of the revolution. In any case, the southern electorate had viewed the threatened revolution with increased fear, particularly after the killing of a British car manufacturing executive, Geoffrey Armstrong, while giving a lecture at Trinity College, Dublin, brought the violence home. Playing with cultural nationalism came at a price many were unwilling to pay. The northern card was now operating at a discount and, as in 1970, those most associated with entrenching southern involvement in the conflict paid the price.

The difficulties were magnified by the increasingly intolerant position adopted by the British government in its own war of position with militant republicanism. The election of Bobby Sands moved that conflict onto a higher plane, demonstrating to all sides in the conflict that the IRA could no longer be classified as an unrepresentative clique but rather an integral and dedicated part of the nationalist community. It created a paradox at the heart of British government policies in relation to Northern Ireland, between the contemplation of constitutional innovation and an over-reliance on security measures.[112] Mindful of safeguarding her tough stance on the need to criminalise the Provisionals, Mrs Thatcher was later to downgrade the December 1980 Anglo-Irish summit with Haughey and call it 'a red rag to the Unionist bull'.

> This meeting did more harm than good because, unusually, I did not involve myself closely enough in the drafting of the communiqué and, as a result,

---

[111] Oliver Crilly, interview with the author, Derry, February 2001.

[112] See Paul Arthur, *Special Relationships: Britain, Ireland and the Northern Ireland problem* (Belfast, 2000), p. 173.

> allowed through the statement that Mr Haughey and I would devote our next meeting in London to "special consideration of the totality of relationships within these islands".[113]

But another imperative was also at work, one that was to severely debilitate the search for a solution. London maintained it was caught in a deadly vice occasioned by the nationalists' refusal to accept an internal settlement, which unionists argued would provide the answer if only the government cracked down on terrorism. The British response was to develop an uneasy strategy based on making the justice system more malleable to criminalise the republican movement while simultaneously embarking on closer relations with the Irish State. Monsignor Faul, who played a pivotal role in persuading families to take their sons off the strike, ruefully remembers the consequences of British obduracy masquerading as steadfast policy.

> The funerals were gigantic things at the start and of course recruiting a lot of people. Fellows felt inspired to go and join the Provos as a result of those funerals. We made the point repeatedly to the British government. We said, "Do you think you are winning? But you're not winning. Go and look at the wakes, go and look at the funerals, look at all the young people queuing up to see these emaciated corpses. You're not winning. You're losing," but of course they couldn't see that. [114]

A network of informers and agents was recruited to penetrate the paramilitaries. The official aim was to prevent paramilitary attack. But the campaign went far beyond collating intelligence; how far was only revealed in a series of explosive television programmes exposing the dirty war in the 1980s and early 1990s. The programmes implicated an elite section of the British army called the Force Research Unit in directing terrorism and demonstrated the consequences of giving primacy to Special Branch.[115]

The emergence of FRU can be traced to the Thatcher administration's response to Warrenpoint, the hunger strikes and the intensification of the criminalisation of the IRA, a policy that succeeded only in fuelling republican support. The IRA swelled in the face of what many in the republican community saw as British intransigence and began rebuilding as both a political and military force.

---

[113] Margaret Thatcher, *The Downing Street Years 1979–1990* (New York, 1995 edition), p. 390. An authoritative Dublin source agreed: 'If Thatcher had realised the implications of the phraseology, she probably would not have signed the communiqué.' Interview with the author, 24 July 2002.

[114] Monsignor Denis Faul, interview with the author, Carrickmore, February 2001. See also 'The Hunger Strike: Dying for Ireland', *Insight*, UTV, 27 February 2001. Transcript available at http://www.utv.co.uk/insight

[115] 'Licensed to Kill, The Inside Story of FRU', 30 January 2000, and 'Policing the Police', 17 April 2001, both produced by the author. Full transcripts are available at http://www.utvinternet.com/insight

Accurate intelligence is the key element in any war and the British government went to extraordinary lengths to ensure that FRU had the resources it required to prosecute its war. The *Insight* evidence pointed not only to rogue agents or rogue units, but to widespread institutionalised criminality. A secret report forwarded to the British and Irish governments by British/Irish Rights Watch, obtained by the programme, concluded baldly:

> Agents of the state have been involved, directly and indirectly, in the murder of its citizens, in contravention of domestic law and all international human rights standards. That such alleged activities took place in the context of a bitter sectarian conflict can be no excuse. Governments are expected to operate to higher standards than those adopted by paramilitaries. If they fail to do so, then democracy itself is at risk.[116]

In a crucial finding the British/Irish report suggested that the clear reporting structures belie any suggestion that its activities including the direction of terrorism were not sanctioned at the highest levels.

> FRU was an integral unit within the intelligence corps, with detailed and clear lines of reporting within the army and clear links with MI5 and Special Branch. FRU's intelligence was reported to and relied upon by ministers.

For the Irish government the failure to take into account the political nature of the problem was augmented by an over-reliance on the military instrument as the key policy determinant. As Garret FitzGerald explained:

> They couldn't understand that moreover of course the fact that the army was used in Northern Ireland as a police force meant the support for the morale of the army tended to dominate the policy. I don't think British policy was ever single-mindedly devoted to solving the Northern Ireland problem because [of] concern to protect the army regardless of what happened. What the army was doing constantly undermined British policy.[117]

But it was a high-risk option that left the government prone to ridicule in international courts. Allegations of torture were replaced by suggestions of a 'shoot to kill' policy and, most explosively, of active collusion between FRU and loyalist paramilitaries. Innocent people died to protect paid informants in a dirty war that had no rules.

The problem facing policy makers in the 1980s, however, was that the secret dependency on a military solution served merely to exacerbate tension in Anglo-Irish relations, particularly with a leader like Haughey whose irredentism

---

[116] *Ibid.*

[117] Garrett FitzGerald, interview with the author, February 2001.

in relation to the national question encapsulated his publicly defined political value system.

Just as the search for a solution in the 1990s would be predicated on dealing directly with the Provisionals, so, too, in the aftermath of the hunger strikes a deal was worked out away from the glare of publicity in which the prisoners' core demands were effectively conceded after the fast ended. The secret channel, in turn, served to weaken the position of constitutional nationalism north and south of the border. Within days of the ending of the hunger strikes Danny Morrison posed a prescient question to the party faithful: 'Who here really believes that we can win the war through the ballot box? But will anyone here object if with a ballot paper in this hand and an Armalite in this hand, we take power in Ireland?'[118] In the prison itself, given access to reading materials for the first time since 1976, the Provisionals began the process of moving away from the politics of brute force to the politics of intercession. The strategy was to pave the way for the decommissioning of republican ideology a generation later.[119] Haughey's initiative required a hold over northern politics that had weakened dramatically in the aftermath of the Arms Crisis. The subsequent failure of the diplomatic initiative brokered at Sunningdale, which established the ill-fated 1974 power-sharing Executive, further distanced the south, hermetically sealing the conflict and the Republic's ability to influence it.

The Modern Prince, who had sought to redefine the nature of the problem by forcing the British government to accept (in principle, at least) the necessity for an Anglo-Irish approach to contain the northern problem, even as a form of crisis management, was by then long out of office. Reformulating the problem as one to be resolved by London and Dublin acting in concert was the chief ideological innovation associated with Haughey. He did not content himself with semantics or paying lip service to constitutional change, which had been the leitmotif of previous Fianna Fáil leaders, including Lemass and de Valera. The concept of the totality of relations offered the possibility, at least, of meaningful dialogue that could – and, in fact, did – eventually transform the situation.[120]

---

[118] Brendan O'Brien, *The Long War: The IRA & Sinn Féin from Armed Struggle to Peace Talks* (Dublin, updated edition 1995), p. 127.

[119] For an analysis of reading material, which contained classic left-wing tracts such as Lenin's *The State and the Revolution*, Marx's *Capital* and Frantz Fanon's *The Wretched of the Earth*, see Richard English, 'Library of the Hard Men', *Newsweek*, 31 July 2000, and 'Left on the shelf', *Fortnight*, September 2000. Professor English conducted a structural analysis of the collection and suggested there was 'a strong identification with movement elsewhere in the world pursuing revolution'. See also Kirsty Scott, 'Men of Letters, Men of Arms', *The Guardian*, 2 December 2000. For a cogent analysis of where the IRA stands today, see Eamon McCann, 'Adams Removes Mandate of History', *Belfast Telegraph*, 25 October 2001.

[120] For an examination of de Valera's use of sovereignty as an instrument of domestic 'southern' politics see John Bowman, *De Valera and the Ulster Question 1917–1873* (Oxford, 1990). For an assessment of Lemass, see Henry Patterson, 'Seán Lemass and the Ulster Question 1959–65' in *Journal of Contemporary History*, Vol. 34 (1), pp. 145–159. Patterson held that nationalism was reduced to 'an ideology of consolation' (p. 159).

The irony for Haughey was that the British government's reluctance to endorse his strategy in 1980 meant that the hegemonic conception he articulated and advanced failed because of imperatives beyond his control. Failure to take the British response into account when explaining what went wrong would seriously impoverish our understanding of the ideological cohesion at the heart of Haughey's response to the northern question.[121]

Indeed, throughout the rest of his political career Haughey never deviated from the core vision he established in 1980. He continued to use the northern question as a mechanism to defend his position within Fianna Fáil. Regrettably, with the ideological conception articulated, he turned to more base pursuits in government.

Haughey's defeat in 1981 heralded the collapse of the most ideologically driven government in the history of the Irish State. He was denied power by the separate agenda of the Provisional IRA, the very organisation he had been accused of funding in 1970. The wheel had turned full circle. Haughey was on the outside again and the political wolves were circling.

---

[121] See, for example, Bruce Arnold, *Haughey: His Life and Unlucky Deeds* (1993), p. 173.

Chapter Four

Grotesque, Unbelievable, Bizarre, Unprecedented: The Price of Power and Ambition

> When trouble is sensed well in advance it can easily be remedied; if you wait for it to show itself any medicine will be too late because the disease will have become incurable.
>
> – Machiavelli, *The Prince*, p. 10

The deep divisions within Fianna Fáil were reawakened following the failure of the party to retain power in the 1981 election. Haughey found himself under attack from three separate directions. The failure of the diplomatic initiative to deliver the promised dawn of unity, or even an approximate route map, coupled with the deepening polarisation in Northern Ireland itself as a consequence of the hunger strikes, had weakened his already precarious grip on the party. Haughey's response to the gathering economic crisis – after identifying it in his infamous address to the nation in January 1980 – was to ignore it. As the economic indicators suggested severe recession and spiralling inflation, the government released misleading budgetary figures that implied public finances were healthier than supposed. It was an attempt to buttress the party going into an election temporarily postponed because of, but overshadowed by, the Stardust dance hall fire in North Dublin and the Maze hunger strikes.

Both strategies signally failed. The electorate was not convinced and the lack of success dismayed those backbench TDs who had given their overwhelming backing to Haughey eighteen months earlier in the expectation that his alleged Midas touch could rectify the inertia preventing a balancing of the books. Before his sacking in 1970, Haughey was regarded as an innovative legislator who combined decisiveness with charisma. With the country staring over the edge of an economic precipice, many backbenchers believed that only a politician of Haughey's talents could impose some controls on the calamitous situation facing the Republic. In office he had not delivered on his promise. Taken together, the failure to secure a breakthrough on the north, the desultory efforts to control public spending, and the catastrophic withering of Lynch's twenty-seat majority legacy left Haughey exceptionally vulnerable. Overarching the malcontents was the party establishment, still not under his control and in large part still locked into the overall direction of economic policy. Waiting for an opportunity to strike, but neutral as to the issue chosen, they determined that that issue would result in the removal of Charles J. Haughey.

Through it all, the leader cautioned his party to hold its nerve: the coalition government was inherently unstable; a conversion to fiscal rectitude would destroy it within months. Power, denied by the intrusion of the northern prison dispute, 'a few quirks of the proportional representational system and the erratic behaviour of a few independent deputies'[1] would be returned. Haughey offered a clear-cut strategy to campaign directors.

> We made no rash or exaggerated promises, and we are proud of the fact that we did not... The façade of liberalism and progressiveness adopted by Fine Gael in opposition for election purposes has been swiftly jettisoned. The standards of living of the lower income group, employment for the young, the improvement of our infrastructure, all these must now be subjected to the dictates of harsh monetarism.
>
> The battle-lines are already emerging. The fight is between economic and social progress or doctrinaire monetarism. We must perfect our organisation and inflict defeat on the forces of reaction.[2]

Haughey combined economic criticism with a trenchant objection to the constitutional crusade adopted by Garret FitzGerald to make the republic more acceptable to northern unionists. There was a fundamental difference between the two leaders' respective approaches. FitzGerald was prepared, first and foremost, to make Northern Ireland work. This shift in policy would be buttressed by amendments to the overtly Catholic nature of the southern Constitution that would, in turn, effect long-term changes of attitude north of the border. Unity may have been the *de jure* goal but, the Republic's constitutional claim to the northern counties notwithstanding, the institutionalisation of the twenty-six county State was the *de facto* reality governing policy. Haughey was never prepared to cede an essentially majoritarian approach to resolving the conflict on an island-wide basis. He was prepared to countenance concessions as a gesture of good faith but not the principle of a united state. He derided FitzGerald as being unbalanced to the point of hysteria and of presenting unionists with a 'goldmine of propaganda that they will use relentlessly and remorsefully from here on in.' Speaking to political correspondents on 28 September, Haughey went further in his distrust of an interim internal solution while unionism held a guarantee that its version of society would continue to be underwritten by the British exchequer.

---

1 Charles Haughey, speech at Conference of the Fianna Fáil Constituency Directors of Election, Dublin, 19 September 1981, reproduced in Martin Mansergh, ed., *The Spirit of the Nation: The Speeches and Statements of Charles J. Haughey (1957–1986)* (Cork, 1986), pp. 520–522.

2 *Ibid.*, pp. 521–522.

> A free people can afford to be generous. A struggling people cannot and should not be so... Dr FitzGerald and his allies and can stand on their heads, turn themselves inside out, discard every belief they have ever held and it won't make any difference as long as that guarantee remains.[3]

FitzGerald's propensity to favour an internal settlement first and then make southern society more acceptable to unionism was based, according to Haughey, on:

> the remnants of that colonial mentality that still linger on in Irish life, a mentality that cannot come to terms with the concept of a separate, independent Irish Ireland... Once again we are being asked to accept a jaundiced view of ourselves. Once again we are asked to look only at our faults and to believe that somewhere else things are ordered much better than they are here and there exists a superior form of society which we must imitate.[4]

Haughey was not being unduly hawkish in this regard. The strategy drew on the support of the SDLP, now under the 'greener' leadership of John Hume and Seamus Mallon, who, like Haughey, believed that peace could only be achieved by harnessing international support to effect a change in British policy. This stood in stark contrast to the proposals put forward by Fine Gael, Labour and the dissidents within Fianna Fáil who argued that Northern Ireland was best handled at a distance.[5]

Denied a mandate from the people, Haughey was depicted in the southern media as being slow to engage in meaningful policy formulation, preparing instead for the imminent demise of the coalition government. An article in *Magill* magazine dismissed Haughey as an arthritic vulture brooding about the loss of power and waiting sullenly for the opportunity to regain it.[6] The article's author, Olivia O'Leary, poured scorn on the difference in approach towards Northern Ireland between Haughey and FitzGerald, and saw in the Fianna Fáil leader a carping, malign presence in the Dáil chamber.

---

[3] Quoted in Martin Mansergh, ed., *ibid.*, p. 522.

[4] Charles Haughey, speech at the Unveiling of the de Valera Memorial, Ennis, 11 October 1981, reproduced in Martin Mansergh, ed., *ibid.*, p. 524. See also speech at the Ógra Fianna Fáil Conference on Northern Ireland, 17 October 1981, pp. 529–532. Haughey argued that accommodation must be two-way.

> I must say very frankly that the Unionist establishment has not made any real efforts over the years to come to terms with the rest of the inhabitants of this island, and to live in peace and unity with them. They cannot totally disregard and defy the wishes of the majority of the people on this island indefinitely, and the stark consequences of trying to do so have become acutely apparent in the last twelve years. (p. 530)

[5] The key role played here was by Seamus Mallon, Haughey's appointee to the Dublin senate in 1983. For details of how the alliance worked in practice see Olivia O'Leary, 'Haughey at the Forum', *Magill*, May 1984.

[6] Olivia O'Leary, 'Charles Haughey: Waiting, Watching and Waiting', *Magill*, December 1981, pp. 8–14.

Haughey's critics within Fianna Fáil were prepared to countenance change but Haughey was not prepared to even debate it. It was a choice that was to exacerbate the smouldering divisions within the party, intensifying the animosity towards him felt by Colley, O'Malley and Seamus Brennan. When Brennan sought to sketch out Fianna Fáil policy on constitutional change in an address to a party meeting in Cork, Haughey made him withdraw the speech. Haughey's considered response to the murmurings of discontent was to retreat into silence, where only the leader could enunciate policy. Olivia O'Leary reached for Dickens to extend her scathing metaphor: 'Like Miss Haversham and her wedding cake, he concedes nothing. Expectations intact, he waits, and watches, and waits.'[7]

Not prepared to wait, a backbencher, Charlie McCreevy, launched a coruscating attack in a newspaper interview in December 1981, condemning the lack of economic coherence in Fianna Fáil policy. McCreevy argued against the nihilism he identified as stultifying a response to the country's economic woes: 'We seem to be against everything and for nothing.'[8] He had long despaired of the malign consequences of economic policy adopted by the party. In January 1980 he observed that 'general elections seem to be developing into an auction in promises. We are so hell bent in assuming power that we are prepared to do anything for it'.[9] As seasoned political commentator Vincent Browne pointed out, the speech, delivered in the immediate aftermath of Haughey's television address admonishing the people of Ireland that they were living beyond their means, received little interest.

Two years later McCreevy was no longer a Haughey acolyte. While adopting a hard line on Northern Ireland, along with his friend Síle de Valera, he regarded his leader's broken promises on the economy a gross betrayal. Disillusion with Haughey had set in. Browne, himself an early supporter of Haughey, regarded his tenure as both 'insipid' and nothing short of disastrous. In the article he listed twenty-nine deputies hostile to Haughey's continued tenure. As late as July 1982, Browne still felt it important to note mitigating factors for a lack of decisiveness. On balance, Haughey was unfairly treated. 'It is certainly true that he has disappointed those expectations but his failure to live up to them hasn't been entirely of his own doing and it is only fair that this should be acknowledged.'[10]

Then he was merely re-articulating party policy, but by December he had identified his leader as the barrier to progress. It signified the open declaration of a civil war within the party that was to consume the Soldiers of Destiny for the next decade. Haughey was fighting not only for the support of the electorate

---

7 *Ibid.*, p. 14. For an assessment of O'Leary's attitude to Haughey see J.J. O'Molloy, 'Pioneers of Tough Adversary Political Journalism', *Magill*, January 1982, a profile of O'Leary and Geraldine Kennedy. According to O'Molloy, O'Leary regarded Haughey as a 'political degenerate' (p. 13). Both women were to become pivotal figures in Irish political journalism.

8 *Sunday Tribune*, 27 December 1981, in Vincent Browne, 'Charlie McCreevy: An End To Political Hedonism', *Magill*, January 1982, p. 19.

9 *Ibid.*

10 Vincent Browne, 'What's Bugging Haughey?', *Magill*, July 1982.

but political survival within Fianna Fáil itself. It was only to conclude with the final resignation of Charles J. Haughey a decade later because of actions taken in what was to become his nightmare year: 1982.

The collapse of the coalition government in January of that year, over an ill-judged decision not to make children's shoes exempt from VAT on the spurious grounds that it would be advantageous for women with small feet, provided the 'arthritic vulture', in O'Leary's vitriolic terminology, an opportunity to reclaim power. The spat with McCreevy over the lack of economic focus, which had led to the withdrawal of the whip from the outspoken Kildare TD, was set aside as power beckoned. Once again, Haughey was denied an overall majority in one of the most divisive election campaigns ever witnessed in Irish politics. Although the result has often been characterised as a failure on Haughey's part, in fact it is better described as inconclusive. The breakthrough of Sinn Féin/the Workers' Party and an array of independents shattered the political mould and led to a fundamental change in voting strength, ensuring that no single party, even Fianna Fáil, would ever be in a position to govern alone again.

In the interregnum between the election and the first meeting of the Dáil, as the main political parties attempted to cobble together an administration with the help of ideologically disparate partners, Des O'Malley now positioned himself to battle for the leadership of Fianna Fáil. What precisely he was standing for, other than widespread antipathy towards Haughey, was unclear.

As Haughey's critics began pushing stories of dissent and fear into the media, Ray Burke and Brian Lenihan tried unsuccessfully to get O'Malley to withdraw. The publication of a list of forty-six TDs said to be hostile to Haughey's continuing leadership backfired dramatically.[11] It exposed many TDs who may have been prepared to vote against Haughey but did not want to appear disloyal. It also served to provide Haughey with useful background intelligence on those he needed to turn. Haughey brought a number of young TDs into his office and outlined the potential for advancement. It was a clear intimation that advancement was predicated on voting in support of Haughey if a challenge was to materialise.

As the plotters plotted, Haughey estimated that the best form of defence was to attack. Ray MacSharry went on RTÉ radio to warn publicly that the party would not forgive anyone whose actions led to the denial of power. In the absence of a formal announcement, McCreevy, by then managing Des O'Malley's undeclared campaign, was reduced to speaking in hypothetical riddles on the lunchtime bulletins. The marked difference in the performances effectively ended the contest before it even began. Liam Lawlor, an astute reader of the political barometer, who was instrumental in the behind-the-scenes lobbying of TDs in support of O'Malley, met Haughey and effectively resigned from the proto challenge.[12] Despite the fact that Fianna Fáil again failed to secure a commanding

[11] Bruce Arnold, *Irish Independent*, 24 February 1982; Stephen Collins, *The Haughey File: The Unprecedented Career and Last Years of The Boss* (Dublin, 1992), p.56.

[12] See Joe Joyce and Peter Murtagh, *The Boss* (Dublin, 1997), pp. 37–39. It remains unclear whether Lawlor was acting as an emissary for Haughey from the start or whether he saw the potential of

electoral majority in a contest centred on Haughey's fitness for office, his rivals lacked demonstrable courage in their convictions.

Ultimately, Haughey's position as party leader was safeguarded because of the clash of egos in the ranks of those opposed to him. The major players, along with O'Malley, were George Colley and Martin O'Donoghue. All three desperately wanted the leadership: each needed the support of the others because none had the political wherewithal to mount an overt challenge. It was a weak and decidedly amateurish performance that stood in marked contrast to what the party leader was potentially offering: power and the patronage that comes from it. As a combination, it made Haughey impossible to beat, a fact acknowledged by Martin O'Donoghue, the chief co-conspirator, who, at the last moment, disassociated himself from the challenge, leading to O'Malley's ignominious withdrawal.

As the horse-trading for real power – the formation of a government – began in earnest, with Haughey now once again at the helm of his party, the negotiating prowess of the two main political leaders came into play. The deal brokered, conducted against a backdrop of a divided Fianna Fáil and hostile bids from Fine Gael, was, as even Haughey's most ardent critics conceded, a superb piece of political machination.[13]

The key lay in negotiating with three TDs returned for Sinn Féin/the Workers' Party (SFWP) and a Dublin activist representing the heroin-infested, decayed north inner-city, an area long ignored by the political mainstream since the slum clearances of the 1930s. What made the deal all the more remarkable was the fact that SFWP was a parliamentary party that had shared ideological principles with the Official IRA in the past. The Official IRA had claimed publicly in 1969 that Haughey, then Minister for Finance, had sought to split the republican movement.[14] Now SFWP wanted assurances from Haughey that the northern question would be handled sympathetically.[15] This would be a

---

advancement evaporating because of the amateur nature of the challenge and switched support in pursuit of his own self-interest. Either way the Dublin TD received nothing from Haughey for his information and lost the trust of the alternate leadership for his betrayal.

[13] For a detailed summary of the deal and how it was brokered see Joe Joyce and Peter Murtagh, *ibid.*, pp. 45–62. See also Bruce Arnold, *Haughey, His Life and Unlucky Deeds* (London, 1993), pp. 194–195. For a contemporaneous assessment of its implications see Pat Brennan, 'A Short Measure?', *Magill*, April 1982, pp. 20–22.

[14] *United Irishman*, October 1969. For discussion of the importance of these revelations, see Justin O'Brien, *The Arms Trial* (Dublin, 2000), pp. 75–76. The leader of SFWP, Tomás Mac Giolla, was to repeat the allegation in 1999. 'It will all come out, but I will be long in my grave at that time. But I can assure you that they did set up the Provisional IRA.' For full details see Justin O'Brien, *ibid.*, pp. 93–94.

[15] See Vincent Browne, 'In the Shadow of a Gunman', *Magill*, April 1982, and 'The Secret World of SFWP', *Magill*, May 1982, a series of exposés of Sinn Féin/the Workers' Party. As Browne noted: 'the fact that the Official IRA is still active, while the leadership of the movement persists in denying knowledge of it, is a manifestation of the many contradictions at the heart of the party.' Surprisingly, the articles omit any mention of the fact that SFWP support was instrumental in propping up the minority government.

difficult promise to make, given Haughey's need to keep on board Neil Blaney, a co-accused at the initial stage of the Arms Trial, who not only relished his involvement in establishing the Provisional IRA but who had consistently advocated the single-minded pursuit of unity. The price for Blaney's support was that Haughey would translate the rhetoric of opposition into policy in power.[16] That Haughey could square these competing imperatives was a remarkable achievement.

The kingmaker was the independent TD Tony Gregory, a tough-talking activist from the inner city who knew that power came at a price that all political parties were prepared to countenance but only Haughey was prepared to pay up-front. Meetings were arranged with Haughey, Michael O'Leary of Labour and the Fine Gael leader, Garret FitzGerald, in which the stall was set out and prices set. Haughey attended the meetings with a retinue of advisors and presented Gregory with a bound folder containing detailed costing of the plans he was prepared to underwrite (although he did not give any real indication of how the government was going to pay for such largesse).

Haughey's success lay in taking Gregory seriously. He was helped by a chance meeting between the negotiating team behind Gregory and the Irish Transport and General Workers Union (ITGWU) general secretary, Michael Mullan. Mullan was a close confidant of Haughey's who had organised the union's brass band to play Haughey onto the stage for his first presidential Árd Fheis in 1980.[17] In some respects Haughey was the only option for the activists. Michael O'Leary of Labour appeared uninterested and, to some observers, FitzGerald's approach was 'slow and misdirected'.[18] By contrast, not only did Haughey respond to the activists with detailed spending commitments on housing in the north inner-city, they exceeded Dublin Corporation's budgetary capacity for the entire metropolitan area. According to Gene Kerrigan, Haughey was so messianic in his desire for power that some concessions were simply forgotten about in the final document. These included a potential freeze on bus fare increases, an issue that in normal circumstances would have been fundamentally important to perceptions about the effectiveness of political representatives in deprived areas.

---

[16] See interview with Peter Taylor, 'The Spark that lit the Bonfire', *Timewatch*, BBC, 27 January 1993. Full details of Blaney's role are included in Justin O'Brien, *The Arms Trial* (Dublin, 2000).

[17] Haughey had longstanding links with the ITGWU. In the midst of the Arms Trial he fulfilled a prior commitment to address the union on the fiftieth anniversary of Liberty Hall: Charles Haughey, 'Tribute to the ITGWU', 6 October 1970, reproduced in Martin Mansergh, ed., *The Spirit of the Nation: The Speeches and Statements of Charles J. Haughey (1957–1986)* (Cork, 1986), p. 141.

[18] Gene Kerrigan, 'Pushing on the open door: How Haughey came to terms with the Gregory team', *Magill*, March 1982. The editor of *Magill*, Vincent Browne, was so indignant that Fine Gael was prepared to sell its soul for power that he commissioned a caricature of FitzGerald as a prostitute. Browne lost his opportunity to print this, however, because of 'Haughey's astounding deal' (p. 15). This was not a compliment. Browne had campaigned for years against the policies that were threatening the nation with bankruptcy. In the same issue Kevin Boland, who had resigned from Fianna Fáil in the aftermath of the Arms Crisis, traced the rot in both parties to the Arms Trial. See Kevin Boland, 'The Tree We Planted is Rotten', *Magill*, March 1982.

Throughout the negotiations Haughey kept repeating the phrase: 'You're pushing an open door.' As Kerrigan astutely pointed out:

> For once, due to a freak result and a second hung Dáil, a group of people who had for years fought a hard fight in an area – both geographically and politically – which had got the short end of the stick, found the going easy. They merely had to point again at the issues at which they had been pointing for years – and this time they got more than platitudes.[19]

In return, Haughey captured the Department of the Taoiseach, heading a minority administration propped up by ideologically disparate factions. Haughey defended his decisions in a speech to the Dáil that revealed the true extent of the price paid. Blaney's continued support was assured by Haughey's commitment not only to the right to national self-determination but for the British to commit to a date for a final withdrawal from Northern Ireland. Again, the Taoiseach maintained that although improved communal relations should be welcomed, they alone could not replace the underlying dynamic for change: 'overall responsibility for satisfactorily resolving the problem lies with the two sovereign Governments and must be exercised by them.'[20] A key advisor to Haughey at this stage suggested that Haughey calculated the trade-off to be feasible because no movement on Anglo-Irish policy was going to be possible as a consequence of the hunger strikes. The polarisation of the communities within Northern Ireland meant that the British government was not going to return to the template agreed at the December 1980 summit. Haughey was not prepared to settle for less, partly because of Blaney, and parked the initiative. This apparent hardening of policy was, therefore, a rhetorical republicanism designed for domestic consumption rather than a wilful lurch towards destabilisation.

The ideological balancing act needed to accommodate the wildly disparate positions enunciated by Blaney and Sinn Féin/the Workers' Party, while singularly impressive, was not the focus of media attention. Instead, it centred on the Gregory deal, derided as 'squandermania' in *Magill*. Haughey was unapologetic.

> The revival of the inner city of our national capital is in the interests of the whole nation. Our aim is to recreate a Dublin of which the nation can be proud, and to provide an imaginative approach to a problem which exists in many other countries.
>
> Our success in dealing with these problems will be a headline for similar areas in every part of the country.[21]

---

[19] Gene Kerrigan, 'Pushing on the open door: How Haughey came to terms with the Gregory team', *Magill*, March 1982, p. 14.

[20] *Dáil Debates*, vol. 33, col. 38, 9 March 1982.

[21] Charles Haughey, speech at Nomination of Members of Government, Dáil Éireann, 9 March 1982, reproduced in Martin Mansergh, ed., *The Spirit of the Nation: The Speeches and Statements of Charles J. Haughey (1957–1986)* (Cork, 1986), pp. 597–598.

Des O'Malley, the putative challenger, was sidelined during the negotiations which heralded a return to office. Still in the Cabinet and locked into the economic decision-making process, his presence was de facto acceptance that the price for Fianna Fáil remaining in power involved Haughey and his spending commitments. O'Malley, in attempting to obtain the leadership in the midst of what for the party was a more important struggle (i.e. that of securing power), had demonstrated, yet again, a failure to understand the reality of playing internal party politics. It was a flaw he never managed to overcome. O'Malley's problem was, always, timing. True, he managed to force Haughey's final expulsion from the leadership a decade later but, by that stage, it was as a destructive power from without. O'Malley had been expelled from Fianna Fáil long before then. Despite his undoubted political flaws, Haughey was simply too able for his internal political opponents. At every stage he outwitted them with audacious political manoeuvres and bullied them into submission. He displayed not only a much better understanding of the ideological underpinnings of Fianna Fáil outside the confines of Leinster House, but in this period also demonstrated his astute ability to use that knowledge to curtail any nexus of power developing independent of his control within the parliamentary party itself. In short, his mastery of the black arts of political persuasion was second to none. Albert Reynolds was in no doubt that 'Haughey was the most brilliant politician of his generation, a master strategist.'[22]

The penalty for such dexterity was the infamous GUBU period, an acronym coined by Conor Cruise O'Brien from Haughey's blustering response to the fact that a man later convicted of a brutal murder was apprehended in the private apartment of the Attorney General. Haughey had variously termed the course of events 'grotesque', 'unprecedented', 'bizarre', and 'unbelievable'. In O'Brien's estimation, that just about summed up the defeated Haughey administration.[23] In some ways it was fair. Crisis management became, of necessity, the leitmotif of an inherently volatile administration in which the dominant party was itself hopelessly divided. The behaviour of Haughey's 1982 government would raise serious questions about the nature of the democratic process in the Republic. It made a mockery of Cabinet government, planted the seeds for Haughey's final downfall a decade later, blurred the dividing line between the executive and the police, and institutionalised a culture of political corruption that is only now becoming apparent.

The government fell within eight months, hopelessly wounded in its final stage specifically by the refusal of Jim Gibbons to participate in a vote-pairing arrangement with a Fine Gael TD. If he had acquiesced to a ruse involving a threat to return to the Dáil from his hospital bed, the government would have been saved from defeat on a finance Bill. In more general terms, an open revolt

---

22 Interview with Albert Reynolds, Dublin, December 2001.

23 The most detailed exposition of travails facing the 1982 administration can be found in Joe Joyce and Peter Murtagh, *The Boss* (Dublin, 1997).

around the Cabinet table exacerbated matters.[24] Charlie McCreevy again became the stalking horse in an unplanned challenge over economic policy. Haughey demanded not only his expulsion but also a public display of Cabinet solidarity at the next meeting of parliamentary party. According to O'Malley, this was presented as an ultimatum.

> He informed the Cabinet that every member of the Cabinet would have to sign a document pledging total unwavering loyalty to him as leader and of course I pointed out to him that this was not a Cabinet matter but a parliamentary matter and every member of the parliamentary party, whether they were a minister or a backbencher, had an equal voice and equal vote there. I was not prepared to transfer a parliamentary matter to a Cabinet matter so he more or less told us that if we did not he would not retain us in the Cabinet.[25]

O'Malley and Martin O'Donoghue preferred resignation to declaring loyalty to the leader under whom they served and which had fallen primarily because of the withdrawal of support by the government's partners.

Haughey finally identified and began to advocate tough spending controls. As a consequence, he lost the crucial backing of Sinn Féin/the Workers' Party for the forthcoming election. He went to the country on the economic blueprint, *The Way Forward*, a document formulated in part and endorsed by the departing ministers. For O'Malley, the issue at stake was a parliamentary matter and not the preserve of the executive. His resignation was portrayed, rather incongruously, as a point of principle when in fact the leadership challenge was based on an open assault by outside, leftist forces on the economic manifesto agreed by the Cabinet of which he was a member. There appeared to be little or no difference in economic or social policy and therefore no real basis for success. In this last matter Haughey showed an adroit and scheming handling of the political process, a fact acknowledged by O'Malley, who has since suggested, somewhat naïvely, that Haughey did not play by the rules.

> Many of the votes in the parliamentary party during that GUBU period were not genuine votes at all because he used to insist, contrary to the rules, that the votes were open even though the rules prescribed that they were to be secret. The way he sought to justify that was by having an open vote as to whether or not we should have an open vote but that, of course, was intimidatory.[26]

---

[24] The difficulties Haughey faced mirrored John Major's problems with what the British Prime Minister memorably described in an unguarded moment as the 'Euro-sceptic bastards' inside the British Cabinet 1995–97. For a riveting examination of British Cabinet government see Michael Cokerell's superlative documentary *Cabinet Confidential*, BBC2, 17 November 2001.

[25] *Des O'Malley: A Public Life*, RTÉ 1, broadcast April/May 2001.

[26] *Ibid.* This view is dismissed contemptuously by senior Fianna Fáil figures. 'O'Malley is guilty of acute moral hypocrisy' was the considered opinion of one former Taoiseach, presumably because if O'Malley had demonstrated loyalty to the administration, no rules would have been broken: interview with the author.

For Haughey and his dwindling supply of declared allies, however, such thinking as O'Malley's was simply unacceptable in any system of Cabinet government. The refusal to back the leader on an issue of economic policy going into an election suggested a certain degree of stubbornness, despite the provocation. In an interview three months later, on the eve of a crucial party meeting to decide his fate, Haughey suggested as much in a softly-spoken but devastating attack on the ambition of O'Malley. This was achieved by declaring simply that he would leave it to the judgment of ordinary people to decide 'whether two men who accepted positions in the Government from me should have not have left at that critical juncture'.

> I must accept some blame for the present state of the party, to what extent again I think only history will decide. All I can say about that is that I have tried. . . . I have been patient with people. I have put up with a great deal, and as I said I kept people in my Government and in positions of authority in the party when every political instinct would have told me not to do so. In fact I am now blamed that I didn't put people out of the party long ago, but I've tried as I say to preserve the unity of the party, to try and keep it together as best I could, keep the diverse factions together. Now if I didn't succeed in that, then of course I must accept some of the blame, but I believe the blame lies primarily elsewhere, in those who from the word go, from the day I became leader, refused to accept that position and fought this battle ever since, which is now culminating.[27]

As a result of the feuding, the party went into a third general election campaign in eighteen months demonstrating a pathological propensity towards internecine feuding. It was hardly surprising in these circumstances that the party failed to gain an overall majority; remarkably, in fact, support only slipped two percentage points, enough on previous occasions to form a majority government.[28] What was unusual, however, was Haughey's ability to reassert control in spite of the dissidents' diagnosis that electoral calamity could be traced directly to Haughey's failure to unify the party and hence the country. As a mobilising strategy for his opponents, not only did it have the advantage of being self-fulfilling, it allowed for an unctuous display of political posturing.

Simultaneously, nowhere was Haughey's political dexterity more acutely displayed than in the chaotic months surrounding the fall of the government, in which the true extent of the feuding within Fianna Fáil was ruthlessly exposed by the Fine Gael Minister for Justice, Michael Noonan. Noonan had called for an investigation into media allegations that his predecessor, Sean Doherty, had

---

[27] Charles Haughey interview with Gerald Barry, *This Week*, RTÉ, 6 February 1983, reproduced in the following day's *Irish Times*.

[28] See James Downey, 'The hidden achievement of Fianna Fáil', *Irish Times*, 1 December 1982. Downey argued that the divisions within the Fianna Fáil party and its loss of the no-confidence motion on a key economic policy Bill rendered meaningless the party's 'trump card' of stable government. A unified party under Haughey or his opponents could have made the difference.

abused his position and unacceptably politicised the gardaí. The reports, revealing illegal telephone tapping of prominent journalists and Cabinet-level bugging, re-lit the touchpaper within Fianna Fáil. It was only a matter of time before the explosive divisions within the party detonated.

It is by assessing how Haughey extricated himself from his government's failings before being ensnared by its dubious legacy a decade later that another key facet of the enigma that is Charles J. Haughey comes into view: the desire and ambition for power and its maintenance at any price. The omens for Haughey's survival in the confused months of January and February 1983 were, to say the least, inauspicious. He appeared, if press reports were to be believed, destined for political obscurity. It was Haughey's ability to tap into the mood of rejection within the broader party following the loss of power in 1982 that ultimately paved the way for his retention of the leadership. It was an ability underestimated by reporting at the time, particularly after the traditionally loyal *Irish Press* published what was, in effect, a political obituary.[29]

The publication of the Department of Justice report was damning in the extreme. Haughey's appointee at Justice had engaged in the illegal phone-tapping of two influential journalists, Bruce Arnold of the *Irish Independent* and Geraldine Kennedy of the *Sunday Tribune*.[30] The appointee had run the Department of Justice like a personal fiefdom and stood accused of unacceptable political interference in the day-to-day operations of the gardaí, thereby drawing it into disrepute. More evidence of the paranoia and distrust that characterised the administration emerged when it was disclosed by Michael Noonan that a further Fianna Fáil Cabinet Minister, Ray MacSharry, had taped a conversation with fellow Minister Martin O'Donoghue immediately after the leadership challenge in October. He stated that the equipment was provided by the gardaí and transcribed by civil servants.[31]

---

[29] *Irish Press*, 27 January 1983. For detail on the decision to publish see Mark O'Brien, *De Valera, Fianna Fáil and the* Irish Press: *The Truth in the News?* (Dublin, 2001), pp. 176–177. O'Brien quoted the editor of the paper, Tim Pat Coogan, saying the obituary 'was put aside with a note attached telling the printers to include it in a supplement if Haughey was ousted, but it was put in by mistake. It was a cock-up rather than a conspiracy.' Yet O'Brien quoted Michael Mills, the paper's political correspondent, saying that he had informed the news editor on duty that Haughey had not resigned, as 'I knew Haughey was not of the resigning character'. Interestingly, the day before the fiasco Mills had written a front-page lead adopting a diametrically opposed position with the legend that 'the resignation of Mr Charles J Haughey as leader of the party was imminent'. Stephen Collins suggested that Haughey made the decision to stay after a meeting with Neil Blaney and P.J. Mara in which he declared in earthy language: 'I think we'll fight the cunts.' Quoted, unsourced, in Stephen Collins, *The Haughey File: The Unprecedented Career and Last Years of The Boss* (Dublin, 1992), p. 64.

[30] Bruce Arnold, 'Why they bugged me', *The Times*, 23 January 1992.

[31] The transcript of an hour's conversation between Ray MacSharry and Martin O'Donoghue on 21 October 1982 was published in Joe Joyce and Peter Murtagh, *The Boss* (Dublin, 1997), pp. 369–382, Appendix D. The full statements issued by the Department of Justice under Michael Noonan on 20 January 1983 are reproduced in Appendix E, pp. 385–396.

In a crucial exchange O'Donoghue suggested the possibility of a deal with Labour to safeguard the stability of the government – but only if Haughey was removed from office. That deal would be impossible to broker with Haughey in place because 'there is too much history'. Labour would not interfere in the leadership election, as long as the winner was not Haughey.

> They say that it is obviously our business, that certainly if [*sic*] their point would be if there was any change in the Fianna Fáil leadership that would put them in the position where they could say that this is a new situation give the new man a chance, let's see what policies they are going to put forward.

O'Donoghue then suggested that money could be made available to get people to switch allegiance. 'What was being said was if there was any suggestion of somebody being compromised financially that it would be sorted out.' Crucially, that money would only be payable to Fianna Fáil if Haughey was deposed. 'There is a lot of money allright [sic] but not for CJ [Haughey] not for him to stay.' O'Donoghue also suggested that Haughey himself might be compromised and could be forced to go.

> I would see the easiest way of doing it is that yourself and a 4 or 5 other senior cabinet people went to CJ and said time to resign.
>
> *MacSharry*: You that man better that I do [sic].
>
> *O'Donoghue*: Then allright you have to face him and say of [sic] you will not go peacefully do you want to be humiliated because there is a way of doing that too. I agree once you agree to make the decisions there is no turning back.[32]

By February that threat to expose Haughey's precarious financial position had not been followed through. His opponents, however, believed that this time, finally and inevitably, the palace coup would usurp the Modern Prince. It was, they claimed, an administration in which the dining room of the Abbeville estate had become the dangerous nexus of political and security power: defending the nation conflated into defending Charlie.

The death of Clement Coughlan, TD, in a road accident on the way to a crucial meeting of the parliamentary party, provided Haughey with much-needed respite. The dissidents wanted the meeting on the leadership issue to go ahead the day after the funeral but were prevented from even making their case by the party chairman, Jim Tunney, who deemed the discussion of such matters, in the immediate aftermath of a TD's death, inappropriate. The dissidents, whose numbers had now swelled to include the two former ministers George Colley and Bobby Molloy, each with reason to despise Haughey, were furious.[33] Sources

---

[32] All quotations from the MacSharry/O'Donoghue recording transcript, *ibid.*

[33] *Irish Times*, 3 February 1983.

quoted in the *Irish Times* suggested that Tunney had literally 'run out the door' rather than permit the parliamentary party to vote no-confidence in Haughey. Tunney stood accused of outrageous partisan behaviour.[34] A petition was circulated, which eventually included the names of forty-one TDs and seven senators, demanding an immediate meeting to discuss the leadership.

The number far exceeded the twenty-two TDs who actually voted against Haughey. The discrepancy can be explained, in part, by the fact that senators and European TDs were able to sign but not vote in the key issue of the leadership no-confidence debate. That being said, it has been consistently alleged that Haughey supporters only pledged allegiance to the motion in order to ascertain the tactics to be deployed by the Opposition. Although the issue has never been settled satisfactorily, the behaviour of Liam Lawlor in the earlier challenge suggests that both sides were involved in intrigue and subterfuge.

Attempts by the chief whip, Bertie Ahern, to broker a compromise failed to cool the political atmosphere. Ahern had argued for a delay until the following week to allow the party to make an informed decision, based on the publication of an internal report into the ministerial bugging incident involving O'Donoghue and MacSharry. Senator Eoin Ryan maintained that Haughey should go, as 'to allow the matter to stay unsettled through another long weekend would put intolerable strain on the party and on individual deputies'.[35] Despite their fury, however, there was little the dissidents could do but make their way to the village of Frosses in County Donegal for the interment of Coughlan, where talk of the impending political demise of Haughey was expected to overshadow their grief. The *Irish Times* editorial called for Haughey to put an end to a spectacle best characterised as 'vaingloriousness shading into narcissism'.[36] The clever use of propaganda and news management, which the paper identified in Haughey's response to the leadership crisis from the beginning, but which was in truth was mainly driven by the dissidents, was now reaching a critical denouement.

Haughey resolved to hit back before the grave had been filled, determined not to be buried too. He authorised the Fianna Fáil press office to release a statement at half-past five in the evening, too late for opponents to arrange a counter-response for publication in the following day's papers. The appeal for unity would provide the backdrop of the funeral at which the party leader would give the oration. Petty squabbles over power would contrast with Haughey paying his respects to a former colleague, an honour bestowed upon him by virtue of his office; the image would be rendered more powerful precisely because Coughlan had openly declared his hostility to Haughey. The statement called on the entire organisation to row in behind Haughey's leadership.

---

[34] Tunney denied he was acting in a partisan manner and accused the media of 'frightening distortions': *Irish Times*, 4 February 1983, p. 5.

[35] *Irish Times*, 3 February 1983.

[36] Editorial, 'Better now', *Irish Times*, 3 February 1983. See also Maurice Walsh, 'The word according to whom?', *Irish Times*, 1 February 1983.

> The issue that faces Fianna Fáil today goes to the very heart of its existence. Are its policies and its leader in future to be decided for it by the media, by alien influences, by political opponents or worst of all by business interests pursuing their own ends?... If the forces hostile to Fianna Fáil and everything it stands for were ever to taste the triumph of bringing down one Fianna Fáil leader by these tactics[,] no future leader could ever again hope to withstand them successfully.[37]

Haughey himself denigrated what he termed 'a largely hostile media and political opponents at home and abroad'. He had an appointment with destiny. 'I have decided that it is my duty in the best interests of the party to which I have devoted all my political life to stay and lead it forward out of these present difficulties.' This time the stakes could not be higher. Haughey concluded with a warning.

> I am therefore calling on all members of the party to rally behind me as their democratically elected leader and give me that total support that I need to restore unity and stability, to re-organise the party, to give it a new sense of purpose, to restate our policies, to re-establish and implement the traditional code of party discipline, and to make it clear that those who bring the party into disrepute, cause dissension or refuse to accept decisions democratically arrived at can no longer remain in the party.[38]

Given the fractious nature of the parliamentary party, Haughey came across as effectively appealing to local constituencies, where his support remained strong despite the scandal permeating Leinster House. The message was clear: declare fidelity to his leadership, leave or be dismissed. It was, as one deputy told Dick Walsh of the *Irish Times*, 'High Noon' for the Soldiers of Destiny.[39] Des O'Malley, who had been widely touted as the main beneficiary of Haughey's downfall, intoned that '[t]he implications for the party and for parliamentary democracy generally are very serious'.[40] Without a trace of irony, he was reported as saying that the 'incredible and amazing' statement he had heard on the car radio on the way back from the Donegal funeral was confirming evidence that 'Mr Haughey obviously wants to split the party'.[41]

It was a view shared, in public at least, by two of Haughey's up-and-coming lieutenants, Ray Burke and Liam Lawlor. The two TDs, whose careers were later to suffer disgrace with revelations at the Flood Tribunal into allegations of planning corruption in Dublin, had personally delivered the petition earlier

---

[37] Charles Haughey statement. Full text published in *Irish Times*, 4 February 1983, and reproduced in Martin Mansergh, ed., *The Spirit of the Nation: The Speeches and Statements of Charles J. Haughey (1957–1986)* (Cork, 1986), pp. 725–727.

[38] *Ibid.*

[39] *Irish Times*, 4 February 1983, p. 1.

[40] Quoted in *Irish Times*, *ibid.*

[41] *Ibid.*, p. 5.

in the week to Haughey. Burke reasoned that the decision to jettison Haughey was as essential to the survival of the greatest political organisation in Ireland as it was personally painful. Burke conferred with Haughey again in Donegal Town and advised him to step aside, before attending a very public lunch with Lawlor. Burke posed a rhetorical question to an *Irish Times* reporter.

> What I cannot understand at this stage, and I wish somebody could explain it to me, is why Charlie Haughey himself does not see that the great majority of the party want him to stand aside – not as a matter of disgrace or dishonour but simply to allow somebody new to take over. It is nothing at all personal against Mr Haughey.[42]

But for Haughey this was the central point. His leadership had been undermined by a damaging campaign of information leaking and innuendo emanating from the Cabinet table, a situation that had made effective government all but impossible. One senior minister at the time suggested that the country was rendered ungovernable because of the stasis at Cabinet, a responsibility he laid firmly at the door of the dissidents who had never given Haughey a chance.[43] The dissidents, through their contracts in the media, were not acting in the interests of the party but in their own cause by undermining the leader. The extent of this manipulation became apparent as the crisis unfolded and, paradoxically, was central to how Haughey created his strategy for survival. With the Árd Fheis only weeks away, Haughey was seen as attempting to usurp the power of the parliamentary party; the cult of the personality was being taken to absurdly Maoist levels. The *Irish Times* editorial writer chose a different international comparator.

> Are we in the world of the Hitler *Bunker* of the last days of the 1939–45 war when the Fuehrer, scores of feet below ground in Berlin, thought he could guide the fortunes of his country to a successful close?
>
> As we know from diaries of the survivors and war records, he pored over out-of-date maps and frantically sent divisions that did not exist to stop the Russian advance; he despatched what were little more than platoons of boy scouts to fulfil the role of whole armies.
>
> Is Mr Haughey playing the same game?...
>
> He may split Fianna Fáil into two parties. But the wonder is, to the outsider, how one man fights so hard and forty fellow-members of the same party are so obviously mesmerised. He is in so many ways a record-breaker.[44]

---

[42] *Ibid.*

[43] Albert Reynolds, interview with the author, Dublin, December 2001.

[44] Editorial, 'Bunker Politics?', *Irish Times*, 4 February 1983. It did not go unnoticed that the week marked the fiftieth anniversary of Hitler's accession to the German chancellery. A benign reading of events is that the Nazi reference was unintended by the *Irish Times*. The Colley family, however, took a much more propagandist view, comparing Haughey to Hitler. The paper discreetly quoted Mrs Mary Colley saying that people were ringing her with messages of support and were drawing

The poisonous atmosphere intensified over the weekend when Charlie McCreevy gave an interview describing Haughey as a 'disgrace to the democratic tradition of Fianna Fáil and the Irish Nation' and as a man who led a 'self-centred, advance-seeking cabal of opportunists.'[45] The editor of the paper later defended the interview on the basis that, although the *Sunday Press* was generally supportive of Fianna Fáil, the Haughey era had placed it in an acute dilemma: 'Which part of the party were the papers to support?'[46]

The day before the parliamentary meeting Haughey gave a lengthy interview to RTÉ. He castigated his critics, arguing that it was unacceptable that 'any small rump in the party, combined with friends in the media and other people outside the party, should be in a position to dictate who is leader of Fianna Fáil.'[47] Haughey conceded that he would give up the leadership and the presidency of the party should he lose. In so doing he removed in an instant what journalist Dick Walsh termed 'a threat, implicit in last Thursday's statement that he would take his case to the organisation and the Árd Fheis if the parliamentary party rejected him'.[48] Haughey, in turn, dismissed this as nothing more than the fantasy of the media.

> That's ridiculous, and that's wrong, and it's just part of this campaign that's going on both by a group inside the party, aided by their friends in the media, to confuse the situation and to try and undermine me and my position, and accuse me of all sorts of things which never even entered my mind.

The interviewer, Gerald Barry, made the cogent point that the perception extended beyond the media and included former stalwarts such as Ben Briscoe, who had declared the Thursday statement dictatorial, and Charlie McCreevy, who argued it was a fascist in tenor and content.[49] Haughey responded indignantly.

> But they are opponents of mine. Why don't you quote from what some of my friends say? These are opponents of mine, and of course they say these things... [T]hese people are making these false accusations against me, but I'm rebutting them. I'm saying they're not true. I never intended to depart from the well-

---

parallels with a drama on the fortunes of a Jewish family under Nazi rule called 'The Oppermanns', screened in a number of countries to coincide with the anniversary. '"They asked did I see 'The Oppermanns' and said they were frightened by the dictatorship aspect of it, and how easy it was for such things to happen when people weren't alert," said Mrs Colley, adding that her phone was buzzing the whole time.': *Irish Times*, 4 February 1983.

45 *Sunday Press*, 6 February 1983.

46 Michael Keane, editor of *Sunday Press* from 1986, quoted in Mark O'Brien, *De Valera, Fianna Fáil and the* Irish Press*: The Truth in the News?* (Dublin, 2001), p. 178.

47 Charles Haughey interview with Gerald Barry, *This Week*, RTÉ, 6 February 1983. Full text reproduced in the *Irish Times*, 7 February 1983, p. 6.

48 *Irish Times*, 7 February 1983.

49 *Sunday Tribune*, 6 February 1983.

> established practices and procedures of the party, and I don't intend to do so, there is nothing in my statement to that effect or that could be interpreted in that way.

At the same time Haughey repeated his determination to remain at the helm, not for personal advancement, but because of a desire to serve the State.

> [I]t's not me wanting to stay there for my own sake, it's my reluctance and my unwillingness to walk away, to walk away from those people, to let them down by resigning. If I am to be defeated in the parliamentary party, I will accept that fully and that will be that, but I don't want of my own volition to walk away and leave these people, that's not my character, my nature. I'm not going to do it.

For Haughey, there was no room for equivocation; responsibility for the mess the party was in could be laid at the door of individual ministers. He was making it clear that there would be no prisoners. Significantly, Haughey did not publicly concede the illegality of the phone taps – only that the mechanism adopted amounted to a potential abuse of power that he would not have countenanced. The emphasis instead was in stopping the need for them in the first place, once and for all. 'It can be stopped in a number of ways. But if it was to continue, the only final ultimate way of stopping it is to put the matter to the test in the parliamentary party, on the basis of expelling people who won't abide by the central democratic decisions of the majority of the party.' The warning, concealed in the velvet glove of conciliatory language, was brutally frank.

> If these recent events hadn't happened, there would be some other occasion when they would have mobilised to try and put me out of the leadership. That is their total motivation in political life – they're not concerned with the good of Fianna Fáil. They're not concerned with the success of Fianna Fáil. They're concerned primarily with their own position in Fianna Fáil and to remove me from the leadership.

Censuring the ambitious within the party was ironic, given how he had encouraged junior Ministers to support him with promises of advancement only a short while ago. Haughey went on to complain bitterly about a cabal in which the prime mover was George Colley, his opponent for the leadership for more than a decade. Colley had not only 'tried to mobilise a movement inside the party to unseat me as leader, [but] then he still expected to be made Tánaiste and deputy leader in the Government.'

The interview served a number of key purposes and provided an important pointer as to how Haughey would handle his defence at the parliamentary meeting the following day. First, the ambiguity at the heart of his statement appealing for the support of the entire Fianna Fáil organisation was used to walk his detractors into a carefully laid trap. As if on cue, they proclaimed that this was evidence of

Haughey's dictatorial leanings. By openly accepting the will of the parliamentary party he was exposing them to ridicule for engaging in hysterical comment masquerading as fact. Secondly, while careful to disassociate himself from openly sanctioning of the tapping and bugging incidents, Haughey provided a context in which blame for the travails facing the party could be laid at the door of those in the Cabinet who refused to accept the democratic will of the party. Thirdly, he suggested that TDs should await the publication of the Tunney report into the allegations before passing judgement, implying that the report would exonerate him. The fact that this defence was based on a falsehood would not become apparent for a decade.[50]

The findings of the internal inquiry into the telephone and bugging controversies were leaked to Peter Murtagh of the *Irish Times*. The conclusions of the investigation, which had no legal power and whose authors had not been given immunity from prosecution for libel should they accuse anyone, were therefore well flagged in advance of the meeting, a more important dynamic than the terms of reference of the probe. Murtagh, the newspaper's security correspondent, cleverly implied a causal connection between Haughey and the Deputy Garda Commissioner Joe Ainsworth that implicated the Taoiseach in the bugging controversy. He cited a meeting at Kinsealy between Haughey and Ainsworth in mid-October, a time when there was no known subversive activity taking place. It suggested the Taoiseach was more involved in the campaign to stop Cabinet leaks than heretofore understood.[51]

But it was a detail lost in the furore of the time. On the basis of the evidence put forward before the parliamentary party conclave – as opposed to whether Haughey had ordered the tap or utilised the information arising from them – there was simply no evidence to indict Haughey. Nevertheless, the media in general was convinced that even Haughey could not survive such an assault.[52] Alone among the commentators, John Healy sounded a note of caution, warning humorously that there might yet be 'a troupe of coffin-dancers who are free due to a last-minute cancellation'.[53]

The order of business reflected Haughey's desire not to leave anything to chance. He ensured that the report by the Tunney committee into the bugging and tapping controversies should be the first item on the agenda. The dissidents failed to block this course of action, forced through because those eligible to

---

[50] See below, pp. 133–134.

[51] Peter Murtagh, 'FF inquiry into phone tapping not to lay blame', *Irish Times*, 7 February 1983, p. 1.

[52] The *Irish Times* editorial on the day of the vote did sound a conciliatory note. It pointed out that Haughey had disarmed critics by speaking 'boldly and in suitably dignified fashion' in his radio interview. It viewed the dispute within the party as not having derived from high-minded principle but as characterised by 'resentment and envy and often plain childish huffiness': Editorial, 'Yes or No', *Irish Times*, 7 February 1983.

[53] John Healy, 'Sounding off', *Irish Times*, 7 February 1983, p. 11. This, in turn, was a reference to an earlier admonition by Haughey in the October 1982 challenge for the media to 'go and dance on someone else's grave'.

vote on the order of business, if not participate in the election of a new leader, included Fianna Fáil Members of the European Parliament and Senators representing the party in the Seanad. The loss of this initial vote made manifest the likely result of the proceedings. Haughey was secure. The question was: by what margin?

The day before the vote O'Malley visited Albert Reynolds, convinced that he had the numbers to succeed. The meeting, which took place after Haughey had given the RTÉ interview, provided further evidence of O'Malley's inability to read the party. He maintained that he had the core support to provide a majority and tried to persuade Reynolds to back him. Reynolds demurred, saying that if O'Malley had such numbers, then he would not need Reynolds's support. O'Malley countered that he wanted Reynolds as a member of the team. Reynolds was not impressed. He told O'Malley that he would never be leader of Fianna Fáil quite simply because he had never demonstrated an ability to read the party, nor demonstrated the propensity towards understanding it.[54] O'Malley then requested that Reynolds at least abstain. Reynolds declined, but gave an assurance that he would not be present for the first vote, 'whatever that might be'.[55] The exchange not only demonstrated Reynolds's awareness of how Haughey intended to run the meeting, but also suggested that O'Malley was lacking in political judgment by confiding in the Longford entrepreneur.

The report was read into the record by the Chief Whip, Bertie Ahern, an exercise that alone took over thirty minutes. Crucially, copies of the report were not circulated to the meeting, although members were subsequently allowed to go to a private area to examine it. Despite a dissenting report issued by David Andrews blaming Haughey for the fiasco under the rubric of collective Cabinet responsibility, these findings also exonerated Haughey of any wrongdoing. Again, Haughey was protected from meaningful attack from the dissidents because Lynch had used exactly the same defence of making individual members responsible for their own transgressions to justify staying in power at the time of the Arms Crisis. Next, before the meeting broke for lunch, Haughey announced that he would introduce a motion at the next meeting of the parliamentary party to withdraw the whip from Doherty and O'Donoghue. The procrastination was presented as not wanting to confuse two issues but, as with every decision taken by Haughey, there was a secret, politically astute agenda designed to further his own self-interest. Two distinct but inter-linked factors were therefore at play.

First, it demonstrated that Haughey was taking decisive action on the issue at hand, dispensing, albeit on the basis of a very incomplete evaluation of facts, what appeared to be even-handed justice to both transgressors. Secondly, and more importantly, in the short term it guaranteed an extra vote for Haughey in the leadership no-confidence debate. Doherty was allowed to vote, as he was

---

54 Interview with the author, Dublin, December 2001.

55 Reynolds was involved in a dispute with a U.K. supermarket chain, Sainsbury's, because of the death of a cat that had allegedly eaten a tin of cat-food made by his company.

a serving TD. O'Donoghue, despite being elected to the Seanad, had failed to retain his seat in the aftermath of the 1982 election. Doherty would be sacrificed to ensure the continued rule of his leader, but not before he had served his usefulness. Haughey was, as usual, leaving nothing to chance.[56]

To the consternation of observers at the secret vote on 7 February 1983, Haughey triumphed by a margin of seven votes. It was a slender victory but, in the circumstances, a rout. Haughey appeared indestructible. Political commentators were perplexed. As Bruce Arnold recounted in 1993: 'It was an astonishing outcome. Commentators had run out of comment. The press corps was punch-drunk. Prediction was a futile exercise. Logic seemed an entirely un-Irish pursuit. Chaos was the political order of things.'[57]

A senior source interviewed in Dublin suggests that one of the key reasons for O'Malley's failure was his inability to understand the Fianna Fáil parliamentary party. According to the source: 'After O'Malley gave his speech, he departed the room – he did not work it. A touch and go situation was transformed.'[58] This characteristic, mirroring O'Malley's own admission to Vincent Browne that he found 'the self-projection aspect of politics somewhat repellant',[59] was to prove his undoing.

Serious questions surrounded just why the press got it so wrong. The problem centred on sources and the dangerous admixture in political reporting that blurred the line between fact and comment. There is no doubt that Haughey was deemed fair game to journalists, whom he derided as a form of gullible sub-species, below his intellectual par and therefore not worth talking to. He preferred to talk directly to the people or, more precisely, the Fianna Fáil grassroots via RTÉ interviews than risk being distorted by opponents in the press. As a result, the antipathy between the Fianna Fáil leader and the press corps was mutual and predated the current crisis, which coloured the adjective-laden copy. In addition, the political correspondents made a calculated but erroneous decision that there was no way in which Haughey would survive. This was precisely the problem.

The range of journalists' contacts was too narrowly drawn, not enough emphasis was given to challenging the assumptions of a vocal minority and the confident predictions of Haughey's high-profile supporters were viewed with scepticism because the momentum seemed impossible to turn around. The press corps was covering the most exciting political story in a generation, but Haughey's imminent demise was a mirage; the media's prophecies were delusions not supported by the facts.[60] Indicative of the blurring of the line between fact and

---

[56] By supreme irony, it was Doherty's decision on 21 January 1992 to expose this that paved the way for the ultimate destruction of Haughey's political career. See below, p. 135.

[57] Bruce Arnold, *Haughey, His Life and Unlucky Deeds* (London, 1993), p. 215.

[58] Confidential source, interview with the author, Dublin, 24 July 2002.

[59] Vincent Browne, 'O'Malley's Prospectives', *Magill*, December 1979, p. 53.

[60] One argument about the failure of political journalism made cogently by the veteran Washington correspondent for the *Baltimore Sun* serves to illustrate the problem. He suggested that concentrating on who's up and who's down on the basis of partisan sources reinforces 'our inability to give

comment was the news coverage of the *Irish Independent*, which as early as 28 January headlined its edition 'The Final Days'. It not only drew comparison with the corruption in Nixon's White House but also set the paper's political line. Chris Glennon somewhat overstated his case by claiming: 'Charles Haughey begins his final days as Fianna Fáil leader after a party summit yesterday which has finally left him with little option but to resign.'[61] Glennon's counterpart at the *Irish Times*, Dick Walsh, also allowed the drama of the story and his contacts within the dissident wing of Fianna Fáil to drive his coverage.[62] Their colleague Bruce Arnold of the *Irish Independent* went even further as polemics replaced analysis. He nailed his colours firmly to the mast as early as 6 February when he suggested that the parliamentary party had to do the right thing, for 'neither the electorate nor the media can help in that'.[63]

John Horgan's 1984 analysis of the press coverage made clear that the alarmingly poor predictive power could have been avoided if standard journalistic procedures had been followed.[64] Not only were the majority of Fianna Fáil TDs unwilling to commit in public before the vote but 'even the most generous allocation of TDs to the anti-Haughey camp by the journalists concerned falls significantly short of a majority of the Fianna Fáil parliamentary party'.[65] With everyone following the same anti-Haughey agenda, breaking ranks in a localised competitive media market became all but impossible as a tremendous force rained down on the beleaguered Fianna Fáil leader.[66] As a result, the coverage was not Irish journalism's finest hour. It was to prove pivotal.

---

readers-viewers-voters an accurate and round editorial picture of the candidates and the dynamics of the campaigns': see Jack Germond, 'No sense of proportion', *Colombia Journalism Review*, November/December 1999; http://www.cjr.org/year/99

61 Chris Glennon, 'The Final Days: A succession battle looms', *Irish Independent*, 28 January 1983.

62 Dick Walsh, 'Secret ballot on Monday likely to oust Haughey', *Irish Times*, 5 February 1983.

63 *Irish Independent*, 5 February 1983.

64 For a useful summation of the perils involved in handling political sources, see John F. Kelly, 'May the Source Be With You', an executive summary of the 1999 Watchdog Journalism Conference at the Nieman Foundation for Journalism, Harvard University; http://www.nieman.harvard.edu/events/conferences/watchdog2/index.html

65 John Horgan, 'Vilification Once Again', *Magill*, January 1984, p. 37. Horgan asked the key question: 'did reporters allow themselves to be used by anti-Haughey sources, and, if so, why?' He argued persuasively that allegations of news management were made only against Haughey's campaign to survive

> [b]ut it is undeniably true that Mr Haughey's opponents were never accused of press management throughout this period... This leads to the conclusion, with which presumably both the journalists concerned and Mr Haughey's supporters would agree, that there was in the media throughout this period a pronounced and consistent anti-Haughey emphasis (p. 39).

See, for example, Conor Cruise O'Brien's articles on Fianna Fáil in the *Irish Times* during this period.

66 For a devastating attack on the peer pressures exerted in pack journalism see Paul Starobin, 'A Generation of Vipers, Journalists and the New Cynicism', *Colombia Journalism Review*, March/April 1995; http:www.cjr.or/year/95. No serious analysis has been conducted into the handling of the leadership crisis by the media and the media itself was not going to hold itself open to ridicule by analysing its own failures. Instead, it retreated into moral indignation at the seeming irrationality

The media simply got it wrong by failing to recognise the reality of Fianna Fáil politics with its emphasis on loyalty to the leader, a reality that had cost Haughey ministerial office in 1970 and which he now turned to his own advantage a decade later. Important dissidents who had a clear agenda that went unchallenged by many of those charged with providing impartial reporting, used sections of the media to their own advantage.

Haughey's strategy for survival was based on a diametrically opposed and more realistic reading of the situation. The dissidents were successfully, and skilfully, represented as the agents of chaos who fundamentally weakened Fianna Fáil as it entered the election. In Fianna Fáil parlance, their actions amounted to treason. Those who were to challenge for the leadership in the future determined not to make the same mistake and, thereafter, political journalism was even less useful in determining what was actually going on within Fianna Fáil leadership circles. That was in the future: in 1983, the churlishness of the Colley-O'Malley-O'Donoghue faction was writ large in banner headlines and the poison rendered more acute by the scale of the defeat that followed.

If Haughey thought his address would silence the critics within the party and stop members' private deliberations appearing on the front pages of the national newspapers, however, he was totally mistaken. According to the *Irish Times,* the atmosphere at the next parliamentary meeting was 'as close and uncomfortable as the arguments, which, with every contribution, exacerbated the division in the party and rendered less likely the healing of its now gaping wounds'.[67] The morning newspapers presented lurid details of accusations of dictatorship, divisiveness and the malign influence of Haughey shattering the credibility of the party. Ray Burke, previously one of Haughey's chief lieutenants,

of Fianna Fáil, the recurring theme of the urbane political correspondents and editorial writers. Only two articles seriously questioned the media at this time, both in *Magill*: Gene Kerrigan, 'Charlie and the Press Gang', *Magill*, February 1983; and John Horgan, 'Vilification Once Again', *Magill*, January 1984, pp. 34–39. Within the daily press only one unsigned article in the *Irish Times*, tucked away on page six, addressed the crucial question of why commentators, including its own, got the story so spectacularly wrong: 'Did tactics beat predictions?', *Irish Times*, 8 February 1983. Even the considered treatments advanced by political correspondents in books, notably by Bruce Arnold and Stephen Collins, blithely pass over their predictive failings. Arnold regarded it as unfathomable, 'extraordinary and frightening': *Haughey: His Life and Unlucky Deeds* (London, 1993), p. 215. Collins suggested that the media merely 'overestimated the support for the anti-Haughey faction while the Fianna Fáil organisation rallied to the support of the party leader and intense pressure was applied to any TD believed to be wavering against the leadership. Dissident TDs again had stories about intimidating phone calls and threats from Haughey supporters in their local organisations': Stephen Collins, *The Haughey File: The Unprecedented Career and Last Years of The Boss* (Dublin, 1992), p. 61. Readers will look in vain for a reassessment in Collins's latest oeuvre *The Power Game: Fianna Fáil since Lemass* (Dublin, 2000). In no case was independent corroboration found of, nor any Fianna Fáil member brought to book over, the alleged intimidation. This is not to say it did not happen, but scepticism, the first refuge of investigative journalism, was inexplicably withheld.

[67] *Irish Times*, 8 February 1983, p. 7.

was quoted as saying that 'Fianna Fáil under Mr Haughey had lost its identity and was now incapable, in his view, of winning an election'.[68]

After all the planning to oust him, Haughey had still managed to outwit his opponents. Brian Lenihan, one of the few Haughey loyalists to openly campaign for his leader throughout the short campaign, informed the *Today Tonight* programme that valuable lessons should be learnt by dissidents and media alike about the true nature of Fianna Fáil. There could not be:

> a repetition of recent days, which I acknowledge, has not done the party any good. We must recover from that position, and we can recover and unite behind Mr Haughey, who has been positively confirmed as party leader and that is the end of the matter as far as I am concerned. A lot of the talk that he would be defeated was exaggerated, completely wrong forecasting and this has happened before. I am not going to engage in any attack on the media, but the media in this instance seemed to get their forecasts wrong or seemed to get forecasts from people who did not fully understand the position.[69]

That position was just how far Haughey was prepared to go to remain in power. An indication was apparent in Lenihans's curiously framed response to questioning surrounding the planned removal of the whip from Doherty and O'Donoghue. Bugging on grounds of national security was to be defended; the problem for Doherty was in the way he had gone about it. More profoundly serious, in his eyes, was the action of Martin O'Donoghue.

> The condemnation in regard to Mr Doherty was not in relation to the whole "bugging", as it is called, which is related to national security, but telephone tapping was. The criticism was in relation to the manner in which he did it. In regard to Dr O'Donoghue that is where the really serious criticism came, because it struck at the very roots of the party.'[70]

Conor Cruise O'Brien was aware of the stench emanating from both wings of Fianna Fáil. There was the fact that the conversation recorded seemed to be of

---

[68] *Irish Times*, 8 February 1983, p. 1. This fits in with Burke's interview with the same paper on 4 February quoted above, pp. 109–110. However, many of the dissidents believed that Burke and Lawlor were in fact *agents provocateurs*: see John Healy, 'The sleepers and the heave', *Irish Times*, 12 February 1983. This interpretation was borne out on mature recollection by Mary Harney on 15 November 2001. She also accepted that Haughey out-manoeuvred them and there was considerable weight to Haughey's argument that the media campaign was not only orchestrated but counter-productive. Dick Walsh, political correspondent of the *Irish Times* at the time and now a senior political analyst, vehemently disagreed. He argued that the bi-weekly columns of John Healy in the *Irish Times* more than compensated for his own copy. See Dick Walsh, 'Strongman Haughey looked after his interests', *Irish Times*, 22 May 1999. Little *Irish Times* coverage at the time could support this contention, however: Haughey and his shenanigans, real or exaggerated, clearly made good reading.

[69] Brian Lenihan interview, *Today Tonight*, RTÉ, 7 February 1983; *Irish Times*, 8 February 1983.

[70] *Ibid.*

such a nature that a prudent person might wish to have a record of it. Standards on both wings of Fianna Fáil seem to have got so low that bugging may have come to seem no more than a reasonable precaution: 'A bug never flew on one wing.'[71] For the moment Haughey was secure and all that remained was to negotiate the terms of the surrender. Dick Walsh accepted, grudgingly, the scale of the victory. 'I'm not about to join the cult of the cute hoor, but there's no denying Mr Haughey's adroitness and craft. If he's to apply the same energy and guile to running the country, we would not be in the mess we're in now.'[72] A snapshot poll conducted by the *Irish Times*/MRBI seemed to suggest that the electorate viewed events in a similar vein.[73] The key, however, was to manage the Árd Fheis without further exacerbating the crisis within Fianna Fáil. A resolution was passed on 16 February that 'condemned the practice of the tapping of telephones of persons not engaged in subversion or serious crime, the recording of a private conversation and any proposition to compromise with funds any member or members of the party'.[74]

Simultaneously, Des O'Malley and Bobby Molloy were brought back to the frontbench. Haughey hoped to control them by locking them into the hard decisions made and keeping them away from the backbenchers. Colley neither sought nor received an appointment with Haughey; the locus for dissent transferred to O'Malley alone. The most significant change, other than Colley's wounded retreat to the backbench, was the demotion of Ray Burke, chastised for disloyalty. O'Malley pledged full loyalty to Haughey but expressed disappointment that Burke and Colley were passed over. In return, he saw his Cabinet responsibility extend with the addition of Energy to his portfolio. Haughey now felt that the time had come to be magnanimous. 'I justify myself in saying that I believe I have a totally integrated front bench and a party in which the mood is for unity of purpose and for effective opposition.'[75]

The management of the Árd Fheis still provided a potential policy headache for Haughey. Two diametrically opposed motions threatened the fragile newly-constructed unity: one called for McCreevy to be expelled; another for Blaney to be re-admitted. The political correspondents, so wrong-footed before the no-confidence motion, were about to again find predictions of potentially 'explosive scenes' off the mark. The mood evinced by the sketch writers placed the journalists not at a party conference but in a war zone. Haughey mischievously played on their insecurity in his opening address. 'Ours is an open, democratic

[71] Conor Cruise O'Brien, 'A bug never flew on one wing', *Irish Times*, 15 February 1983.

[72] Dick Walsh, 'Through thick and thin', *Irish Times*, 10 February 1983.

[73] According to the poll Haughey's approval ratings increased by eight per cent to thirty-nine per cent: *Irish Times*, 16 February 1983.

[74] Fianna Fáil parliamentary party statement, 16 February 1983, quoted in *Irish Times*, 17 February 1983. The paper quoted sources within the party saying that the resolution passed actually went much further, repudiating not only the tapping but also the recording of conversations.

[75] Quoted in *Irish Times*, 22 February 1983, p. 5.

organisation. We welcome fair and objective reporting of our affairs. We ask for no more and expect no less.'[76] For Olivia O'Leary, the implication was clear: 'Very loud. Deafening, it was. Loud enough to frighten you, if you didn't know how welcome you were. We knew how welcome we were.'[77]

Behind the scenes, however, party managers withdrew both divisive motions; Haughey and Haughey alone would be centre stage in Monday's papers. And that was just how he liked it. The crowd was warmed up by Albert Reynolds and Haughey emerged to tumultuous applause. 'The difficulties we have had are now behind us. We are back again on the high road as a great unified party; there will be no turning back; we face the future eager and determined.'[78] Des O'Malley retreated behind a very public cigarette as the crowd roared their approval, but his humiliation by the party was not yet complete. Despite pledging obeisance to a leader he clearly despised, his attempt to build an independent power-base within the party was signally rebuffed. He had put himself forward unsuccessfully for election to the largely ceremonial post of vice-president. It was an indication that he was in Cabinet on sufferance. O'Malley was, as Haughey's gambling argot would have it, 'a busted flush'. Eighteen years later O'Malley was to describe the period as deeply sinister and totally contrary to the norms of parliamentary democracy. He called the acceptance of Haughey's leadership and patronage by others incomprehensible, yet at the time he had also accepted that very reality.

> I know you are supposed to respect everyone but it is very hard to respect people whom you know know themselves they are doing the wrong thing but they are prepared to do it for some personal advantage which they hope will accrue to themselves.[79]

In order to further his case, he even went so far as to imply his own phone had been bugged.[80] In O'Malley's account, Haughey's supporters and, by extension,

---

76 Quoted in *Irish Times*, 26 February 1983, p. 1.

77 Olivia O'Leary, 'The Winner Takes All', *Irish Times*, 26 February 1983. See also Peter Murtagh, 'Charlie warms to the media', in the same edition. Murtagh reported that Haughey allowed himself to laugh to the press. Both knew who had won. The scale of the rout only became apparent at the close of the Árd Fheis, as O'Leary conceded: see Olivia O'Leary, 'Sun shone on Charlie's heaven', *Irish Times*, 28 February 1983.

78 Charles Haughey, Presidential Address to the Fianna Fáil 51st Ard-Fheis, 26 February 1983, reproduced in Martin Mansergh, ed., *The Spirit of the Nation: The Speeches and Statements of Charles J. Haughey (1957–1986)* (Cork, 1986), p. 734.

79 Desmond O'Malley, *A Public Life*, RTÉ, 6 May 2001.

80 *Ibid.* O'Malley claimed to have been told by the head of the IDA, Michael Killeen, that his telephone had been bugged. According to O'Malley, Killeen delivered the warning in a handwritten note that allegedly emanated from a source in An Garda Síochána. Given the positioning of the revelation in the documentary, it seemed to back suggestions that the tap had official sanction. In the aftermath of the programme, Martin O'Donoghue alleged that George Colley told him he had good reason to believe his (Colley's) phone had also been tapped. Michael Noonan, the Minister for Justice at the time, introduced an important caveat. In an interview with the *Irish Times* he made clear that there was no evidence to back up these assertions and that the only taps were on

Haughey himself were guilty of intimidation. He characterised the attitude of the delegates to the Árd Fheis as being a relationship more akin to 'a cult member to a cult leader'.[81] Yet, at the time neither O'Malley nor any of the other challengers overtly questioned Haughey on either tactics or policy. The commentary for *A Public Life* unquestioningly accepted O'Malley as a principled politician derided by fanatics who only understood the language of the school bully. Other members of the Cabinet at the time do not subscribe to such a charitable reading. One senior figure regarded the amateurish antics of O'Malley and his cohorts as totally unacceptable.

> They never accepted Haughey's leadership. You couldn't have a situation going on and on and on. No matter who the leader was, no matter what the provocation. There was only one way you can decide as far as a democratic party is concerned and that is by majority vote. Who gave anybody else the right to be undermining anybody? They had put their views forward time and time again within the parliamentary party. They had been rejected by a majority. So whether you like it or whether you don't, you are expected to tow the line. But George Colley never accepted his leadership. He had reservations on it from day one and Haughey made a big mistake in accepting those reservations when he called in everybody for their views. It's not that I have anything against George Colley but for the benefit of the party and the country and the government you couldn't carry on a government with people with reservations. He [Haughey] put himself unnecessarily in a very weak position.[82]

Arnold and Kennedy. See Mark Hennessy, 'Colley "feared phone taps on Cabinet"', *Irish Times*, 8 May 2001. For a scathing assessment of *A Public Life*, see Vincent Browne, 'O'Malley TV series is a disgrace', *Irish Times*, 16 May 2001.

81 *A Public Life*, *ibid.* Haughey himself was to claim the personification of the nation. When asked a year later to define the Celtic tradition, Haughey replied: 'What is the Celtic tradition? Why the Celtic tradition is Croke Park, Fianna Fáil and myself.' Quoted in Olivia O'Leary, 'Haughey at the Forum', *Magill*, May 1984.

82 Interview with the author, Dublin, December 2001. Reynolds would not make the same mistake. When he succeeded Haughey in 1992 he sacked a number of influential senior ministers. The reshuffle was of such severity that it gained the sobriquet 'the Valentine's Day Massacre'.

Chapter Five

Decline and Fall: The Collapse of Authority

Whoever believes that with great men new services wipe out old injuries deceives himself.

– Machiavelli, *The Prince*, p. 27

Charles J. Haughey's survival in 1983 was, by any reckoning, a staggering political comeback. Thereafter, as O'Malley and his allies knew, taking Haughey out of power in the foreseeable future would be an almost impossible task. His position in the parliamentary party was buttressed by the adroit cultivation of the SDLP, particularly the deputy leader, Seamus Mallon, whom Haughey had appointed as a senator in the dying days of the 1982 administration. When FitzGerald convened the New Ireland Forum in May 1983, to discuss 'the way in which progress may be made towards ending the violence and the reconciliation of the two traditions in Northern Ireland in the context of a New Ireland', Haughey used the ensuing debate to mark out a distinct Fianna Fáil policy platform. A key element of the strategy was to use the divisions within the SDLP to buttress Haughey's own position in Dublin by ensuring there could be no dilution of the goal of the unitary state, much less joint authority or federalism, the two other options discussed.[1] It was a measure of Haughey's success that the final report owed more to his formulation than FitzGerald was initially prepared to permit.[2] Indeed, as FitzGerald himself pointed out, from the very beginning the endeavour was viewed with deep suspicion not only by his coalition partners but, crucially, also from within his own party. 'They feared that if my proposal went ahead my deep concern about Northern Ireland could distract me from what they saw – with some reason – as exceptionally pressing domestic problems.'[3] Fianna Fáil

[1] For Haughey's opening gambit see Martin Mansergh, ed., *The Spirit of the Nation: The Speeches and Statements of Charles J. Haughey (1957–1986)* (Cork, 1986), pp. 752–758. For a detailed examination of the mechanics of the Forum see Paul Arthur, *Special Relationships: Britain, Ireland and the Northern Ireland problem* (Belfast, 2000), pp. 184–208. For the difficulties within the SDLP at this time see Olivia O'Leary, 'The John Hume Show', *Magill*, March 1984. Mallon was significantly more inflexible than Hume, but because he was a permanent delegate he was ultimately more pivotal, a fact that played into the hands of the Fianna Fáil strategists.

[2] Olivia O'Leary, 'Haughey at the Forum', *Magill*, May 1984.

[3] Garret FitzGerald, *All in a Life* (Dublin, 1991), pp. 464–465.

had no such compunction, as a disciplined team unerringly followed the party line sketched out by Haughey and given intellectual cogency by the formidable Martin Mansergh.

> Anyone who stands back from the situation can see clearly that it is the British military and political presence which distorts the situation in Northern Ireland and inhibits the normal process by which peace and stability emerge elsewhere. That process can only develop, and peace and stability be secured, under new all-Ireland structures in the context of which an orderly British withdrawal can take place.[4]

Haughey made clear that he would not apologise for the constitutional framework of the Irish Republic but acknowledged the possibility of devolved government. 'We accept without reservation the right of the people of Northern Ireland to retain the way of life to which they are accustomed and to the full expression of their identity and their beliefs.' As with his first speech to the Dáil as leader of Fianna Fáil, Haughey was offering a devolved administration compromise but only under an all-Ireland framework underwritten by the two governments, a template sketched in outline form at the Dublin summit in December 1980.

> It was here in Dublin Castle, two and a half years ago [the December 1980 Dublin summit], that a British Prime Minister acknowledged that the problem of Northern Ireland could be solved by joint action of the two sovereign Governments. It is with that truth clearly in our minds that this Forum takes the first steps along the road to a final constitutional settlement.[5]

It was this determination that only a unitary state was acceptable, coupled with a desire throughout the 1980s to conjoin with the Catholic Church on doctrinal matters, particularly the vexed questions of divorce and abortion, that re-ignited the conflict within Fianna Fáil. After Colley's sudden death in September 1983, Des O'Malley became the sole focus for dissent within Fianna Fáil but still failed to develop sufficient alliances. O'Malley was horrified at Haughey's endorsing only the unitary state option for the future and argued that this hardline approach undermined the final report before it could even be debated. He received backing from the editorial writers of the *Sunday Independent* newspaper, who condemned Haughey for engaging in what they termed 'an act of national sabotage'.[6]

Haughey demanded and received a mandate from the parliamentary party that he alone would articulate northern policy. When O'Malley criticised both the policy and the rendition of events portrayed to the media of the meeting,

[4] Charles Haughey, speech at the Opening of the New Ireland Forum, 30 May 1983, reproduced in Martin Mansergh, ed., *The Spirit of the Nation: The Speeches and Statements of Charles J. Haughey (1957–1986)* (Cork, 1986), p. 753.

[5] *Ibid.*, p. 757.

[6] *Sunday Independent*, 6 May 1984.

Haughey pounced with alacrity. He again demanded obedience. O'Malley was suspended from the parliamentary party in a vote carried fifty-six to twelve. P.J. Mara emerged from the meeting declaring the political legend that from now on there would be '*uno duce, una voce*. We are having no more nibbling at my leader's bum'.[7] In an infamous interview with the *Sunday Press*, O'Malley criticised what he termed the 'air of paranoia' surrounding Haughey.[8] The challenge, however, was now academic, as O'Malley was finished within the party and he knew it. The following February he used a debate on family planning law to commit an act of political self-immolation.

> "Republican" is perhaps the most abused word in Ireland today. In practice what does it mean? The newspapers do not have to explain it because there is an immediate preconceived notion of what it is. It consists principally of anglophobia. Mentally, at least, it is an aggressive attitude towards those who do not agree with our views on what the future of this island should be. It consists of turning a blind eye to violence, seeing no immorality, often in the most awful violence, seeing immorality in only one area, the area with which this Bill deals... I do not believe that the interests of this State or our Constitution and of this Republic would be served by putting politics before conscience in regards to this. There is a choice of a kind that can only be answered by saying that I stand by the Republic, and accordingly, I will not oppose this Bill.[9]

O'Malley was out. A week later he was summoned to Fianna Fáil headquarters in Mount Street, Dublin, to hear his fate. O'Malley was expelled for 'conduct unbecoming'. When the circumstances finally came together in 1992 to depose his nemesis, O'Malley, long denied the opportunity to destroy his opponent from within Fianna Fáil, gleefully waved the knife. The man who was to take possession of the leadership was the same man who had welcomed Haughey onto the stage at the 1983 Árd Fheis: former dance hall manager and pet food

---

[7] The comment was first published by Geraldine Kennedy and later reported in T. Ryle Dwyer, *Short Fellow: A Biography of Charles J. Haughey* (Dublin, 1999), p. 291.

[8] See also Bruce Arnold, *Haughey: His Life and Unlucky Deeds* (London, 1993), p. 221.

[9] *Dáil Debates*, vol. 356, col. 277 and col. 285, 20 February 1985. For an uncritical assessment see Bruce Arnold, *Haughey, His Life and Unlucky Deeds* (London, 1994), p. 224. Arnold lauds the speech as:

> brilliant...O'Malley had enough of the pusillanimous subservience of Fianna Fáil to the Roman Catholic Church and self-interest, in whatever order these powerful motivations for politics in Ireland chose to arrange themselves... It was a moment of deep humiliation for Haughey and for the Fianna Fáil party. Their attitude towards the bill had been callously political. They had sought only to shame and defeat the moves to give freer access to contraception and to advice. They had aligned themselves with the most entrenched conservatism of Roman Catholic Church teaching.

Arnold suggested that the Forum typified the intellectual limitations of Haughey, who was undermined by Ray MacSharry. This contention is palpably untrue. MacSharry was still under a cloud because of the bugging controversy the year before. The Forum report was unquestionably consistent with Haughey's entire ideological thinking on the national question.

entrepreneur, Albert Reynolds. The wheel had turned full circle. Charles Haughey, the great survivor of Irish politics, had finally lost his grip on power. But the demise had little to do with principle or moral certitude and owed everything to the vicious factionalism which, along with ambivalence towards violence in Northern Ireland, has been the chief characteristic of Fianna Fáil politics since Seán Lemass.

The roots of Haughey's downfall can be traced back to the private deal Haughey had conducted with O'Malley to forge the 1989 coalition in the first place, thereby sacrificing what had been a cardinal principle for Fianna Fáil. The fact that the deal was conducted secretly, despite the opposition of chief negotiators Albert Reynolds and Bertie Ahern, meant that Haughey alone took the risk for acceding to O'Malley's cold embrace. The Progressive Democrats leader had justified his participation in the government on the basis that only he could keep Fianna Fáil in check. In truth, from its inception in 1989, following Haughey's failure to win an overall majority for the fifth time, the coalition functioned only to reveal the sordid reality of power politics.

Haughey's survival depended on a succession of humiliating concessions to O'Malley, each serving to undermine the integrity of the Taoiseach. The malign potency of the GUBU period was demonstrated yet again with the betrayal in May 1990 of Brian Lenihan, Haughey's trusted lieutenant and the Fianna Fáil candidate in the presidential election. It emerged that Lenihan had attempted to persuade the President not to dissolve the Dáil following the collapse of FitzGerald's government in 1982 but proceed directly to the elevation of Haughey as Taoiseach without the inconvenience of an election. O'Malley argued that this revelation demonstrated an abuse of due process and he demanded Lenihan's sacking as the price for remaining in coalition. Haughey's acquiescence added to the restiveness within the Fianna Fáil parliamentary party, large sections of which now regarded the exorbitant price of power as too demeaning. The noxious air of scandal permeating Leinster House intensified throughout 1991 as a succession of corruption inquiries were ceded. The allegations left many in the party unsure about their seats and convinced that there would be no ministerial advancement in the current climate. Haughey retreated into a siege mentality, a character trait he so despised in its unionist manifestation across the border.

The irony was that his unwillingness to translate the rhetoric of opposition into concrete policy changes when he returned to government at the head of a minority administration in 1987, and again after ceding the cardinal principle of majoritarian government by accepting coalition in 1989, weakened his apparently distinctive position. This dilution of purpose was crucial in providing the very possibility of a successful challenge. The Anglo-Irish Agreement was a case in point.[10] Haughey had vehemently opposed it as an act of folly 'repugnant to the

---

[10] See Frank Millar, 'The man who looked most likely to succeed', *Irish Times*, 31 January 1992. See also Mark Brennock, 'From republican rhetoric to patient pragmatism', in the same edition.

Constitution'.[11] Speaking in the Dáil in the immediate aftermath of its signing, he argued that Fianna Fáil alone now represented continuity with a revolution betrayed by a misguided government and by what he viewed as a media-inspired conspiracy of silence on the abdication of *de jure* Irish sovereignty over the six counties.

> In effect, what is proposed in this Agreement is that the Irish Government, accepting British sovereignty over part of Ireland, will involve itself in assisting and advising the British Government to rule that part of Ireland more effectively, to help make it more amenable to the authority of the British Government... As a responsible, political party, regardless of whether it costs us votes or popularity, we are not prepared to surrender by desertion the constitutional nationalist position.[12]

But this is precisely what he was prepared to do when returned to office two years later. Faced with the potential collapse of the government should he depart from the terms of the Anglo-Irish Agreement, he instead worked its provisions assiduously. Although it was true that Haughey was prepared to utilise ideology to buttress his position within Fianna Fáil, the gap between rhetoric and reality had been progressively exposed from 1987 onwards. The failure of the national question to reunify a split electorate and give Haughey the majority he required severely curtailed his room for manoeuvre.[13] Furthermore, the minority government, in which a coalition of opposition forces could bring down the vulnerable administration, had become a forced coalition, in which the Progressive Democrats had an actual veto on attempts to derogate from the Anglo-Irish Agreement. This further tied Haughey's hands politically, making it less likely that the chasm between rhetoric and policy could be bridged.

The failure to deliver on issues Haughey had repeatedly deemed of profound importance was perhaps the greatest paradox of his political career. Defined for a generation by reference to his republicanism, in the end he was unprepared to risk power to achieve a breakthrough. Herein lay the truth behind Conor Cruise O'Brien's caustic observation of the compromises needed to tame the Modern Prince.

---

11 *Dáil Debates*, vol. 361, col. 2581, 19 November 1985.

12 *Dáil Debates*, vol. 361, col. 2600ff, 19 November 1985. The Dáil speech is reproduced in Martin Mansergh, ed., *The Spirit of the Nation: The Speeches and Statements of Charles J. Haughey (1957–1986)* (Cork, 1986), pp. 1012–1025.

13 See Peter Mair, 'Breaking the Nationalist Mould: The Irish Republic and the Anglo-Irish Agreement', in Paul Teague, ed., *Beyond the Rhetoric: Politics, the Economy and Social Policy in Northern Ireland* (London, 1987), pp. 81–110. Mair made the interesting point that while nationalism is 'genuinely the bottom line in politics... the commitment to unity appears to play a much more questionable role in the mobilisation of electoral support' (p. 84). For an assessment of how the political winds have changed further since 1987, reducing the chances of any party achieving single party governance, see Richard Sinnott, *Irish Voters Decide: Voting Behaviour in Elections and Referendums since 1918* (Manchester, 1995), p. 107.

> The Haughey who now leaves the stage is a more or less tamed politician, battered into a kind of respectability (except in some financial dealings). Ten years ago he was extremely dangerous. The politician who used the top level of the police as spies in the service of his own party leadership would have turned the Republic into a one party state. He was tamed as a result of being denied an overall majority.[14]

It is a view that holds considerable sway within Fianna Fáil. One senior minister believes that, following the expulsion of O'Malley, Haughey had the potential to mould the Fianna Fáil party into his own image and became at that stage

> as close to being a dictator as not to matter. His problem was that power was ultimate to him. Power was everything. You can analyse it in retrospect but it wasn't obvious then. He needed power to maintain a lifestyle that wasn't obviously maintainable.[15]

Mainly through the speechwriting of Martin Mansergh, Haughey was always assumed to have strategic vision; to personify the Spirit of the Nation. It was slow to be recognised, when he finally got to power, that he clearly exercised his authority for the pleasure of that exercise, rather than to achieve an integrated set of national objectives. This was neither appreciated by his party nor the public at large at the time. Deconstruction of the Haughey myth would later establish his propensity for the high-profile, singular attention-getting act, whether that be tax-free status for artists in 1969 or a free toothbrush for every child in the nation in 1977. It would also reveal that during his years as Taoiseach from 1987 there was simply no evidence of his preparedness to risk power to achieve a strategic breakthrough on the northern question, the very issue that defined his political life. Once the ambiguity was exposed over time, Haughey stood accused of desiring power for its own sake, thus rendering him susceptible to the charge that he should be best understood as a cynical theoretician of power rather than a true Machiavellian, using all necessary means only in the pursuit of a noble objective.[16]

Simultaneously, Haughey's currency *within* Fianna Fáil was devaluing with each succeeding compromise with O'Malley. Loyalty and advancement, the two sides of the Fianna Fáil coin, were bettered served by the pretenders to the throne. By 1991 the monolithic party had degenerated into feudal baronies more interested in self-preservation and self-promotion within the twenty-six-

[14] See, for example, Conor Cruise O'Brien, 'The rogue who ruled Ireland', *The Times*, 4 February 1992.

[15] Confidential source, interview with the author, Dublin, December 2001.

[16] For a reading of Machiavelli insisting that this differentiation must be addressed see Louis Althusser, *Machiavelli and Us* (London, 1999). Althusser maintains that the means can only be justified if they are in pursuit of a noble objective. This he terms 'the antipodes of vulgar pragmatism. The result alone counts: but the *goal* is the sole arbiter of the result that counts' (p. 93, emphasis in original).

county State than supporting a substantive ideology. The most powerful of these mandarins were Lawlor and Burke in Dublin, with Reynolds and Flynn operating a nexus stretching from the midlands to the West. Haughey was, quite simply, expendable. He was now without an over-arching profile at local constituency level because of the string of compromises to the Progressive Democrats. With his ability to invigorate Fianna Fáil weakened, Haughey found it impossible to counteract the growing stature of his lieutenants. Devoid of a demonstrable, distinctive position on the national question in particular, Haughey had outlived his usefulness.

In October 1991 a group of four TDs issued a statement critical of Haughey, partly prompted by their leader's response on RTÉ radio to allegations of corruption in the semi-State sector. During the interview Haughey had also indicated mischievously his intention of remaining at the helm of his party by remarking on the longevity of Chinese leaders, who stayed in power 'til they are eighty or ninety'.[17] Although the dispute failed to catch fire, it signalled the beginning of open hostilities between Haughey and Reynolds, the powerful Minister for Finance. As early as February 1990, Reynolds had dismissed the coalition with the Progressive Democrats as 'a temporary little arrangement' and intimated that he would be a candidate if a vacancy for the leadership arose.[18] He told Haughey privately that he would not openly agitate for his removal but should a further heave materialise, then his support would end. Reynolds was too seasoned a politician not to prepare in advance for the moment 'the boil would have to be lanced'.[19] These secret plans gathered pace from early summer as the crisis of confidence within Fianna Fáil intensified. Organised in a series of cells, secrecy was the defining characteristic of the Reynolds campaign and adroit political management central to its strategic direction.

Tom Savage, a director of influential Dublin media strategists Carr Communications, was instrumental in sketching out a possible course of action.[20]

---

[17] See Stephen Collins, *The Power Game: Fianna Fáil since Lemass* (Dublin, 2000), p. 212.

[18] The full quote was: 'I hope that the temporary little arrangement which we have with our junior partners won't be there all that long and that we'll be back to where we were at the start.' See T. Ryle Dwyer, *Short Fellow: A Biography of Charles J. Haughey* (Dublin, 1999), p. 373.

[19] Albert Reynolds, interview with the author, Dublin, December 2001.

[20] Carr Communications, in its early years, specialised in finessing the public image of the country's top politicians. It had developed programmes to enhance the Lynch government's media presentation as early as 1977. Presentation programmes were also developed with Fine Gael, a relationship that continued when Fianna Fáil lost power in 1981. When Haughey assumed the Fianna Fáil leadership he banned members of the front bench from attending the consultancy. Whether this derived from personal suspicion about the political allegiances of Carr executives or the possibility that his ministers might develop alternate media strategies to the detriment of his own is uncertain but it is more likely to be the latter. In 1981, Haughey revisited that decision after being advised by Dr John O'Connell to make use of professional advice to improve the presentation of Fianna Fáil policy. Haughey asked Tom Savage if he could ensure that the grooming service would be kept confidential. Savage replied by telling Haughey that members of the Fianna Fáil front bench had been clients consistently throughout the fatwa and that nobody, including

His advice was to forsake courting publicity on both personal and party political matters. The corollary of this was that the political journalists were kept out of the loop. There was recognition within the Reynolds camp that the only way in which its candidate could position himself for assuming the leadership when Haughey left office was if there was no suspicion of betrayal. Reynolds would not make the same mistake as O'Malley and Colley before him, nor would he rely on the fickle embrace of the political lobby to sway the parliamentary party. This tactic had already proved a failure at creating the circumstances for Haughey's demise and incapable of deconstructing the myths assiduously built up by him as the personification of the nation.

Savage had been approached by a senior group of Fianna Fáil TDs who intimated they were aware that the Haughey years were drawing to a close. The group included Maire Geoghegan Quinn, Padraig Flynn, Michael Smith and Charlie McCreevy. They had a proposition for the media strategist: 'We believe that Reynolds can be and will be the next leader of Fianna Fáil but only if you agree to work on aspects of his communications strategy, public statements: the whole range.'[21] Savage's job, in essence, was to prepare the putative challenger for office, rather than prepare the challenge. Given Reynolds's reputation as a nouveau riche 'political fixer', his supporters feared he would appear gauche after Haughey's self-consciously regal presentation.

Savage took control of every aspect of Reynolds's media presentation, guarding against gaffes and pushing forward an image of the man far removed from the dismissive 'country and western' brigade epithet so beloved by Haughey loyalists. It was imperative that the initiative not only remained secretive but that there would be no suggestion that Reynolds was out to destabilise Haughey's leadership by creating yet another factional cabal. Extraordinary measures were taken to maintain the integrity of the operation. The strategists never socialised together, nor congregated in the Dáil tearooms or bar. Meetings were held at Reynolds's house and further precautions involved never leaving messages on the telephone. Reynolds had studied past form. Knowing that loyalty to the party leader was a trait he himself would want to utilise, he did not want to be associated with destabilisation or the perception by political commentators that that was the focus of his campaign.

By November 1991, following Sean Power's demand for a secret ballot to depose Haughey, Albert Reynolds resolved that the time had come for an open challenge. 'The well-being of our country requires strong and decisive leadership of government and of the Fianna Fáil party, I am not satisfied that such leadership now exists. In the circumstances, I will be supporting the motion tabled for the party meeting,' he declared in a statement.[22] Key to his decision to make the

---

Haughey, had discovered – or would ever discover – their names. Irritated but reassured, Haughey issued the contract: Tom Savage, interview with the author, Belfast, December 2001.

[21] Tom Savage, interview with the author, Belfast, December 2001.

[22] *Irish Press*, 8 November 1991.

challenge was the blunt advice imparted to him by Tom Savage. 'I remember saying to him: "if you challenge Haughey there is a risk that you will never be leader of Fianna Fáil. If, however, you do not challenge him you *certainly* will never be leader of Fianna Fáil."'[23] Haughey responded by sacking Reynolds and a day later the Minister for the Environment, Padraig Flynn, for having the temerity to back his dismissed colleague. But as the bonfires in the west to welcome Maire Geoghegan Quinn home following her subsequent sacking demonstrated, it was the Haughey court itself that was facing immolation.

Reynolds recognised that the political game involved defence as well as attack; the ability to predict not only the moves the opponent was likely to take but also the recognition that sacrifices could – and should – be made to ensure final victory. It was a skill that marked Haughey out as the most accomplished political operator of his generation. Haughey had survived so long because of an acute ability to manage the conflicting factions of the party, a fact acknowledged by his major opponent, who had evidently learnt the lesson well. It appeared that Reynolds lacked the vision or the political skills required when he was despatched with what appeared to be relative ease, securing only 22 votes in a no-confidence debate. But a much deeper and complex political game was being played out which can only now be revealed.

Reynolds and his team had prepared their ground, recognising that, although they did not have the wherewithal to win outright, there was a capacity to mortally wound. Their primary consideration was to lull Haughey into a false sense of security, while positioning the board to ensure Reynolds became heir apparent should the final humiliation take place. Timing, strategic thinking and the maintenance of a media blackout – measures singularly lacking in previous heaves – were everything. According to Reynolds, this was crucial. 'The strength of the party is such that it was never going to allow the media to elect a leader. The solid mass [the middle ground] was not going to be dictated to. That was my view, my calculation.'[24] On the night before the vote, key emissaries in the party were instructed to tell supporters to vote *in favour of* Haughey.

The parliamentary party meeting lasted fourteen hours. Haughey began by using the demand for an open vote to flush out the dissidents. He succeeded by a margin of eleven. He was determined that, should he go, he would do so at a time of his own choosing and would anoint a successor. It was not be the flamboyant Reynolds but Bertie Ahern, the loyal lieutenant. Haughey's problem was that he had met his match with the new generation of politician, typified by Reynolds and Ahern, brought in with the Fianna Fáil landslide of 1977 and now hungry for power. Unknown to his political master Ahern had held two meetings in Reynolds's Dublin apartment *before* the November challenge to carve out the leadership of Fianna Fáil over the next decade.

Ahern was able and willing to play both sides knowing that the current

[23] Tom Savage, interview with the author, Belfast, December 2001.

[24] Albert Reynolds, interview with the author, Dublin, December 2001.

game was drawing to a conclusion. Indeed, even after Haughey offered Ahern the Finance portfolio, the appointee discussed the merits of taking it at considerable length with Reynolds. It was indicative of Ahern's own strategic ability that, given his own close association with the Boss, he recognised the need for an interregnum before he could accede to the leadership without carrying an inordinate amount of political baggage. It was indicative, too, of Haughey's own political judgement that he famously described Ahern as the most cunning of all his lieutenants.[25]

Far from being a rout, the strategic thinking behind the Reynolds campaign nevertheless ensured that the denouement was imminent. Just how fragile Haughey's hold over the party had become was cruelly demonstrated when O'Malley blocked Haughey's nominee for the ministry of Defence in the reshuffle following the sacking of Reynolds. At the last minute, in the Dáil chamber, Haughey chose not to protest O'Malley's refusal to endorse Jim McDaid. The reason O'Malley gave for his defiance was that McDaid had had the temerity to be photographed outside the Four Courts with one of his constituents, James Pius Clarke, a member of the Provisional IRA who had escaped from the Maze Prison and who had successfully appealed to the Supreme Court to prevent extradition to Northern Ireland.[26] In 1988 he had ruled that extradition should be allowed in order to preserve the integrity of the Anglo-Irish Agreement and had ensured the passage of an Extradition Act, despite vocal opposition from many in the party, including Charlie McCreevy.[27] Now that the junior partner in the government was pushing the Taoiseach to overrule the court, Haughey meekly acquiesced. The climb-down was a desultory reminder of the earlier compromises on northern policy that Haughey had made to stay in power. It

[25] The notorious remark was made in the wake of agreement on the renewed programme for government in 1991. According to Stephen Collins, who was among a group of journalists present, Haughey applauded Ahern's deal-making skills with the words: 'He's the man. He's the best, the most skilful, the most devious and the most cunning of them all.' See Stephen Collins, *The Power Game: Fianna Fáil since Lemass* (Dublin, 2000), p. 213.

[26] Politics is unquestionably a brutal occupation. For a touching account of the impact this had on the McDaid family, see Marguerite McDaid, 'Day the prize was snatched away', *Sunday Independent*, 25 November 2001. Jim McDaid was elated when Haughey brought him into his office late on 12 November 1991 to offer him the Defence portfolio. 'I've just left the boss's office. I'm in. He's bringing me right in at the top. . . For God's sake, don't tell anyone,' he told his wife breathlessly. She, in turn, was elated. 'I lay back and the tears started. Tears of absolute joy, happiness and disbelief. Five minutes later, I jumped out of bed and ran up and down the long hallway of our bungalow talking to myself. I needed to thank God out loud.' As she made her way to Dublin to watch her husband accept the accolade, she was unaware that O'Malley had vetoed the appointment. According to Mrs McDaid, when her husband withdrew citing 'the broader national interest', she saw him 'suddenly transformed into a tortured soul before my eyes'. Bertie Ahern subsequently made McDaid Minister for Tourism in 1997 but, according to his wife, her husband had already paid an unacceptably high price. 'An impermeable barrier was erected, leaving a body of stone. Sadly, when that goal was achieved six years later, the warmth and the smiles had long disappeared, and only a shell remained.'

[27] T. Ryle Dwyer, *Short Fellow: A Biography of Charles J. Haughey* (Dublin, 1999), pp. 328–335.

was clear that the end of the Haughey era, predicted by Flynn and Geoghegan Quinn in the early summer, was now only months away. It was simply a matter of timing. The questions were: when and on what basis?

It was, perhaps, apt that Haughey's final fall from grace began to be played out in Hell's Kitchen, not the tough, lower west-side, meat-market Manhattan neighbourhood, itself an approximate facsimile to the reality of Fianna Fáil politics, but a bar situated in the County Roscommon town of Castlerea. Castlerea typified the 'country and western' heartland so despised by Haughey, an area of modern Ireland far removed from both its mystical roots and thrusting cosmopolitanism. The county bordered the power-base of Albert Reynolds, who had made his fortune tapping into the dreams of the 'ballroom of romance' generation. It was also the retreat of Haughey's erstwhile Minister for Justice, Sean Doherty, whose actions in 1982 had so tarnished the administration. Following 1982–1983 scandal, Doherty retreated into the wilderness. He was readmitted into the parliamentary party in late 1984 but never considered for promotion from the backbench. In 1989 he lost his seat in the Dáil after a misjudged attempt to raise his profile by standing simultaneously for the European parliament over-stretched his local political machine. He did secure a position in the Senate and was elected Speaker largely through the non-intervention of Haughey who, for the first time, gave his tacit approval for the partial rehabilitation by breaking with tradition in not nominating a candidate. Nevertheless, the two men remained estranged; there was unfinished business between them. In late 1991 their paths crossed again when the imminent passage of a Phone Tapping Bill threatened to reawaken the ghosts of 1982.

In the autumn of 1991, as Haughey once again faced political challenge from within Fianna Fáil, Doherty made the independent decision to visit Carr Communications, looking for guidance and a way to articulate his rage. He was unspecific about the details. In retrospect, but unknown to the company at the time, it is clear that the former Special Branch detective was seeking a legitimate channel for his frustration. Doherty had long been brooding on the way in which he had been sidelined from the upper echelons of Fianna Fáil, particularly after Haughey's return to power in 1987 did not lead to even a junior ministry being offered. He sought recognition from his former mentor; he also wanted to be compensated for having taken sole responsibility for the 1982 debacle; and revenge for watching Ray MacSharry rise to the heights of the European Commission while he languished in political purgatory, a salutary reminder of the excesses of GUBU.

To coincide with the launch of John Waters's idiosyncratic memoir, *Jiving at the Crossroads*, the RTÉ arts programme *Nighthawks* recorded an edition in Hell's Kitchen. The Doherty interview for the programme was supposed to be light-hearted, but its consequences continue to reverberate to this day. The former Minister for Justice maintained that the breaching of Cabinet confidentiality in 1982 was an issue that was raised 'in the highest boardroom in the country'. He alleged he was detailed to ascertain how to stop it by whatever means necessary.

> There was a decision taken in Cabinet that the prevention of the leaking of matters from the Cabinet must be stopped. I, as Minister for Justice, had direct responsibility for doing that – I did that. I do feel that I was let down by the fact that people knew what I was doing.[28]

After the recording, to underscore the importance of the revelation, Doherty reiterated to the presenter that he had imparted significant new information. The presenter, Shay Healy, decided to contact Bruce Arnold, one of those bugged in 1982, to alert him in advance of the broadcast. Arnold splashed the story in the *Irish Independent*.

> The latest revelations add further damage to the Taoiseach's credibility, revealing a deliberate misrepresentation of the facts at the time and a subsequent concealment of formal Government knowledge of both the phone tapping and the actions taken against political journalists and colleagues within his own party.[29]

Following the *Nighthawks* programme, as the media frenzy developed around him, Doherty began looking for support. He talked to several senior Fianna Fáil figures, including Brian Lenihan, who had had experience of dealing with the political consequences of lying.[30] Lenihan is believed to have recommended that Doherty visit Carr Communications, 'who may be able to come up with a formula of words to get you out of the problem'.[31] Doherty arrived at the company's offices without warning. Savage was on his way to another appointment and introduced Doherty to his wife, Terry Prone, who had not yet had any dealings with the disgraced politician. It was predictable that Prone, who had no involvement in the Reynolds planning and who had not seen *Nighthawks*, would refuse to come up with the 'required form of words' if that meant deliberately setting out to mislead. Then Managing Director of Carr Communications, she had a reputation for ensuring the integrity of her firm by never assisting business leaders or politicians in lying. Instead of a formula designed to move Doherty away from his *Nighthawks* claim, what emerged was a statement that elaborated on that claim, presented with exquisite timing at a news conference at the Montrose Hotel close to RTÉ's television studios. Prone gave the statement to her husband, adding that the news conference would begin within minutes. 'As soon as I read it, I realised that this would bring Haughey down within days,' Savage remembers. 'All you had to do was to plot the fallout. It was as easy to predict as that.'[32]

---

[28] See *Irish Times*, January 1992.

[29] *Irish Independent*, 15 January 1992; Bruce Arnold, *Haughey: His Life and Unlucky Deeds* (London, 1993), p. 276.

[30] See above, p. 126.

[31] Tom Savage, interview with the author, December 2001.

[32] *Ibid.*

The State broadcaster's journalists were on strike and the station was being run by a skeleton staff. The timing of the statement, less than an hour before the news screened, meant that the entire event went to air unedited, thereby significantly adding to its dramatic impact.

> I am confirming tonight that the Taoiseach, Mr Haughey, was fully aware, in 1982, that two journalists' phones were being tapped, and that he at no stage expressed a reservation about his action... I did not seek nor did I get instruction from any member of the Cabinet in this regard, nor did I tell the Cabinet that this action had been taken. Telephone tapping was never discussed in Cabinet. However, as soon as the transcripts from the taps became available, I took them personally to Mr Haughey in his office and left them in his possession. I understand that the Taoiseach has already denied that this happened, so I wish to reiterate it in specific terms... Each and every one of those relevant transcripts were transported by me to Mr Haughey's office and handed to him directly. He retained all but one of them, making no comment on their content. At no stage did he indicate disapproval of the action which had been taken.[33]

The true significance of Doherty's statement became apparent in the following passage.

> The tapping of the journalists' phones was revealed and before I commented on it Mr Haughey stated on RTÉ radio that he would 'not have countenanced any such action', and described it as 'an abuse of power'. When I was later interviewed I felt pressured to support Mr Haughey's stated position.
>
> Not only did I take the blame, but when Mr Haughey claimed not to have been aware of the tapping while it was in progress I did not correct this claim, and indeed supported it.
>
> However, the truth is that the Taoiseach, as I've already said, *had* known and had not expressed any reservation during the several months in which he received from my hands copies of the transcripts of the taped telephone conversations.

The impact of the Doherty statement was magnified by its clinical dissection of Haughey's contention in a RTÉ radio interview ten years earlier that the telephone tap was an abuse of power he would not have countenanced.[34] The exposure of the strategic thinking that lay behind both the interview and the tactics for survival over the next few months were central to the structure of the statement, a hint that it served a deeper purpose than catharsis. Its strength lay not just in the clearly emotional rendition in front of the television cameras, nor even in the exclusive targeting of Haughey; rather, it reposed in the cogency of the entire argument. It apparently revealed that the tactical brilliance deployed by

---

[33] Sean Doherty press conference, 21 January 1992. Full text reprinted in *Irish Times*, 22 January 1992.

[34] *This Week*, RTÉ Radio, 19 December 1982.

Haughey in the pursuit of the maintenance of power in 1983 involved an elaborate, and ongoing, deception.

> I agreed to a proposal from Mr Haughey to let him call for the removal of the whip from me. This he did at a parliamentary party meeting. The other half of this arrangement was that I would then resign the whip voluntarily, so that the motion didn't have to be passed. This I duly did – again in loyalty to the party leader.

But did the new claims stand up to serious scrutiny? More seriously, what were the strategic imperatives at work? Doherty presented his revelations as an act of remorse. He was confessing the truth because the proposed Phone Tapping Bill would shortly have forced him to compound the lie. The measure had been introduced by the Minister for Justice, Ray Burke, as part of the Programme for Government agreed between Fianna Fáil and the Progressive Democrats. As a consequence, Doherty wanted to unburden himself once and for all in a sort of Pauline conversion. The journalists present did not doubt the raw emotive power evinced by a politician stripped of equivocation.[35]

There are, undoubtedly, a number of ways of reading the Doherty recantation. On one level it could be ascribed to cynical remorse. It is certainly true, as the *Irish Times* editorial pointed out, that Doherty's claim that he had nothing to gain and everything to lose was, at best, disingenuous. The retraction served to provide a 'last chance' launch pad for Doherty's campaign to re-enter the Dáil.[36] At the same time, he was clearly aware that in speaking out he risked bringing the party into further disrepute and severing all residual contact with Haughey loyalists, all without any guarantee that his actions would endear him to the Reynolds camp.

The account contained a number of inconsistencies. First, Doherty maintained that there was concern within government about leaks to the press and that 'it was the function of the Minister for Justice to prevent such leaks'. It is unclear from the text alone – and Doherty would not elaborate then or since – where the imperative basis of that function lies: the office of state or the head of government? It would appear Doherty believed that it was an act of treason for a government minister to deliberately leak to destabilise his own administration. In those circumstances, given Haughey's declared position that the leaks had to stop, it was therefore his responsibility to trace the source by whatever means possible, even if that meant breaking the law.

Secondly, without providing any evidence to sustain his claim, he suggested that Mr Ainsworth, the Deputy Garda Commissioner in charge of security, had agreed that the Cabinet leaks were a national problem, thereby transferring the

---

[35] John Waters, 'Nobody was spared – least of all himself', *Irish Times*, 22 January 1992. See also Jimmy Walsh, 'Emotional drama of "betrayal" at the top', *Irish Press*, 22 January 1992.

[36] Editorial, 'Sean Doherty 1982–1992', *Irish Times*, 22 January 1992.

blame for the operation onto a civil servant. Thirdly, he maintained that he was merely following advice, a position in stark contrast to the relevant documentation released by the Fine Gael-Labour coalition government. It was a matter of public record that the order to tap Arnold's phone was initially vetoed by officials within the Department of Justice.[37] Finally, he admitted that he did not seek nor got any instruction from any member of the Cabinet, which included Haughey as head of government, a significant dilution of the wide-ranging allegation broadcast on *Nighthawks*.

The most difficult aspects of the statement were the disparaging references to the phone-tapping legislation, measures he decried as lacking in 'legislative urgency' and claimed were forced through by the capricious Progressive Democrats. At no stage did he accept the need for such legislation to prevent the kind of action he took in 1982. The omission was the weakest element of a statement supposedly girded with a desire to return to a moral high ground. As Bruce Arnold pointed out, the phrasing throughout was exceptionally careful. '[It] does not preclude knowledge among colleagues, at the time, of what he was doing. Nor does it rule out the involvement of others in his decision to make the statement in the way he chose, without any question from the press.'[38] Nevertheless Arnold was in no doubt that Doherty was now telling the truth, if only out of spite for not being rehabilitated earlier by Haughey.[39]

Neither for the first time in his political career – nor the last – was Haughey to find there was a blatant contradiction between his version of events and that of his accusers. His closest advisors remained convinced that he could ride out the political storm, but privately Haughey intimated that this time there could be little chance of success. Martin Mansergh telephoned the Taoiseach at his home immediately after the *Nighthawks* programme and detected a rare and momentary sense of 'total resignation' in his boss's reaction. After the televised statement by Doherty, the Taoiseach briefed Mansergh, who returned to Government Buildings and spent five hours preparing a detailed response. Despite the energy expended, there was a sense that the fight was over.

Haughey maintained that his first knowledge about the tapping of the journalists' phones was when Peter Murtagh of the *Irish Times* broke the story on 18 December 1982 but that his anxiety about Doherty's handling of the Justice portfolio predated this, a fact he argued was made manifest by the arrangements he had made for a judicial inquiry.

> I have never felt beholden in any way to Mr Doherty for statements he made in

[37] The gardaí experienced difficulties identifying the second tap on Kennedy because the telephone was not registered in her name.

[38] Bruce Arnold, *Haughey: His Life and Unlucky Deeds* (London, 1993), p. 277.

[39] Bruce Arnold, 'People's verdict awaited on Haughey culpability', *Irish Independent*, 23 January 1992. Arnold was doubtful that Haughey would let go of power. He equated the Fianna Fáil leader to 'an aging wrestler once again committing himself to well-worn and familiar tricks and sleights of hand, in the ring.' Arnold concluded with an appeal to the people to act as jury.

> 1983, nor have I acted as if I were... Is it not obvious to everyone that he has become obsessed with the belief that it is in his electoral interest to present himself to the people of Roscommon as an innocent victim or scapegoat, who was made to carry the can for others? The truth of the matter, however, is that he was the author of his own downfall in 1982. Having been given a position of high responsibility and the utmost sensitivity, requiring correct behaviour at all times, he engaged in a multiplicity of actions which, when a full picture of them emerged at the end of the 1982 administration he could not convincingly justify or explain and which no one else could defend...
>
> I am forced to the conclusion that Mr Doherty is attempting to bring down both the present FF/PD Coalition Government and the Taoiseach for personal political gain, and perhaps for other political motives, regardless of the short or long-term consequences for his party. It is clear from the debate on the motion of confidence in me at the parliamentary party that renewed allegations of illegal phone-tapping or surveillance are now regarded as the most effective means of achieving this objective, even though such allegations were unsubstantiated and untrue.[40]

In order to present the best possible interpretation of events Haughey left himself, however unnecessarily, a hostage to fortune he could ill afford to be. He claimed that the first knowledge he had of the taps was when Doherty attended a meeting at his office attended by another Fianna Fáil minister, whom he identified as Ray MacSharry. MacSharry, however, failed to substantiate this version of events. Although confirming that he was present at a meeting on the day in question, MacSharry stated that he did not hear what was being discussed, adding enigmatically 'what he was discussing was a matter for Mr Doherty'.[41] It was a less than ringing endorsement, as was the decidedly neutral contribution made by the former Deputy Garda Commissioner Joe Ainsworth, that the controversy represented 'total and absolute politics between two political people at the present time'.[42] Haughey's further suggestion to journalists that they should read the intervention by Padraig Flynn on RTÉ radio the previous weekend as confirming evidence of an elaborate leadership plot similarly backfired. Flynn angrily riposted with a transcript from the interview which showed he had merely said that Doherty should clarify his remarks. Flynn then made Haughey's response a leadership issue.

> Mr Haughey has misquoted me to portray Mr Doherty's statement as part of an elaborate leadership challenge. This conspiracy theory has no basis in fact but serves to distract from the issues raised. It should not be allowed to serve as a distraction from these serious issues, nor should the Taoiseach indulge in public misquotations of colleagues to create distractions where none exist.[43]

---

[40] *Irish Times*, 23 January 1992, p. 8.

[41] James Downey, 'MacSharry can't back Haughey's story', *Irish Independent*, 23 January 1992.

[42] *Irish Times*, 22 January 1992, p. 7.

[43] Quoted in John Foley, 'Flynn blasts conspiracy link', *Irish Independent*, 23 January 1992.

What made matters worse was that Haughey appeared to renege on an earlier commitment to stand aside in the short term by noting petulantly that he alone would decide when to vacate the leadership. Bruce Arnold admitted the grittiness of the performance but could not resist seeing further Machiavellian impulses in its staging. 'He was seated against the backdrop of a dark curtain, which gave the occasion some of the atmosphere of a Jacobean theatre set – rich, primitive, faintly sinister, as though hidden figures were monitoring the conviction and mapping further speeches of defence.'[44] As Dick Walsh pointed out, those who had for years followed Haughey looking for a smoking gun eventually found one, with two sets of prints.[45] Yet, despite the clear inconsistencies in Doherty's story and very serious questions over its timing, the media frenzy centred on whether Haughey could survive the censure of the Progressive Democrats. This issue became the sole focus of media now running, as in 1983, in a pack.[46]

Although the ritual slaughter may have had its public origins in Hell's Kitchen, it can only be rendered explicable by reference to the private decision to cede the principle of single-party government to the Progressive Democrats in 1989. Haughey proved incapable of quelling the suspicion and distrust of senior Fianna Fáil strategists towards even the concept of coalition, never mind with O'Malley. The Modern Prince found himself locked in a loveless political marriage, and each side was aware that the electorate viewed neither as an eligible suitor should one obtain a decree nisi. Although they formed a working arrangement, the divisions within and between the coalition partners rendered it susceptible to the latest crisis.

The accusations from Doherty, whom the *Sunday Times* described as 'hopelessly compromised',[47] had tapped into a widespread credence that O'Malley seized upon. The final push was publicly delivered not because of principle within Fianna Fáil but rather the self-interest of the junior coalition partner, the Progressive Democrats. O'Malley saw in the dispute an opportunity to demonstrate his abiding aversion to the politics of Haughey. His strategy, if he had planned one, was also beginning to emerge. He was distancing himself from Fianna Fáil politics at the time while keeping his options open should he seek to demand Haughey's dismissal. It fitted into a pattern of behaviour.

---

[44] Bruce Arnold, *Haughey: His Life and Unlucky Deeds* (London, 1993), p. 278.

[45] Dick Walsh, 'Two sets of prints on the smoking gun', *Irish Times*, 25 January 1992.

[46] See T. Ryle Dwyer, 'Haughey's trial by media continues', *Irish Independent*, 23 January 1992. For a more considered analysis see T. Ryle Dwyer, *Short Fellow: A Biography of Charles J. Haughey* (Dublin, 1999), pp. 425–432.

[47] Peter Millar, 'Time and patience run out for Ireland's tainted "Boss"', *Sunday Times*, 26 January 1992. With few notable exceptions, the deficiencies in the Doherty case and the rationale for jettisoning Haughey were not seriously tested in the domestic media. See also John Waters, 'Exit our last leading character', *Irish Times*, 28 January 1992; Eoghan Harris, 'CJ more convincing but probably doomed', *Irish Independent*, 23 January 1992; T. Ryle Dwyer, 'Haughey's trail by media continues', *Irish Independent*, 23 January 1992; and Martin Mansergh, 'C.J. Haughey and the phone tapping saga', *Irish Independent*, 24 January 1992.

The junior partner in the government had already successfully demanded the sacking of the Tánaiste, Brian Lenihan, for allegedly lying over a highly contentious attempt to persuade the President not to grant the dissolution of the Dáil following the collapse of FitzGerald's 1981–1982 administration but to appoint Haughey Taoiseach without the inconvenience of an election. Acceding to that request not only torpedoed Lenihan's campaign as Fianna Fáil's nominee for the presidency of Ireland eighteen months earlier but also further undermined Haughey's position within the party. Now, the re-awakening of the GUBU scandal added significantly to both the fissure within the party and its relationship with the Progressive Democrats. As usual, the conflict centred on the persona of Charles J. Haughey.

In the wake of the *Nighthawks* programme O'Malley issued a vehement denial that the need to use all necessary means to stop the leaking of Cabinet details was ever raised at Cabinet within his knowledge. 'That's not to say that some members of the Cabinet did not know about the matter, but clearly it was not going to be raised in front of the Cabinet as a whole.'[48] Reynolds, who recalls Haughey's plaintive attempts to persuade his internal critics to protect the integrity of Cabinet confidentiality, challenges that recollection. Careful, however, to remain neutral on the issue of whether Haughey ordered Doherty to tap the phones to prevent publication of sensitive information, Reynolds maintains that the deleterious effects of the leaks were raised a number of times.

> It was a very unhappy period in government because there were leaks after leaks after leaks with the result that in the end you didn't feel like speaking your mind and government became at a large extent crippled by all those leaks. Nobody wanted their business bandied around like that which was happening. That wing of the party were being blamed and those members of the Cabinet that represented that wing were being blamed by the party. It got very nasty.
>
> Q.: *But was it ever discussed in Cabinet? Did Haughey ever say that this has got to stop?*
>
> To my best recollection I would have said a few times. Anybody would have to say it, you just could not tolerate it going on day after day, week after week. It was undermining the government; it was undermining the party.[49]

Almost immediately after Doherty's televised statement, O'Malley let it be known that he was 'devastated' by the 'chilling account' now offered by the former Minister for Justice; an account he inferred – but did not explicitly state – meant that Haughey had authorised the tapping.[50] To emphasise the point, Progressive Democrats tacticians began to brief heavily that the survival of the government was at stake. The following day a statement was released suggesting that it was 'not for the Progressive Democrats to decide as between the conflicting accounts'.

---

[48] *Irish Times*, 17 January 1992.

[49] Albert Reynolds, interview with the author, Dublin, December 2001.

[50] Emily O'Reilly, 'Haughey knew says Doherty', *Irish Press*, 22 January 1992.

The statement expressed exasperation at how the effectiveness of government was being constantly undermined. The unspoken common denominator was Haughey. The price for the maintenance of the government was then set out in unsubtle language.

> The situation which has now arisen is one which we view with the utmost gravity. It calls for an immediate response in order that the credibility and stability of the Government be immediately restored.
>
> While the Progressive Democrats will not interfere in the internal affairs of another party, we are anxious to see that the acute dilemma facing the Government is speedily resolved. [51]

An *Irish Press* editorial asked rhetorically whether 'the resurrection of these ten-year-old allegations by a man, who has been untruthful about them in the past, merited the downfall of this government'.[52] Haughey's defence, Progressive Democrats sources conceded to the *Irish Times*, was, quite simply, 'no longer the issue'.[53] The following day the *Irish Press* advised, cautiously, that Haughey should go for the benefit of the national interest, a justification Haughey himself had used to excuse the sacking of Lenihan.[54]

Haughey had already made up his mind. He had determined that he would not fight another general election as leader of Fianna Fáil. O'Malley came to his office to spell out an altogether unnecessary ultimatum. It was agreed that Haughey would stand down the following Thursday, after the budget had been voted on. To ensure that the deal was followed through, the Progressive Democrats took the precaution of seeking public witness by releasing its terms.

> The support of the Progressive Democrats for the Government will be withdrawn if the necessary step to restore the authority and effectiveness of the Government is not taken during the immediate aftermath of Budget Day.[55]

---

[51] Progressive Democrats statement, quoted in *Irish Times*, 23 January 1992, p. 9.

[52] *Irish Press*, 23 January 1992.

[53] Denis Coughlan, 'Haughey terminally damaged by Doherty, PDs conclude', *Irish Times*, 23 January 1992. The PD leadership was taking the line that the coalition government had to be maintained while allowing the Fianna Fáil party to make its own decisions 'without obvious or overt pressure from the Progressive Democrats'. The Progressive Democrats were presented as a natural party of government, 'a policy-driven party', that had delivered 'a good deal of input' into the formulation of the Budget. There was no questioning as to why a coalition partner should not support the head of government if he was being unjustifiably accused. But this was not the issue. The protestations from O'Malley remind one of a bastardised Augustinian maxim: Lord, make me chaste, but not yet. A more measured analysis was provided in a special contribution by the anonymous commentator Drapier, who suggested that the scandal placed the 'mould breakers' on the horns of a dilemma as O'Malley wanted to remain in power at almost any cost. The introduction of various tribunals of inquiry were an attempt to 'sidle out' of its responsibilities: see Drapier, 'PDs have had enough but will the Club of 55 act?', *Irish Times*, 23 January 1992.

[54] *Irish Press*, 24 January 1992.

[55] Progressive Democrats statement of 23 January 1992, quoted in *Irish Times*, 24 January 1992, p. 1.

According to Collins, there was nothing personal in the ultimatum, 'it was just business however brutal'. However, given the history between O'Malley and Haughey stretching back to the Arms Crisis in 1970, this seems simplistic.[56] After the final Cabinet meeting Haughey allegedly signalled his impending departure to colleagues with the words: 'you can't keep on refuting allegations all the time.'[57] It remains to be asked what had changed in the intervening years to make the defence appear so threadbare? By 1992, few within the party were prepared to give Haughey the benefit of the doubt. He ran out of political cover despite a spirited press conference in which he plaintively asked journalists to compare his own openness and availability to the manufactured performance put forward by Doherty and what he termed the 'country and western alliance'. For him to resign would allow people to get to power 'by totally illegitimate means'.[58] Later, at a meeting of the Fianna Fáil national executive, Haughey proclaimed: 'We have nothing to fear from our enemies without, it is the enemies within we must fear.'[59] It became the epitaph for his political career. The remark was a veiled reference to the political manoeuvrings of Albert Reynolds that were infinitely more damaging than the dubious and flawed pedigree of Doherty and which was the real reason why the Modern Prince consented to fall on his sword at last.

The unanswered question was whether Doherty was working to his own agenda or to that of Flynn and Reynolds. Doherty stated explicitly that Reynolds was blameless in both the timing and the execution of the retraction.

> I want to add emphatically that I have never discussed this with Albert Reynolds, nor have I talked to him in the past fortnight. This statement flows out of the events of nine years ago. It is about me, my reputation, my loss of faith in the Taoiseach, and my resignation.[60]

As with much of the reporting on Haughey, the complexity of who stood to gain both inside Fianna Fáil and inside the government by the *volte-face* and its curious timing was inexplicably reduced to an irrelevant debate on whether Haughey knew – a question only the two men could answer and which neither would.[61]

---

[56] In one of the most entertaining contributions to the entire debate over Haughey's role in Irish politics, John Waters likened him to J.R. Ewing, the Machiavellian oil baron anti-star of the hit television series *Dallas*. O'Malley was described as a bit player, a facsimile of the embattled and embittered Cliff Barnes character, who was always bested by J.R.'s cunning and style. See John Waters, 'Exit our last leading character', *Irish Times*, 28 January 1992.

[57] Stephen Collins, *The Haughey File: The Unprecedented Career and Last Years of The Boss* (Dublin, 1992), p. 232.

[58] *This Week*, RTÉ, quoted in the *Irish Times*, 24 January 1992.

[59] Stephen Collins, *The Haughey File: The Unprecedented Career and Last Years of The Boss* (Dublin, 1992), p. 233.

[60] Sean Doherty press conference, 21 January 1992; *Irish Times*, 22 January 1992.

[61] According to Stephen Collins's 1992 account, the incident provided confirming evidence of the

Reynolds, in fact, remained pointedly neutral as Dublin politics went into overdrive. Tom Savage maintained that neither Reynolds nor any of the senior members of his team, including Flynn, McCreevy and Geoghegan Quinn, knew anything about the visit of Doherty to Carr Communications until, in Reynolds's case, an hour before broadcast, and in the case of the others, until it went out unedited. 'Albert knew nothing about it whatsoever. In fact nobody in the political mainstream knew anything about it.'[62] According to Haughey the allegations were explicable only with reference to the machinations of a clique determined to depose the leader of Fianna Fáil by subterfuge.

> I wish to state categorically that I was not aware at the time of the tapping of these telephones and that I was not given and did not see any transcripts of the conversations... Unfortunately, when Senator Doherty seeks long afterwards to substitute for what he now claims to have been a premeditated blanket of lies an entirely new version of events, the public have no means of judging the truthfulness of any of his statements by themselves. It is perhaps significant that four years ago, Mr Doherty admitted to a journalist that his "memory about that period is getting a bit hazy."[63] I also regard it as significant that Mr Doherty, if he has an interest in telling the truth, the whole truth and nothing but the truth, declined to be questioned by the press yesterday about the inconsistencies between his different versions of events.[64]

---

fact that Doherty felt personally aggrieved at the failure to rehabilitate his career and felt the passage of the Phone Tapping Bill 'could push him over the edge': Stephen Collins, *The Haughey File: The Unprecedented Career and Last Years of The Boss* (Dublin, 1992), pp. 226–227. When the Bill was published, Doherty reportedly 'blew a gasket' (p. 226). Collins surmised that Doherty's decision to go on *Nighthawks* and subsequently clarify his statement probably had nothing to do with the new generation of plotters; rather, events took a turn in Reynolds's favour. However, in his 2000 survey of Fianna Fáil politics, using an interview conducted by Whelan and Masterson that implied that Doherty was acting as a cipher for a further Reynolds challenge, Collins accepted that the truth behind the Doherty intervention has never been adequately explained (p. 223): Whelan and Masterson, *Bertie Ahern: Taoiseach and Peacemaker* (Dublin, 1998), p. 89. Bertie Ahern is quoted saying:

> The first time Albert, Flynn and the boys had a go in November I led the campaign openly to keep Haughey in power and we succeeded. The second time they came after him with the Doherty interview about the telephone bugging Haughey was gone... I don't know who set it up but Albert, Flynn and the boys obviously knew about it, because Flynn had gone on the radio the previous Sunday about the same thing.

See also Flynn's interview with the *Sunday Tribune*, 19 January 1992. Interestingly, the international press took a more balanced view of the affair. The *Times* reported that there seemed to be 'some substance in his [Haughey's] claim that Mr Doherty, who had admitted he had lied in the past, might be lying again for political ends in his Roscommon constituency': 'Dissidents urged to act on Haughey', *The Times*, 23 January 1992.

62 Albert Reynolds confirmed this account separately in an interview with this author, December 2001. He tried to persuade Savage to stop Doherty from going ahead with the broadcast.

63 *Sunday Tribune*, 24 May 1987.

64 Charles Haughey statement, 22 January 1992; reproduced in the *Irish Times*, 23 January 1992. Interestingly, Haughey told the subsequent press conference that his statement was prepared rapidly and that he would have liked time to elaborate on it. Haughey retreated from this by 4

It is certainly the case that Doherty's intervention threatened the entire Reynolds enterprise. Reynolds feared, correctly, that given serious question marks over the credibility of the former Minister for Justice, if it could be established that his team had wilfully revisited the turmoil of 1982, he might be portrayed as a man willing to bring the party into disrepute for narrow sectional gain.[65] Haughey was right was about a leadership plot but it did not centre on Doherty; in fact, the disgraced former Minister for Justice threatened to derail months of secret planning. It was precisely for this reason that Reynolds refused to become involved in the melee immediately after the confession. Evidence to back up this assertion comes from Savage, who had called Reynolds as soon as he read the statement that was to be televised. He was amazed at the reaction.

> At five minutes to eight I rang Reynolds and said where are you going to be at half eight and afterwards. Down in Longford. OK I need to let you know, I think the phrase I used was the balloon was going up from Sean Doherty at quarter past eight tonight. There was dead silence. 'Holy Sweet Jesus, can you stop him!' That to me was a very interesting conversation but it took me years to work it out. He was absolutely deeply threatened by what was going to happen. I knew that he had some other way of knowing when Haughey was going and that this was going to cause a problem.[66]

Albert Reynolds does not dispute the inevitable inference that he had some undertaking in advance of that confession that Haughey would go on an agreed date, and feared that the undertaking would be unravelled by Doherty's unexpected move. Reynolds confirms the plan involved 'to some degree, shall we say,' Dr John O'Connell, a former confidant of Haughey's who was – unexpectedly – to become Minister for Health in Reynolds's first administration. But the former Taoiseach refuses to elaborate on the details of that plan, remarking mischievously that 'it may never be known'.[67]

Dr John O'Connell was a millionaire who had a lifelong ambition to serve in a major ministry. He had been long promised a significant political position by Haughey but had never attained it. His social and business contacts ensured that Haughey and his stud-owning daughter Eimear gained entrée into the lucrative international racing circuit but no political patronage was ever delivered in return. O'Connell had given Haughey £50,000 in 1985, the day he joined Fianna Fáil, ostensibly the proceeds of a horse sold by the Abbeville stud to the Saudi Arabian billionaire Prince Mahmoud Fustok. O'Connell progressively lost confidence in the Modern Prince and transferred allegiance to Reynolds, calling him occasionally as late as two a.m. in early January 1982.

February, reading the pre-prepared statement into the Dáil record unchanged: *Dáil Debates*, vol. 415, cols 764–771, 4 February 1992.

[65] Albert Reynolds, interview with the author, Dublin, December 2001.

[66] Tom Savage, interview with the author, Belfast, December 2001.

[67] Albert Reynolds, interview with the author, Dublin, December 2001.

The first public indication that O'Connell played any role in the downfall of Charles J. Haughey came in an article penned by Sam Smyth for the *Irish Independent* to mark the tenth anniversary of the Doherty allegations. Smyth, one of the best-informed political commentators in the Irish media, reported that Haughey had arranged to meet O'Connell in an intermediary's house in Sutton.

> Haughey was seeking an assurance from O'Connell that he would keep the [£50,000] payment from Fustok, and other details of their business dealings secret. Dr John O'Connell couldn't accede to his old friend's request and told Haughey he was a serious liability to Fianna Fáil and urged him to resign the leadership.[68]

Smyth further reported that O'Connell sought and received a written assurance from Haughey that he would retire in March. In these circumstances, the intervention of Doherty served no strategic interest for either of Haughey's opponents.

Reynolds justified the appointment of O'Connell on pragmatic grounds: a health professional with a track record of social concern, he was well placed to sort out the failing health service in the Republic. However, the undertaking had a further and deeper purpose. It had been won as the price of delivering a stark message to Haughey: go, or be exposed. At stake was the potential disclosure that Haughey was secretly utilising his position for self-interest and that substantial gifts from a golden circle were needed to fund his increasingly grandiose lifestyle. Despite the lack of any hard evidence to substantiate the long-held belief that Haughey was the spider at the centre of a corrupt web, the potential threat to the Fianna Fáil leader's self-belief was acute. Re-opening the Pandora's box of questions about the funding of his lifestyle at a time when he had run out of ideological ammunition would have amouned to political suicide.

It was this threat of exposure rather than the discreditable testimony of the former Minister for Justice or the righteous indignation of Des O'Malley that ultimately caused Haughey to reconsider his position. The political leverage of Albert Reynolds meant that Haughey had been left with no alternative. Haughey had tried to contrive the circumstances of his departure, allowing time for his chosen successor, Bertie Ahern, to gather support. But this time it was too late; Reynolds had done the groundwork well in advance In fact, Reynolds only wanted to serve one term at the top. The modesty of this ambition had in its favour the promise that Fianna Fáil factionalism of the past could be averted by the presentation of a dream interim leadership ticket. There was also a threat. If Haughey's personal skeletons were exposed, Ahern would be tarred with its legacy. It was a risk that the shrewd Minister for Finance calculated not worth taking. Reynolds had Ahern over a barrel and Ahern accepted it.

Following Reynolds's elevation to the leadership in February 1992, he

---

[68] Sam Smyth, 'The end for Charles Haughey', *Irish Independent*, 26 January 2002.

immediately began moves to work for a breakthrough on the national question, against all expectation and in conditions of great secrecy. He did not tell O'Malley about his secret contacts with the Provisional IRA, nor did he risk informing the established civil service. Instead, the operation to transcend the Anglo-Irish Agreement that had so constrained the possibility of movement was formulated within Fianna Fáil and specifically within the Department of the Taoiseach. Reynolds, a pragmatic politician who eschewed nationalist rhetoric, approached the North as a business problem and delivered undreamed of results. His perseverance and ingenuity was rewarded with an IRA ceasefire in August 1994. Despite the fall of Reynolds over a maladroit handling of the internal dynamics of coalition within months of that triumph, the IRA cessation and the loyalist ceasefire brokered six weeks later stand as his greatest achievement: the defining cornerstone of his stewardship of the nation and a reflection of the powerful subterranean republican impulses informing Fianna Fáil's internal politics.

The irony was that the possibility of a breakthrough was first mooted in 1986 when the Redemptorist priest Fr Alex Reid, from Clonard Monastery in West Belfast, first approached Garret FitzGerald's administration with the message that the Provisional IRA wanted to move away from violence. The offer was made again to Haughey in 1987 and 1988, at a time when John Hume was being pilloried for engaging in talks with Sinn Féin north of the border. A number of meetings were arranged between Bertie Ahern, Martin Mansergh and prominent members of the Provisional IRA. Haughey, however, remained aloof, telling Ahern that if the discussions were made public he would be 'on his own'.[69] Without the backing of higher authority the contacts proved inconclusive. It required considerable moral courage to break the logjam, a commodity in short supply as the passage of time had demonstrated. Haughey's administration was not prepared to deliver the radical promise inherent in the republican mystique of the Modern Prince. That Haughey refused to endorse publicly the work of a man he had once pilloried as 'the High Priest of compromise' was a particularly cruel and spineless betrayal. By the time the Modern Prince departed the public arena on February 1992 – quoting Othello, that he had done the state some service – he had, in effect, squandered the vision that had sustained his career and at last propelled him to power.

---

[69] Cited in T. Ryle Dwyer, *Short Fellow: A Biography of Charles J. Haughey* (Dublin, 1999), p. 332.

Chapter Six

Unravelling the Project: The Impact of the Tribunals

> If a prince wants to maintain his rule he must be prepared not to be virtuous, and to make use of this or not according to need.
>
> – Machiavelli, *The Prince*, p. 50

Charles Haughey loved the finest things in life: his Gandon-designed mansion on the outskirts of the capital, which he opined precluded the necessity for an official residence; a private table in Dublin's most exclusive restaurant, Le Coq Hardi; racehorses; his island home off the western seaboard; patronage of the arts. They combined to present an image as carefully tailored as the Charvet shirts he imported through the diplomatic postal service, using money from the public purse designed for party political purposes. This vanity, another key aspect of his enigmatic personality, was to be his undoing. During his years in public office, speculation ebbed and flowed about the source of the wealth he had accumulated while, in theory, surviving since 1959 on a parliamentary salary.[1] Did it derive from the accountancy practice he had founded a decade earlier, from land speculation deals using inside knowledge in the 1960s, or, as suggested *sotto voce*, from the raiding of the public coffers?

Essentially, the Modern Prince was a kept man – and an expensive one at that. Until achieving the pinnacle of power, Haughey bullied his bank into funding a long-term overdraft, in the process tearing up the credit-rating system. Once he became Taoiseach, he was bankrolled by a cartel of prominent businessmen who saw the Fianna Fáil leader as the talisman of their generation. From the

[1] Interestingly, when Jack Lynch was Taoiseach, he maintained that he was still living in a semi-detached house over which the bank held a charge of fifty per cent. This was at a time that Haughey was speculating in a Georgian manor. The speculation surrounding Haughey's personal finances intensified following the leadership challenge in January 1983. One of the first articles appeared under the by-line of Des Crowley in the *Evening Press*, 28 January 1983. It quoted 'well-informed speculation' that 'Haughey owed one million pounds to a major bank and that the bank had held its hand because of his elevated position': cited in Mark O'Brien, *De Valera, Fianna Fáil and the* Irish Press (Dublin, 2001), p. 178. However, by then Haughey had long ago reached a settlement with AIB. The debt was cleared within months of his becoming Taoiseach in 1979. See below, p. 149.

man who self-consciously conflated the interests of the nation with his own, one could extrapolate the interests of those who comprised his 'golden circle'.

Following serious allegations of payments to politicians published in November 1996, four years after he had departed the national scene, judicial tribunals were established to ascertain if there was any corrosive linkage between business and elite politicians. Given Haughey's centrality to Irish politics since becoming Minister for Justice in 1963, it was only a matter of time before it emerged that he was the recipient of over IR£1 million in payments from the country's pre-eminent retailer, Ben Dunne. The total figure of what appeared to be *ex gratia* payments for the period 1979–86 was tabulated at £8.6 million.[2] We now know what Haughey received during his tenure in office; we also know that there was a direct correlation between the level of funding and office bearing. We don't know why.

Although the tribunals have given us a detailed picture of how Haughey was funded, the unanswered question is whether these forensic financial inquiries will prove any more able to find Haughey's fingerprints on the 'smoking gun' than his political opponents. In part, this can be attributed to the focus, similar to that of the media reporting, on direct corruption, always a difficult accusation to prove and one in which the manner of presentation is everything. Therefore, it is necessary to deconstruct the evidence adduced by the tribunals and their modus operandi before turning to an overall assessment of Haughey.

By the time Haughey won the leadership of Fianna Fáil in December 1979, he was on the verge of bankruptcy. His financial address to the nation the following month, in which he set out honestly the true extent of the difficulties facing the Irish exchequer, could equally have applied to himself. Like the country, Haughey was broke. His involvement with the IRA during the Arms Crisis had carried an onerous economic, as well as political, cost. His attempt to reclaim lost ground throughout the 1970s was an expensive affair, which, until he returned to the opposition front bench, was met with scarcely concealed derision by his bankers, Allied Irish Bank. In an internal memo the Regional General Manager stated that Haughey's attitude to his spiralling indebtedness 'could not and would not be tolerated'.[3] After Haughey's political rehabilitation in 1975, however, that is exactly what happened.

In September 1976 Haughey was summoned to meet a senior banking executive, James Denvir, to discuss excessive unauthorised drawings on his account. AIB had privately resolved to ask the recalcitrant shadow Minister for Health and Social Welfare to hand back his chequebook. Bank records detail that, when the moment of confrontation arrived, things did not go according to plan.

---

[2] It is beyond the scope of this book to go into the intricacies of the tribunals in exhaustive detail. The best summaries can be found in Colm Keena, *Haughey's Millions: Charlie's Money Trail* (Dublin, 2001), and Paul Cullen, *With a Little Help from my Friends: Planning Corruption in Ireland* (Dublin, 2002). Ted Harding of the *Sunday Business Post* is another expert chronicler of both the Moriarty and Flood Tribunals. See his articles, available online at http://www.sbpost.ie

[3] Colm Keena, *Haughey's Millions: Charlie's Money Trail* (Dublin, 2001), p. 52.

> At this point Mr Haughey became quite vicious and told Mr Denvir that "He would not give up his cheque book as he had to live" and "that we were dealing with an adult and no banker would talk to him [Mr Haughey] in this manner". Furthermore, he stated that if any drastic action were taken by the bank he could be a "very troublesome" adversary.[4]

The meeting ended, like so many others, with the bank granting Haughey a further extension to his overdraft. His rise from the backbenches was matched with an improvement in his stock with the mercantile class, a process that intensified when Fianna Fáil was returned to office in the 1977 landslide. In evidence given to the Moriarty Tribunal in February 1999, the chief executive of AIB, Gerry Scanlon, explained that despite his flaws – including his scathing contempt for a bank that would ask for its money to be repaid – Haughey was regarded as a 'Key Business Influencer'. Such an appellation in recognition of his prominence ensured that senior management of the bank would remain reticent about calling in Haughey's debts. AIB reckoned that his potential to bring in new business by virtue of his position outweighed the drawbacks of having such a troublesome client on its books. It was a Faustian pact that was to have profound implications. The financial journalist Colm Keena contended that throughout the 1970s that Haughey and his bankers were locked in an escalation imperative and the 'only currency which was to retain its value was the AIB money Haughey continued to spend'.[5] But there were limits, even to AIB's corporate patience.

As Haughey put in place the final moves to position himself as Jack Lynch's successor in late 1979, he faced the recognition that his precarious financial position could prove to be his Achilles heel. On 7 September 1979, Haughey contacted his long-suffering bank manager, Michael Phelan, to 'state categorically' that he wanted to resolve this dangerous situation once and for all. A week later, he told the bank he could reduce his indebtedness by £500,000 but wanted to settle the remaining debt for less than the full amount. What would the bank accept? His trusted friend and personal accountant, Desmond Traynor, moved to find the benefactors who would assuage the bank; detailed negotiations began on 13 September. It was suggested that a named businessman would refund the AIB borrowings in exchange for an arrangement to buy part of Haughey's Abbeville estate.[6]

Following Haughey's triumph over George Colley in the December 1979 leadership contest, Traynor again approached AIB. He explained that, owing to changed political circumstances, the proposal they had been discussing was no longer viable. Instead, he informed them, the merchant bank Guinness and Mahon

---

4 AIB internal memo, quoted by Colm Keena, *ibid.*, p. 61.

5 Colm Keena, *ibid.*, p. 46.

6 For full details of Haughey's relationship with AIB see John Coughlan, SC, Opening Statement to the Moriarty Tribunal, 28 January 1999, p. 22ff. All Moriarty Tribunal statements can be accessed at http://www.moriarty-tribunal.ie. Hereinafter, '*Moriarty Tribunal Statements*'.

was prepared to pay £600,000 for total discharge of £1.143 million of debt. According to counsel for the Moriarty Tribunal, when AIB demurred, Traynor opined that the only other option was 'to leave the debt outstanding indefinitely'.[7] High-level negotiations followed in which the bank progressively lowered its demands for the minimum acceptable final settlement figure. AIB records revealed that Chairman Niall Crowley and Deputy Chief Executive Patrick O'Keefe took the policy decision to bring the matter to a conclusion. Within a month of becoming Taoiseach, Haughey agreed to pay £750,000 in full settlement of his personal overdraft of £1,143,000.[8] The bank meekly accepted the loss of £393,000 from the Taoiseach of the day, despite holding securities on the Abbeville property far exceeding the total amount owed.

Just as surprising to the tribunal investigators was the fact that an account in arrears for a decade was suddenly and inexplicably paid off without any explanation of where the money came from. Haughey had declared to his bankers that he had no other source of income and no other bank accounts. A man with no business interests to justify merchant facilities was now able to call on its services to opt out of retail banking. When the mystique surrounding the financing of Charles J. Haughey's lifestyle is stripped away, a sordid reality is revealed; the most powerful politician in the country effectively prostituted the importance of his public office for private gain.

On the night he became Taoiseach for the first time, Haughey had returned to the former Lord Lieutenant's House on the outskirts of Dublin, where he held court beneath a framed copy of the 1916 Proclamation of Independence. For those present to venerate the new master, the abuse that had been hurled across the chamber of Dáil Éireann over Haughey's 'flawed pedigree' and desire to own the State was already a fading memory. Haughey was lord of all he surveyed, a domestic variant of the Anglo-Irish ascendancy. Through the careful husbanding of political charisma and economic argument, he had at last succeeded in becoming that iconic Fianna Fáil leader who could deliver prosperity to the Irish people and, more specifically, the business class.

Watching proudly as Haughey gained his position at the very pinnacle of Irish society was Patrick Gallagher of the Gallagher Group, a property and construction firm associated with Haughey for over a decade. The late patriarch of the firm, Matt Gallagher, had personally brokered the buying of Haughey's previous residence, the Grangemore estate in north Dublin, in 1969. During Haughey's short tenure, the Grangemore land was rezoned from agricultural to residential and subsequently bought back by Matt Gallagher's company. The transaction made the politician his first fortune and allowed the move to Abbeville. In an interview with the *Sunday Business Post* in 1998, Patrick Gallagher recounted that:

---

[7] John Coughlan, SC, *Moriarty Tribunal Statements*, 28 January 1999, p. 23ff.
[8] See Geraldine Kennedy, 'Haughey's use of power is exposed', *Irish Times*, 30 January 1999.

6 October 1982:
Top: Charlie McCreevy being escorted from Leinster House. *(Derek Speirs/Report)*. *Centre:* Coming out of Leinster House, Jim Gibbons is flanked by the waiting media. *(Derek Speirs/Report)*. *Bottom:* Following the Fianna Fáil parliamentary party meeting, Charles Haughey appears briefly to announce the result. Unsettled party members, among them Bertie Ahern, stand by. *(Derek Speirs/Report)*

Left: Emphasising Fianna Fáil's republican credentials at an exhibition in honour of Éamon de Valera, Ennis, 17 October 1982. The legend 'I arise to complete my task' is echoed *below* by Haughey's supporters at a rally on 31 January 1983. *(Derek Speirs/Report)*
Bottom: Commemorating Wolfe Tone, 11 October 1987. *(Derek Speirs/Report)*

Albert Reynolds emerges from Fianna Fáil election headquarters in Longford, 24 November 1982. *(Derek Speirs/Report)*

Desmond O'Malley and Chief Whip Bertie Ahern, *right*, at the February 1983 Fianna Fáil Árd Fheis. *(Derek Speirs/Report)*

Above: At the New Ireland Forum, 9 February 1984, *from left:* Bishop Cassidy, Dick Spring, Charles Haughey, Bishop Cahal Daly, Bishop Edward Daly, and Garret FitzGerald. *(Derek Speirs/Report)*

Below: Autographing copies of the Forum report, 2 May 1984. *(Derek Speirs/Report)*

Above: P.J. Mara and Martin Mansergh, powerful advisors, at a Fianna Fáil press conference, Leinster House, 28 May 1985. *(Derek Speirs/Report). Below, left:* Michael McDowell in 1986. He went on to become Attorney General and Minister for Justice in the 2002 coalition government. *(Derek Speirs/Report). Below, right:* Frustrating times, 2 June 1989. *(Derek Speirs/Report)*

Top: Michael O'Kennedy, Charles Haughey, and Desmond O'Malley at Áras an Uachtaráin to receive their seals of office, 12 July 1989. *(Derek Speirs/Report)*
Centre: Desmond O'Malley at an early Progressive Democrats conference. *(Derek Speirs/Report)*
Bottom: Charles Haughey shakes the hand of businessman Ben Dunne in 1986. (*Eamonn Farrell/Photocall Ireland*)

Above: Haughey responds to the Doherty allegations. On the table before him is a copy of the *Irish Times* transcript of Doherty's statement, with key passages underlined. Haughey's notes for the press conference read:

'Public will have to decide
Christmas dinner
Cannot escape conclusion
P. Flynn statement
Noonan Statement on T
Over a period of months
~~Done by Doherty~~'
(Derek Speirs/Report)

Left: Charles Haughey considered Ireland's presidency of the E.U. at the time of the summit paving the way for the reunification of Germany to be a highlight of his career. With Helmut Kohl, Dublin Castle, 28 April 1990. *(Derek Speirs/Report)*

Top: Charles and Maureen Haughey after enjoying a day aboard their yacht, the 'Celtic Mist', August 1994. *(Derek Speirs/Report)*

Below left: Leaving Dublin Castle after giving evidence before the tribunal, 15 July 1997. *(Derek Speirs/Report)*

Below right: Coming out of the Four Courts with Maureen, 25 March 1998. Close behind are their children Sean, Conor and Eimear (out of the frame). *(Derek Speirs/Report)*

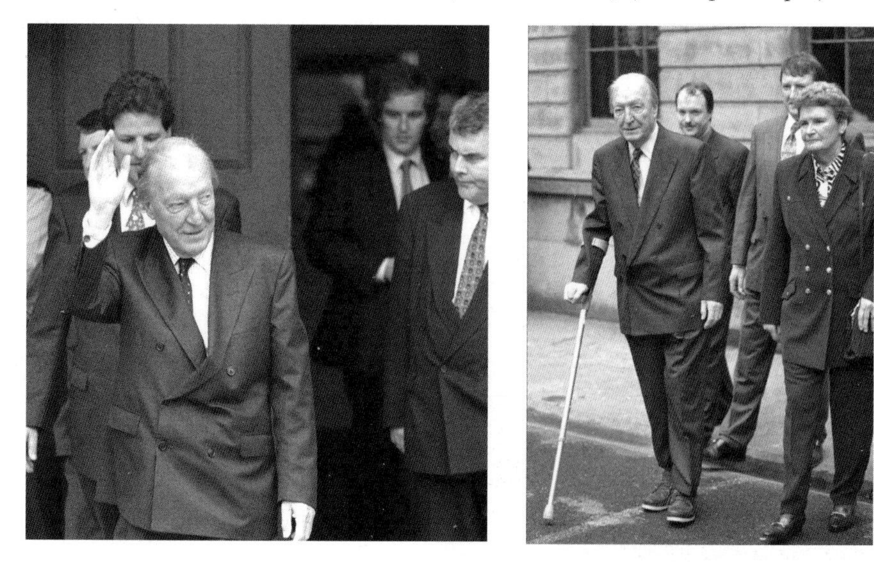

> Haughey was financed in order to create the environment which the Anglo-Irish had enjoyed and that we as a people could never aspire to... Somebody had to live in the big house...[9]

A week after the victory party at Abbeville, Patrick Gallagher was invited back to Haughey's mansion. The new Taoiseach had a delicate financial problem he wished to discuss. Gallagher, following family tradition, decided to help out.[10] Haughey first asked for £750,000. The twenty-eight-year-old chief executive, still in awe of the Modern Prince, whom he had known since childhood, replied that Haughey was 'well in a position to be able to carry a certain amount of that money himself'. Gallagher asked for the bottom line and was told it could be £600,000. Gallagher spoke to his brother Paul about it. 'We were flush with funds and I suggested we would go half. But we would have to get something tangible in return.' This was to be land at the Abbeville estate, the exact measurement to be agreed later, but land that Gallagher conceded would only be relinquished because Haughey was desperate. Again, Traynor was to be the lynchpin in brokering the agreement.

A memorandum of understanding was drawn up, dated 27 January 1980, under which the developers would pay a £300,000 deposit to buy thirty-five acres of the Abbeville estate for £1.225 million. A particularly onerous condition was inserted that called on the Gallagher Group to provide a sixty-acre stud farm within a twenty-mile radius of the General Post Office in Dublin. Furthermore, the Haughey family had a right to reject any proposed site without having to provide an explanation. If the deal was not concluded by 31 December 1985, it would fall through and Haughey would keep the deposit. Given the difficulty of sourcing such prime real estate in close proximity to the city centre, the contract was almost certainly destined to fail. The arrangement was widely considered a ruse, certainly by the Senior Counsel for the Moriarty Tribunal, who noted mischievously that:

> the agreement does not appear to have been prepared by a solicitor. Although it involved a substantial parcel of land and contained some unusual clauses, the agreement ran to only seven paragraphs and did not contain any of the usual conditions to be found in most contracts for the sale of land...[11]

According to Patrick Gallagher's testimony, this course of action was suggested by Traynor to ensure that the agreement remained confidential. The exorbitant cost of the transaction was rendered more curious given that the land in question

---

[9] Quoted in Colm Keena, *Haughey's Millions: Charlie's Money Trail* (Dublin, 2001), p. 29.

[10] For detailed account of Patrick Gallagher's evidence see Charles Mallon and Fergus Black, '£600,000 to save Taoiseach', *Irish Independent*, 22 May 1999, and Colm Keena, 'Land deal not "guise" to give money to Haughey', *Irish Times*, 22 May 1999.

[11] John Coughlan, SC, *Moriarty Tribunal Statements*, 18 May 1999, p. 4ff.

was zoned as agricultural.[12] Patrick Gallagher claimed that, although the primary reason behind the deal was not commercial, the deal made commercial sense. John Coughlan, for the tribunal, dismissed the contract as 'unenforceable in law'. Gallagher accepted this but regarded the deal as 'a matter of honour'; as he delicately put it, he had been helping a family friend out of a serious predicament. For his part, Haughey rejected the suggestion that the deal was an untenable 'sham', telling the tribunal that such an interpretation was 'a very dramatic statement and totally false'.[13]

The money to pay off AIB came from accounts held in Traynor's name at the merchant bank Guinness and Mahon.[14] Of this at least £300,000 was routed directly from the Gallagher Group. It has not been established who else contributed to the refunding of Haughey's debts, but a clear pattern began to emerge from the investigations. The politician had continued to spend extravagantly but subsequent bailouts from corporate benefactors corresponded mainly to periods when Fianna Fáil was in office. Keeping Haughey in the style befitting the new gentry was a price that some of the most influential businessmen in the country deemed worth paying. The question the tribunals wanted answered was: what, if anything, did they get in return?

Haughey was to claim in sworn evidence that he could see no wrong in a group of friends making the corporate decision to help its chosen politicians 'because they are running the country well, because they are engaging in initiatives which are beneficial to everyone, as I think I continually did'.[15] To Haughey there was a qualitative difference between helping a politician one admired and the allegation that such an action implied the recipient became beholden. It was

---

[12] When the Gallagher Group collapsed in April 1982 the receiver, Laurence Crowley, found the memorandum among the files. He sought legal advice on how to either pursue Haughey for the money or challenge the validity of the deal in the courts. He was warned in no uncertain terms that the possibility of succeeding was unlikely. 'Having regard to Mr Gallagher's business style prior to the collapse of the Gallagher Group, there must be a real possibility that his stated reasons for entering into an agreement of this kind would not be disproved.' The Revenue Commissioners took a similar view. In a letter to Crowley in May 1984, the Chairman of the Revenue, Seamus Pairieir, declared that, irrespective of Mr Haughey's 'status', a successful outcome 'would not seem to be great'. Nevertheless, the Revenue charged Haughey £80,000 in capital gains tax. This was duly paid. For Laurence Crowley's evidence see Colm Keena, 'Revenue did not pursue Haughey for £300,000', *Irish Times*, 25 May 1999.

[13] Ted Harding, 'Generous friends who asked nothing in return', *Sunday Business Post*, 24 September 2000.

[14] See also Mark Brennock, 'Impeding Haughey's [*sic*] meant banking on trouble', *Irish Times*, 20 February 1999.

[15] Quoted by Colm Keena, 'Getting by with a little help from his friends', *Irish Times*, 30 September 2000. See also Ted Harding, 'Generous friends who asked nothing in return', *Sunday Business Post*, 24 September 2000, and Gene Kerrigan, 'Truth and Reality are all we need', *Sunday Independent*, 24 September 2000. Kerrigan cut through the verbiage of Haughey's account with the acute observation: '"disinterested", "altruistic" patriots, one and all, Haughey told Moriarty, though of course he doesn't know who they were.'

a question of philosophical ethics. This position prompted Senior Counsel to the tribunal to exclaim: 'This is serious, Mr Haughey.' Haughey argued that he was 'thinking of the sort of situation where a group of friends would come together and, out of purely altruistic motives assist a particular politician in a particular difficulty'. The largesse was simply a unique political contribution; there certainly was 'no big line of differentiation'.[16]

For Allied Irish Bank, the mechanics of the deal, brokered by Traynor through accounts held in Guinness and Mahon, were irrelevant. The arrangement represented the end of a tempestuous and disastrous relationship in which the bank had broken all of its own internal guidelines.

> Allied Irish Bank believed the compromise was commercially justified, having regard to the protracted and difficult history of the accounts, to the fact that it was extricating itself from them and was to have no further dealings with the affairs of Mr. Haughey.[17]

Counsel for the Moriarty Tribunal made clear that the substantial discount negotiated by Haughey's advisor went far beyond commercially justified limits and in the process implied that that the bank had defaulted from its responsibility to the Irish nation by not breaking client confidentiality. According to Coughlan, AIB was negligent in not confirming the essential truth of an article speculating on Haughey's indebtedness, published in the *Evening Press* at the height of the O'Malley challenge for the leadership in 1983. On 1 February of that year the bank had released a statement to the paper in which it described 'any suggestion that Mr Haughey was heavily indebted to the bank in the previous year [as] outlandishly inaccurate.' According to counsel, this was splitting hairs. 'Of course it was correct to say that Mr Haughey's indebtedness for the year prior to the publication of the press article was inaccurately stated in the article but was not inaccurate so far as his historical indebtedness to the bank was concerned.'[18]

---

[16] Haughey did concede that he knew Traynor was locked into a wider circle, which Traynor could turn to for support. The mechanism bonding all together was the Ansbacher accounts system, money ostensibly held offshore and exempt from tax but in reality held in a number of coded accounts in Dublin. See below, pp. 166–169.

[17] Statement from AIB read by John Coughlan, SC, *Moriarty Tribunal Statements*, 28 January 1999, p. 26ff. The tribunal would establish that the credit facilities offered to Haughey far outweighed those offered to other clients.

> From the information available to the Tribunal there seems to have been no case in which the bank permitted borrowings of the order of Mr. Haughey's borrowings unconnected with any investment such as the purchase of new land or the requirements of the agricultural sector for working capital.

See John Coughlan, SC, *Moriarty Tribunal Statements*, 18 May 1999, p. 2ff. The bank was later to provide the tribunal with outline details of a number of cases involving a similar level of indebtedness in order to prove its assertion that Haughey was not treated any differently from other clients, an argument the tribunal treated with scarcely concealed derision.

[18] John Coughlan, SC, *Moriarty Tribunal Statements*, 28 January 1999, p. 25ff.

The implication was that the bank was being deliberately disingenuous and had a duty to reveal details in the public interest. Despite the provocation, this would have been an unlikely course of action for the bank to take and would have set a precedent of doubtful propriety. Furthermore, the case as outlined by the tribunal did not take into account that the messy interaction between politics and finance was a factor in the leadership dispute. Haughey was apparently suspected of dispensing favours for cash, but the tribunal had no power to pursue Martin O'Donoghue, who had hinted to a Cabinet colleague that money could be made available to financially compromised supporters of the plan to depose the leader.[19] This uncomfortable reality was simply not factored into the underlying strategy behind the defence of Haughey's conduct.

The thrust of the investigation was to weaken the defence proffered by Haughey that Des Traynor had taken control of his personal finances as early as 1960 to enable Haughey to devote his energies to politics and the good of the Irish people. The tribunal's counsel aimed to expose how intimately involved Haughey was in the management of his financial affairs and the extent of his knowledge of the business tactics utilised by Traynor in the pursuit of capital. Traynor could not be called upon to question the veracity of Haughey's testimony as, by the time the tribunals were launched, Traynor had died. The legacy of his actions, however, was to cast a heavy pall over proceedings at Dublin Castle.

As the tribunals reconstructed from only partial records the manner in which Traynor did business, evidence was presented which, at the very least, demonstrated sharp practice and, at worst, showed that an orchestrated tax evasion strategy was developed for an entire economic, political and business class that defrauded the Irish exchequer of millions of pounds of revenue. Should it be proven beyond doubt – or even perception – that Haughey knew of the nature of the accounts, not only would it demonstrate the wilful failure of the Taoiseach to collect tax revenue but, even more seriously, convict him of institutionalising political corruption for personal benefit. The smoking gun would be found.

The Moriarty Tribunal lawyers were helped considerably in their task by the experience garnered by Justice McCracken in his earlier investigation into payments made by Ben Dunne, one of Ireland's leading retailers, to Charles Haughey and to the former Fine Gael Minister Michael Lowry. It was Haughey's defence to the McCracken Tribunal that became the pivot on which Moriarty operated: was the former Taoiseach's evidence credible?

The McCracken Tribunal evidence was that within months of returning to office in February 1987, after five years in opposition, Haughey was once again in serious financial difficulties. Guinness and Mahon, the merchant bankers who had facilitated his overdrafts since 1979, had been bought by Japanese investors who demanded that the accounts be regularised. Traynor, who had

---

[19] See transcript of Martin O'Donoghue's telephone conversation with Ray MacSharry, published in Joe Joyce and Peter Murtagh, *The Boss* (Dublin, 1997), pp. 369–384, Appendix D.

become a director of Cement Roadstone, one of the country's largest contractors, set up a satellite banking service in the company's offices, using mercantile facilities operated in the Cayman islands by Ansbacher Cayman. As a matter of urgency he required £700,000 to close the Guinness and Mahon accounts and protect Haughey from possible disclosure. He began a frenzied search for investors. This time, one tycoon in particular offered to take care of the problem, remarking that it would be a big mistake trying to create a consortium. Should the information leak into the public domain, the damage would be devastating. 'I think Haughey is making a huge mistake trying to get six or seven people together… Christ picked twelve apostles and one of them crucified him.'[20] That benefactor was Ben Dunne, the chief executive of Dunnes Stores, Ireland's largest retail chain, a business with a weekly turnover of £1,012 million.

It was to be Dunne's own very public humiliation in Florida in February 1992, when he was arrested for possession of cocaine, that was to destroy the reputations of both men. In a bitter boardroom contest Dunne lost control of the family emporium and news of unorthodox payments to politicians leaked out. Haughey found his legacy under question as a series of tribunals were ceded to ascertain what return, if any, Dunne and others like him had received on their largesse. Although accepting that he could provide no evidence to back up the claim of corruption, Justice McCracken was unequivocal in his criticism of Haughey.

> It is quite unacceptable that a member of Dáil Éireann, and in particular a Cabinet Minister and Taoiseach, should be supported in his personal lifestyle by gifts made to him personally. It is particularly unacceptable that such gifts should emanate from prominent businessmen within the State. The possibility that political or financial favours could be sought in return for such gifts, or even be given without being sought, is very high, and if such gifts are permissible, they would inevitably lead in some cases to bribery and corruption…
>
> There is [however] no evidence of any favours sought of Mr. Charles Haughey by Mr. Ben Dunne, the Dunne family or the Dunnes Stores Group, nor is there any evidence of any attempt by Mr. Charles Haughey to exercise his influence for the benefit of Mr. Ben Dunne, the Dunne family or the Dunnes Stores Group. There appears in fact to have been no political impropriety on the part of Mr. Charles Haughey in relation to these gifts but that does not take away from the unacceptable nature of them.[21]

The McCracken report was littered with withering references to Haughey. For example:

> By allowing himself to be put in a position of dependency, Mr. Charles Haughey

[20] Quoted by Mr Justice Brian McCracken, *Report of the Tribunal of Inquiry (Dunnes Payments)* (Dublin, 1997), p. 43. Hereinafter '*McCracken Report*'.

[21] *McCracken Report*, p. 73.

> failed in his obligations to his constituents and to the citizens of this State, and indeed has devalued some of the undoubtedly valuable work which he did when in office.[22]

Haughey's evasions during the McCracken Tribunal probes served not only to heighten the perception that he was guilty of corrupting single-handedly the entire Irish political system but also to bring him to the dock to face charges of obstruction. The publication in full of Haughey's initial response to McCracken, coupled with a retraction and a grovelling apology in which he effectively accepted that he had lied, reduced his reputation to tatters.[23] The former Taoiseach stood charged with misleading an official instrument of the very Oireachtas he had pledged to serve; the ultimate political betrayal.

The deceits and half-truths demonstrated not only the disdain with which Haughey had treated the Tribunal but also gave an indication of how tenacious he was in protecting his secrets, a fact he finally acknowledged on 15 July 1997.

> I was concerned as to the effect that the publication of these payments would have for me in the public mind and in hindsight I accept that a lot of the problems and embarrassment that I have caused would have been avoided if I had been more forthcoming at each and every relevant period.[24]

In a telling exchange that day, counsel for the tribunal had asked Haughey in sworn evidence the following question:

> "[A]nd would you accept now, Mr. Haughey, that you sat outside the Tribunal in Abbeville waiting to see whether or not the Tribunal would gather sufficient evidence to make it incumbent upon you to make a statement. Would that be a fair summation?"
>
> His reply was: -
>
> "Well, it could be, but I suppose basically I was looking at the fact of the inevitable disclosure."[25]

The recantation was forced upon him by the forensic unravelling of his income and a mistaken expectation that the retraction would provide closure. Much of Haughey's evidence was described as 'unacceptable and untrue'.[26] His argument that Desmond Traynor handled all his financial affairs, despite the urgent need for approximately £1,000,000 in late 1987, was clinically deconstructed. In his first statement to the tribunal Haughey had maintained:

---

[22] *McCracken Report*, p. 51.

[23] *McCracken Report*, Seventh–Ninth Schedules, pp. 100–108.

[24] Statement of Charles J. Haughey, 15 July 1997, reproduced in the *McCracken Report*, Ninth Schedule, p. 107.

[25] *McCracken Report*, p. 65.

[26] *McCracken Report*, p. 57.

> I never had to concern myself about my personal finances as Desmond Traynor took over control of my financial affairs from about 1960 onwards. He saw to it as his personal responsibility to ensure that I would be free to devote my time and ability to public life and that I would not be distracted from my political work by financial concerns.[27]

Yet, the emergence of information about his dealings with AIB demonstrates that Haughey was all too aware of his financial position and only too willing to apply pressure on the bank to ensure compliance with his demands for more cash. McCracken held that:

> [i]f the problem was so serious as to require almost £1,000,000 it is quite unbelievable that Mr. Desmond Traynor would not have told Mr. Charles Haughey in some detail of the difficulties, and it is equally unbelievable that Mr. Charles Haughey would not have asked.[28]

Haughey had first denied that he knew Dunne had provided a total of £1.31 million and then, in an embarrassing *volte-face*, accepted Dunne's evidence. He argued – unconvincingly to the tribunal, which regarded it as unbelievable – that he could not remember the circumstances of the meeting.

> I would like to reiterate that I now accept that I received the £1.3 million from Mr. Ben Dunne and that I became aware that he was the donor to the late Mr. Des Traynor in late 1993 and furthermore I now accept Mr. Ben Dunne's evidence that he must have handed me £210,000 [in three drafts] in Abbeville in November 1991.
>
> I have absolutely no recollection of the November 1991 meeting, but it is clear from the evidence that the late Mr. Des Traynor received the money and that I got the benefit of it. I can offer no other rational explanation to show how the late Mr. Des Traynor could have received these drafts...[29]

Haughey went on to claim that he only became aware of the £1.1 million already paid by Dunne to help with his finances between 1987–91 after his departure from office. Haughey concluded with a plaintive appeal. 'I apologise... but I wish to emphasise that this serious lapse in the management of my personal affairs did not in any way affect the discharge of my public duty when in office.'[30] In a critical assessment of Haughey's evidence, the Chairman of the tribunal noted that he had asked the former Taoiseach if he had ever discussed with Desmond Traynor whether all the money from Dunne had been spent.

---

[27] Statement of Charles J. Haughey, 15 July 1997, reproduced in the *McCracken Report*, Seventh Schedule, p. 100.

[28] *McCracken Report*, p. 58.

[29] Statement of Charles J. Haughey, 15 July 1997, reproduced in the *McCracken Report*, Ninth Schedule, p. 107.

[30] *Ibid.*, p. 108.

Haughey gave the answer:

> "No. I mean, he would have been supplying the statements of account in that regard."
>
> The clear implication is, that despite his earlier denials, Mr. Charles Haughey had in fact received statements dealing with his accounts which he read and noted, and therefore he did not have to ask about his affairs, because he was already aware of them. The Tribunal believes this to be the true state of affairs.[31]

Particularly damaging to the qualified accountant, former Minister for Finance and several times Taoiseach, was the Justice McCracken's rejection of the contention that Haughey had been unaware of the offshore banking scheme. On the contrary, McCracken argued, Haughey had:

> deliberately shrouded the gifts in secrecy and allowed the money to be kept off-shore in an attempt to ensure that the Revenue authorities would never know of the gifts, or indeed presumably of the interest paid on the monies deposited on his behalf.[32]

Details of Haughey's dealings with the tribunal were forwarded to the Director of Public Prosecutions, with a thinly veiled directive that the former Taoiseach be charged with obstruction.[33] McCracken observed that there were many missing links in the sources of Haughey's incomes, particularly in the operation of what he described as an 'ingenious' off-shore system involving some £38 million, some of which went to fund Haughey's lifestyle. This connection ensured that further governmental inquiries would have to be established.[34]

Rather than accept the overall recommendation of the report calling for mandatory disclosure of members' interests and the introduction of a criminal offence to prevent deliberate misrepresentation to the Oireachtas, the Taoiseach Bertie Ahern established a series of more wide-ranging inquiries. Along with a detailed investigation into the funding of Charles J. Haughey under the aegis of Justice Brian Moriarty, a separate Department of Industry and Commerce inquiry was convened to investigate the £38 million Ansbacher tax scheme.[35] A

---

[31] *McCracken Report*, p. 60.

[32] *McCracken Report*, p. 73.

[33] See *McCracken Report*, p. 73. Haughey was charged with obstruction but the trial was postponed indefinitely, following his lawyers' successful arguments that adverse media comment had prejudiced proceedings.

[34] *McCracken Report*, p. 38.

[35] The final report into Ansbacher ran to fifteen volumes and was published on 6 July 2002, after the failure of a court challenge by some of those named. Such was the haste to make the report available that there was no pause to amend the release date on the cover: see *Report of the Inspectors Appointed to Enquire into the Affairs of Ansbacher (Cayman) Limited*, Record Number: 1999/163 Cos (Government Publications, Dublin, 24 June 2002). Hereinafter '*Ansbacher Report*'. For an examination of its findings and implications in relation to Haughey, see below, pp. 166–169.

concurrent probe into planning corruption in Dublin under the chairmanship of Justice Flood was also initiated, following the forced resignation of the Minister for Foreign Affairs, Ray Burke, over allegations that he benefited from corruption within the County Dublin planning process. The aim was apparently to insulate the present generation of politicians from the excesses associated with the past.

The case built up by counsel to the Moriarty Tribunal investigating payments to Haughey was carefully designed to ensnare him in a web of his own making. Haughey had begun by defending Traynor stoutly, a scenario not unlike that presented to McCracken. Yet he claimed that the accounts were all established without his knowledge and were considerably overdrawn for most of their lifetime, thus exposing Haughey to substantial liability. To make matters worse, one of the four accounts was held in the joint names of Haughey and Harry Boland, his former accountancy partner. Boland testified to the tribunal that he had never given Traynor authority to open an account. Would Haughey now back Traynor or Boland? He began by accepting that the state of affairs was 'unusual', but was pressed to elaborate by the question:

> "Would you go as far as to say it was irregular and improper?" . . .
>
> "I would not go that far."[36]

After one gruelling session with John Coughlan, Haughey was forced to admit that he was aware of the existence of secret accounts with Guinness and Mahon through which a total of £1.1 million passed between 1979–87. Haughey had alleged he knew nothing about them but when asked to comment on the fact that at least one had been opened prior to the settlement of the AIB claim, he replied that he had been informed, although 'not in those terms'. Yet Haughey had told AIB he had no other accounts. Which version was true? Could he leave himself open to a perjury charge? The former Taoiseach was clearly rattled. He subsequently retreated to a catch-all defence when asked again about the existence of the Guinness and Mahon accounts in 1979 or subsequently. 'To the best of my knowledge, no. If I was aware of it at the time, I have since forgotten about it, until this Tribunal brought it to by attention.'[37]

In fallow periods, support was forthcoming from a small circle of acolytes,

---

[36] Emphasis added. Quoted in Brian Dowling, 'You can always bank on CJH not being "improper"', *Irish Independent*, 29 September 2000.

[37] See Brian Dowling, 'Time for Haughey to consider his position', *Irish Independent*, 28 September 2000. The following day Haughey returned to the witness box and denied lying.

> I can only suggest I may have been a little fatigued towards the end of the session. I have thought about it. I am as certain as I can be that at the time I was not aware of the existence of this account in my name.

Quoted in 'Haughey "never intended to hide funds from AIB"', *Irish Independent*, 29 September 2000. Haughey suggested the money might have come from a loan taken out in his name by Des Traynor, a scenario strongly rebutted by John Coughlan, SC, who revealed that tribunal investigators had trawled through every financial institution in the State.

including the hotelier P.V. Doyle. Haughey accepted in evidence that Doyle had taken out one loan for £120,000 in May 1985 for his benefit and a second for a further £50,000 that December. The proceeds were subsequently paid into accounts at the bank controlled by Des Traynor for the benefit of Haughey. Both loans cleared in 1988 and £301,138 in principal and interest was paid on them. But when Doyle died his wife spent £150,230 to repay the loans on the advice of Traynor, who also played a key role in managing the affairs of the Doyle Group. Haughey was asked if he would have condoned Traynor's actions. A deputy manager with the Doyle Hotel Group had already testified to Moriarty that not only was Doyle backing Haughey but that after the hotelier's death Traynor told him there was 'no chance that Mr Haughey would pay off the loan and that the Doyle Group would have to do it'.[38] This, according to John Coughlan, was both improper and dishonourable. Haughey said he could not comment, as he was unaware of the loan. 'I was aware PV Doyle was helping out with regard to my finances with Mr Traynor,' he said, but claimed not to have known the detail.[39] As the pressure mounted on Haughey to elaborate, he moved to forestall further probing by citing a deteriorating medical condition and asked to be excused from answering any more questions. His request was rejected by the tribunal's chairman.[40]

The intersection between the Ansbacher accounts and the Fianna Fáil leadership account funded by the exchequer now poses the most serious problems for the former Taoiseach, Fianna Fáil, and indeed for the entire political system. The allegations that Haughey misappropriated money designed to save the life of his best political friend, Brian Lenihan Snr, and looted the leadership account for personal purposes, although not technically illegal, are perhaps the most damaging for Haughey's legacy. Payments from the country's elite for access to Haughey were not regarded as a hanging offence; but bringing the party into disrepute was something that could never be forgiven.

The leadership account is funded by the public exchequer to enhance party political, technical and research capabilities. As noted above, while there is no legal restriction on the operational independence of the requisite leader, it is certainly neither a petty cash account, nor to be used for defrauding the exchequer by evading tax. The tribunal discovered unaccountable streams of revenue moving in and out of the leadership account, some of which, damningly, found their way into the offshore Ansbacher accounts held at Guinness and Mahon for Haughey's personal use. This was a discovery put to Haughey in oral evidence at Abbeville in January 2001.

The tribunal revealed that the leadership account contained significant money transfers over and above the funding provided for by the exchequer. It

[38] 'Top hotelier took loan of £150,000 to help Haughey', *Irish Independent*, 3 October 2000.

[39] *Ibid.*

[40] See Justice Moriarty's ruling, *Moriarty Tribunal Statements*, 14 December 2000, pp. 1–3ff.

amounted, in effect, to a slush fund. Two key sets of lodgments from the Irish Permanent Building Society, then under the control of Dr Edmund Farrell, set out the pattern. The first involved £100,000 donated to Fianna Fáil in two tranches, on 7 April 1986 and 22 October 1986. Both cheques were endorsed by Haughey and deposited into the leadership account. Haughey denied that he had ever asked the IPBS chief executive for funding, in direct conflict with the testimony offered by the banker to the tribunal in July 1999. He accepted, however, that 'Farrell was one of the people anxious to assist or prepared to assist him personally/politically'.[41]

Here again was evidence of a conflation of interests: Haughey believed that he personified Fianna Fáil and its goals to the party's supporters. To reinforce the self-aggrandisement, the Modern Prince repeated the argument that he saw no distinction between 'support in the form of personal political support, political support, that is in a party context, or personal support'.[42] This was a carbon copy of the defence for the funding provided by the Gallagher consortium in 1979 to pay off the AIB overdraft. Having others pay his personal debts, according to Haughey, was part of the necessary price for unleashing creative potential.

Haughey's stock declined further with accusations aired in the tribunal that he had looted a fund established to provide his close colleague Brian Lenihan with a liver transplant at the Mayo clinic in the United States. In one of only two interventions outside of his enforced evidence, Haughey issued a public statement denying the allegation in the most strenuous terms.[43] The tribunal attempted to repudiate him by reference to a further payment from IPBS in 1989 that included money destined for the Lenihan medical fund.

Throughout this period Dr Farrell continued spending on Fianna Fáil lavishly. On the eve of the 1989 general election he provided a further £95,000 in three cheques.[44] One, for £65,000, was lodged directly with Fianna Fáil. The other cheques, for £10,000 and £20,000 respectively, were designed for Haughey's personal electoral campaign and the expenses needed to defray the Lenihan medical expenses respectively. Haughey endorsed both cheques personally. They were then, inexplicably, lodged into an account controlled by Celtic Helicopters, a company formed by Haughey's son, Ciaran, and financed

[41] *Moriarty Tribunal Statements*, 22 May 2001, p. 9ff.

[42] *Moriarty Tribunal Statements*, 22 May 2001, p. 9ff.

[43] The second intervention surrounded allegations that he had misused money intended for the support of artists.

[44] Farrell told the tribunal that Haughey had personally asked him for a contribution because 'the campaign fund was very low'. Farrell said he regarded the approach, made in 1989 at a function in the Berkeley Court Hotel, 'inappropriate and surprising': see Ted Harding, 'The Unravelling of Haughey', *Sunday Business Post*, 23 July 2000. Farrell was to later reject Haughey's contention that the money was destined for Haughey's personal use: see Ted Harding, 'Haughey: where to now?', *Sunday Business Post*, 3 June 2001.

by a cartel of business associates approached directly by Charles J. Haughey.[45] On 21 June 1989, a cheque made out for £30,000 cash was drawn on the Celtic Helicopters account and cashed over the counter at AIB in Baggot Street, the branch where the Fianna Fáil party leadership account was also held. Haughey denied any knowledge of how the two original IPBS cheques, which he had personally endorsed, ended up in his son's company account and of the draw-down from the AIB. Counsel for the tribunal noted, without comment, Haughey's reasoning for this curious turn of events.

> Mr Haughey appears to be somewhat perplexed as to how this cheque was dealt with. He indicated personally that if this cheque was cashed and not lodged, then the money must have been used for some Fianna Fáil purpose or for some Party Leader's purpose. When queried as to what Fianna Fáil purpose would warrant a cash payment of £25,000 in 1989, he responded that perhaps people dealing with the party were looking for cash.[46]

The tribunal counsel simply rejected any suggestion by Haughey that the money for Lenihan was refunded. He contended that although the leadership account was credited with the sum of £36,000 in June 1989 the bulk of this money was not sourced via the Celtic Helicopters account. Rather, a further £25,000 contribution had been solicited from Larry Goodman, the beef baron whose business dealings prompted the establishment of the first of the tribunals in 1989.[47]

By any standards, Celtic Helicopters was an unorthodox enterprise. Its accounting procedures were erratic, the sources of its financing obscure, and its ability to repay investors without declaring such repayments to the authorities was unusual. Alone among the investors to make a profit was Dr John O'Connell, who invested £5,000 in the enterprise at its inception, a payment made on the day he joined Fianna Fáil.

> Mr Haughey stated that he didn't wish to get into a dispute with Dr O'Connell as to what was or was not said with regard to what was Dr O'Connell's investment in the company. [Nor did he wish to debate] whether it was an investment or whether, in other words, it was, as Dr O'Connell believed, some kind of once-off contribution connected with him becoming a member of Fianna Fáil.[48]

There was a profound reason for Haughey not to engage in a dispute with

---

[45] For a scathing profile of Celtic Helicopters and its chief executive, see Ted Harding, 'High-flying chopper pilot into low profile mode over Dunne affair', *Sunday Business Post*, 15 November 1998.

[46] *Moriarty Tribunal Statements*, 22 May 2001, p. 11ff.

[47] For full details of the Beef Tribunal, conducted under the auspices of Justice Liam Hamilton, see Fintan O'Toole, *Meanwhile Back at the Ranch: The Politics of Irish Beef* (London, 1995).

[48] *Moriarty Tribunal Statements*, 22 May 2001, p. 19ff.

O'Connell. On the day Haughey resigned as Taoiseach, he summoned O'Connell to his office and arranged immediate discharge of the debt for £15,000, a profit of £10,000 on the original investment. What made matters worse for the former Taoiseach was that this money was repaid not from Celtic Helicopters but via an Ansbacher account. Haughey conceded the unorthodox nature of the payment and that 'as a matter of probability' the cheque was provided to him by Des Traynor. He sought to portray the repayment as a consequence of a figure suggested by O'Connell's accountants, a fact disputed by the man who within days of receiving the money became Minister for Health in Albert Reynolds's administration.[49] It was indicative of Haughey's entire approach to the tribunals that he sought to significantly downgrade the connections forged between the Ansbacher accounts and Dr John O'Connell, whose machinations were ultimately responsible for forcing the former Taoiseach to resign in 1992.[50]

A further potential misuse of the leadership account surrounded payments totalling £26,000 to Fianna Fáil TD John Ellis, who faced bankruptcy in December 1989. Haughey demonstrated his sensitivity to political consequences by viewing the matter not as one of the party facing up to its corporate responsibility to reimburse creditors, but rather basely calculating that the party would not win an upcoming by-election if bankruptcy proceedings necessitated Ellis's expulsion from the Dáil. Haughey's response to questioning by the tribunal on this matter was direct. This was a political issue and therefore justified. He and he alone had the capacity to decide on the matter.[51] It might have been a politically astute move in order to prevent any erosion of the government's already precarious position, but if its motivation was to stymie an election result, then it would be considered a highly inappropriate use of taxpayers' monies.

The fine line between the past and present continues to intersect, primarily because some of those who played a pivotal role in the Haughey era remain in power. This awkward circumstance was underscored by the furore over Ahern's own role in the handling of the leadership account. The politician charged with restoring confidence in the political system had been the treasurer of the Fianna Fáil leadership account at precisely the same time as Haughey was allegedly looting it to pay for expensive meals with his mistress, the gossip columnist Terry Keane.[52]

For his part, Ahern denied all knowledge of alleged misappropriation of

---

[49] *Moriarty Tribunal Statements*, 22 May 2001, pp. 20–21ff.

[50] See above, pp. 144–145. For John O'Connell's evidence to the Moriarty Tribunal see the *Irish Times* reports, 9 July 1999 and 10 July 1999.

[51] Quoting Haughey's evidence on 8 February 2001: *Moriarty Tribunal Statements*, 22 May 2001, p. 15ff.

[52] Like most people involved with Haughey, Keane knew not only the value of her memoir but also when to cash it in for maximum advantage. As Haughey faced ruin and ignominy in May 1999, Keane revealed all about their thirty-year affair in a tasteless interview that was only rivalled by the cattiness of later reports. She began serialisation of her book on the affair in the *Sunday Times* on 16 May 1999. This was followed by an appearance on the last edition of Gay Byrne's *Late Late Show*, RTÉ, 21 May 1999. It was to provoke a week of invasive reporting never before seen in Ireland;

funds from the leadership account. Speaking in the Dáil in 1999, the Taoiseach declared, oddly, that he had checked with the person who had administered the account and could now declare that there had been no irregularities. Later, in evidence to the tribunal he admitted he had signed whole chequebooks so that the amounts could be filled in at the convenience of Haughey and as required from time to time in his absence. What had happened to those chequebooks was something he could not comment on. The chief lieutenant, sensing the changed political mood, had effectively mutinied against his former mentor. It boiled down to a question of trust – and faith in Haughey was at an all-time low.

As Bertie Ahern made clear in an interview in late December 2001, the tribunals had a very clear mandate and purpose.

> The tribunals were established to address serious allegations of corruption in the political and business spheres. Their job is to get at the truth and to reveal all to the public so that faith in the political process is restored and that people can again have confidence in their politicians.[53]

The constant drip-feed of corruption allegations from Dublin Castle, particularly from the Moriarty Tribunal, has exposed the symbiotic relationship between Fianna Fáil under the leadership of Charles Haughey and prominent businessmen in the State, but it has also served to increase antipathy towards the entire political class. For Colm Keena, one of the most astute chroniclers of the Dublin tribunals, the Flood investigation into planning corruption stems from Haughey's own actions:

> [W]hat Flood is investigating could not have arisen in the first place if Mr Haughey was not himself a beneficiary of large clandestine payments. Low standards in high places infect the whole body politics and all of civic society… suspicion is the inevitable bedfellow of large clandestine payments to politicians.[54]

---

talk shows and columnists condemned the invasion and yet proceeded to cover it in all its unsavoury detail. See the analysis of Liam Collins, 'The indestructible exile, silent in face of betrayal', *Sunday Independent*, 23 May 1999. Given the role played by the *Sunday Independent* for years in publishing Keane's gossip column, the high moral tone it adopted was incongruous. Arguably, the righteous anger of the *Sunday Independent* was magnified by the rivalry between News International and Independent News and Media. The fact that the Murdoch-owned *Sunday Times* not only bought the serialisation rights but also the services of Keane enhanced the sense of betrayal. Readers could be excused for questioning which betrayal mattered more to the executives of Middle Abbey Street. Keane was treated with derision by most media. The former Fianna Fáil Cabinet Minister, Maire Geoghegan Quinn, who was instrumental in hastening the demise of Haughey, declared sarcastically that 'what we have is a long-term mistress who has brought the concept of "the other woman" into disrepute. Now, there's a claim to fame': see Maire Geoghegan Quinn, 'The by-line as brand name is journalistic personation', *Irish Times*, 22 May 1999.

[53] Bertie Ahern, interview with Maol Muire Tynan, *Sunday Business Post*, 30 December 2001.

[54] Colm Keena, 'Getting by with a little help from his friends', *Irish Times*, 30 September 2000. See also 'CJ blurs the line over nature and source of funds', *Irish Independent*, 23 September 2000.

The result is that attention has been diverted from the very real economic and strategic vision that characterised Haughey's last two periods in office. These administrations laid the foundations of the Celtic Tiger economy. Haughey was helped considerably by a cross-party consensus that recognised the necessity for desperate measures to stave off national bankruptcy. This was encapsulated in the Tallaght Strategy, an agreement through which Fine Gael agreed not force a general election on economic matters as along as the government maintained its policy of fiscal rectitude.[55] The decision by the trade union movement to forgo wage increases, by signing up to fiscal restraints in a Programme for National Recovery, also played a pivotal role in guaranteeing the stability of the administration. It is argued that only Fianna Fáil could have brokered such a deal. It was a testament to Haughey's own political acumen that this forsaking of sectional interests was portrayed successfully as a sacrifice for the good of the nation. It was also a deliberate throwback to the arguments advanced by the party in the 1930s and 1940s to create a hegemonic construct for the country that placed Fianna Fáil at its centre.[56] Fianna Fáil might have been responsible for savage cutbacks in public services, but responsibility for recovery cut across the entire political establishment.

Coupled with the restraint came the decision to press ahead with the International Financial Services Centre, decried by the opposition at the time as wasteful. It proved essential in repositioning the Irish economy, yet, rather than acting as a defining legacy in place of his inactivity on the national question, the IFSC and the billions of pounds of revenue it continues to generate for the public purse each year has been reduced to a sordid symbol of the unhealthy relationship between finance and politics. The perception that this was the real reason for proceeding with the complex was reinforced by revelations of the decision of the developer, Mark Kavanagh, to give Haughey £100,000 in the form of four bank drafts on the morning of the 1989 general election.

For all the vulgarity exposed as a consequence of the tribunal hearings, there is not, as yet, any proof of a direct causal connection between the gifts given to Haughey and any criminal offence. Although this is the case and no direct evidence of overt corruption has yet been established, the most damaging

[55] For full details see Ray MacSharry and Padraic White, *The Making of the Celtic Tiger* (Dublin, 2000), pp. 75–100. MacSharry, who was Minister for Finance at the time, regarded the Fine Gael decision as one that benefited both the party and the country. Altruistic it may have been incidentally, but the decision appears to have been designed primarily to make Fianna Fáil unpopular, thus paving the way for a Fine Gael coalition to return to power (see p. 76).

[56] For an enlightening discussion of Haughey's relationship with the wider Labour movement see Kieran Allen, *Fianna Fáil and Irish Labour, 1926 to the Present* (London, 1997), pp. 149–174. Allen argued that the re-achievement of social partnership 'in far more unfavourable circumstances than those which faced Lemass' was central to ushering in 'a new period of stability for Irish capitalism' (p. 172).

of the revelations may well prove to be the true extent of Haughey's knowledge of the Ansbacher accounts used to finance his lifestyle.[57]

The Ansbacher report published in July 2002 provides a damning account of the operation, characterising it as a 'deliberately complex… sham trust structure. There is also evidence to show that [it] facilitated widespread tax evasion'.[58] Noting that 'Ansbacher carried on banking business in Ireland without holding a licence to do so', the report concluded that 'the affairs of Ansbacher were conducted with intent to defraud a creditor of some of its clients, that is the Revenue authorities'.[59] As well as breaching the Companies Act, Ansbacher and its directors are accused of:

> a) The common law offence of conspiracy (with, *inter alia*, some of its clients) to defraud, and
> b) The offence of knowingly aiding, abetting, assisting, inciting or inducing another person to make or deliver knowingly or wilfully any incorrect return, statements or accounts in connection with their tax contrary to the provisions of the appropriate tax legislation, now consolidated in Sections 1056 and 1078(2) of the Taxes Consolidation Act, 1997.[60]

Haughey's chief financial advisor is formally accused of 'knowingly and wilfully' conspiring to 'defraud the Irish Revenue Commissioners. This conclusion may constitute evidence tending to show the commission of criminal offences'.[61] Nowhere was this more apparent than in the handling of Haughey's own account with Ansbacher, described in the report as being designed in such a manner 'which would not immediately identify the beneficial owner of the funds'.[62] According to the analysis put forward by the High Court Inspectors, the funding of the Taoiseach of the day was deliberately obfuscated. Its description of the circuitous route made by payments from Ben Dunne reinforced the point.

> Thus, a cheque which ordinarily could have been lodged by Mr Traynor in Dublin to a client's account or accounts, was directed through a London account and two Irish accounts, none of which were in the name of the actual client,

[57] For an indication of how low that confidence had fallen see Fintan O'Toole, 'Respectable lose "veneer of legitimacy"', *Irish Times*, 25 September 1999. O'Toole's central contention was that:

> we have to adjust our understanding of contemporary Ireland to take account of two startling facts. One is that, at least from the early 1980s onwards, a large swathe of Ireland's ruling elite silently withdrew its allegiance from the State. The other is that organised crime in Ireland, which we used to imagine as the preserve of shifty working-class men with names like the General, the Penguin and the Monk, is also carried on by respectable, beautifully tailored members of the upper middle class.

[58] *Ansbacher Report*, Vol. 1, pp. 489–490.

[59] *Ansbacher Report*, Vol. 1, p. 490.

[60] *Ansbacher Report*, Vol. 1, p. 490.

[61] *Ansbacher Report*, Vol. 1, p. 492.

[62] *Ansbacher Report*, Vol. 1, p. 275.

> before reaching its final destinations. It can be seen from this example that, by deliberately complicating the lodgement and withdrawal system, Ansbacher, through Mr Traynor, made it difficult for anyone to trace the link between the client and their funds.[63]

The central issue of Haughey's use of an illegal banking service is sidestepped. Instead, utilising evidence provided in his testimony to Moriarty, the report seeks to prove he was a client. Letters addressed to Haughey at the Abbeville Stud are used to demonstrate his awareness of the scam. This documentation concerned the approval for an extension to a £400,000 loan sourced in Cayman by Guinness Mahon Cayman Trust, a name used previously by Ansbacher. In a submission to the High Court Inspectors, Haughey's solicitors rejected this interpretation, positing instead a more benign explanation.

> Our client has always categorically rejected any suggestion or conclusion that he is anything other than a person with loan account approval from GMCT [Guinness Mahon Cayman Trust] and as such has always rejected a conclusion that he was a client of Ansbacher Limited.[64]

The difference in interpretation is crucial and is left unresolved in the final report.

> Mr Haughey was himself a client of GMCT (subsequently renamed Ansbacher). Consistent with the Inspectors' approach to the identification of other clients of Ansbacher, once the connection with Ansbacher was established, further investigation of the personal affairs ceased as being not relevant to this Inquiry. The full investigation of these issues is properly left to the Moriarty Tribunal. Two pieces of evidence were, however, disclosed to the Inspectors, which tend to show that at least some of the money available to Mr Haughey was under his effective control. A payment was made from an Ansbacher account of IRL£10,000 to a Mr Conor Haughey [Charles Haughey's son] in September 1992 [after Haughey's retirement from active politics] and a further sum of IRL£15,000 [from a different account operated by Traynor]. . . [65]

Yet, this additional evidence was also hotly disputed by Haughey's attorneys, who argued that it was not causally proven in either case that Haughey had control.

> The balance of the evidence referred to does not allow for a definitive conclusion... It is clear that Mr. Conor Haughey received the two amounts from the accounts from which they were drawn... they may have been give[n]

---

[63] *Ansbacher Report*, Vol. 1, p. 60.

[64] 'Letter from Ivor Fitzpatrick & Co. Solicitors to the Solicitor to the Inspectors', 13 December 2001, reproduced in *Ansbacher Report*, Vol. 6, Appendix XV (54).

[65] *Ansbacher Report*, Vol. 1, p. 333.

> to him by his father. However in the absence of account name details they do not conclusively support without further evidence the conclusion that Mr Haughey was a client of Ansbacher.[66]

Given what was at stake and the legal disputes over the absence of information linking Haughey definitively to control of the accounts, it was perhaps understandable that the High Court Inspectors prefaced their fifteen-volume report with the following caveat:

> It is a matter for others to decide whether, in the light of the available evidence and the standard of proof required in a criminal case and other factors such as delay, any criminal prosecutions are desirable or possible. The Inspectors foresee some difficulty in bringing such prosecutions.[67]

As noted above, the question of Haughey's role in utilising secret funds is studiously avoided by the Ansbacher Inspectors, who argued that he had only 'a marginal involvement in the general Ansbacher scheme, (in so far as it related to the company's alleged wrongs).'[68] Responsibility of the failure to detect the malfeasance is placed partly on lack of regulation at the very time Haughey was at the zenith of his political power.

> A combination of the misleading information furnished by Guinness and Mahon and in particular by Mr Traynor and a failure on the part of the [Central] Bank to test, appraise and gather the information available to it resulted in the true nature of Ansbacher's activities going undetected for longer than ought to have been the case.[69]

At the very least, however, Haughey was guilty of relying on a financial advisor who established a scheme to defraud the exchequer. If it could be proved that Haughey was aware of the intricacies of the operation – and the High Court, utilising the evidence adduced by Moriarty, has failed to do so – a more damaging vista would open up. The Modern Prince would be convicted, in the court of public opinion, if not in law, of presiding over a regime that orchestrated tax evasion for the elite as a matter of policy. It is partly to forestall such an outcome that Haughey has repeated the mantra that Traynor and Traynor alone looked after his personal financial affairs. When confronted with evidence to the contrary, Haughey retreated to a defence of limited mental recall. The question Justice Moriarty must decide is whether this strategy of plausible deniability, borrowed from the Nixon White House, holds credibility.

---

66 'Letter from Ivor Fitzpatrick & Co. Solicitors to the Solicitor to the Inspectors', 13 December 2001, reproduced in *Ansbacher Report*, Vol. 6, Appendix XV (54).

67 *Ansbacher Report*, Vol. 1, p. 18.

68 *Ansbacher Report*, Vol. 1, p. 330.

69 *Ansbacher Report*, Vol. 1, p. 502.

Irrespective of whether Moriarty goes further in his criticisms of Haughey than McCracken, there remains serious doubt whether the tribunal disclosures will result in imprisonment. A recent report by the Council of Europe highlights the very real problems associated with the approach taken by Irish government to avert any further haemorrhage of political support. The report was critical of the fact that the tribunals were established mainly to assuage public concern, noting that the gardaí have already investigated unsuccessfully the allegations of corruption identified by Flood. A serious structural failure was identified in the provisions of the Tribunals of Inquiry Act. It stipulates that:

> a statement or admission made by a person before a tribunal or when being examined in pursuance of a commission... shall not be admissible as evidence against that person in any criminal proceedings.

Given the fact that the tribunal lawyers are not accompanied by police investigators, 'if a criminal investigation is decided in the future, it has to start from the beginning'.[70] The Council of Europe report regarded suggestions that Ireland did not suffer from corruption (because of the low level of detected corruption brought before the courts) as misguided optimism. It concluded to the contrary, that corruption could become a major issue for Irish society, and recommended that 'consideration be given to whether it is preferable to initiate and carry on, at least in some serious cases involving corruption offences, parallel criminal Garda investigations in order to safeguard the necessary evidential material'.[71]

Even if the loophole in the Act was closed, further problems have come into focus with the unsuccessful attempts to try Haughey for obstructing McCracken in 1997. In an interview with the *Irish Independent*, Tánaiste Mary Harney called for Haughey to be 'convicted and jailed'.[72] Haughey's lawyers argued successfully to the High Court that her comments had hopelessly prejudiced the possibility that their client could ever have a fair trial.[73]

In the court of public opinion, however, a trial is unnecessary. Haughey, the young and able minister who promised so much, has been reduced to a pathetic figure. His once great persona has been diminished to that of a man scrounging off the rich, devoid of moral character and engaged in a determined, if futile, attempt to gain acceptance by the monied elite who regarded his ostentation as vulgar pretension. In a telling comment at the height of the disclosures into the extraordinary sums needed to finance his lifestyle, the former Cabinet Minister Maire Geoghegan Quinn, who secured her first step up the

---

[70] Group of States against Corruption (GRECO), *Evaluation Report on Ireland*, adopted by the Council of Europe in Strasbourg, 17–20 December 2001, p. 15. Full text available at http://www.greco.coe.int

[71] *Ibid.*, p. 26.

[72] See *Irish Independent*, 27 June 2000.

[73] Emily O'Reilly, 'Hapless Harney bitten by her own soundbite', *Sunday Business Post*, 4 June 2000.

ministerial ladder in a Haughey administration, remarked sardonically that the coverage was:

> a bizarre testament to the man at the centre of it all. Throughout his reign he was a figure exuding power, a man with the ability to charm or to strike fear into almost anyone. A man elevated to almost mythical status... If Charles Haughey's life were to be viewed as a Greek tragedy then his fatal flaw was not his greed but his overwhelming desire for class. It was what motivated him, what made him the figure he was and ultimately turned him into the figure of fun he is today. He will be remembered not for what he achieved but what he bought.[74]

Charles J. Haughey received more than £8 million in donations since becoming Taoiseach in 1979. In the process he was responsible for dragging into disrepute himself, the party to which he pledged loyalty, and the State to which he pledged allegiance. His final years are likely to be spent selling off parcels of land to fund ever more arcane legal battles to stave off court appearances. Even if convicted, it is unlikely that he will ever see the inside of a prison cell because of his age and state of health. Instead, ignominy and public disgrace will be his life sentence, served in the genteel surroundings of his Abbeville estate.

---

[74] Maire Geoghegan Quinn, 'An emperor stripped down in public', *Irish Times*, 9 October 1999.

Afterword

Burying the Republic

The inherently brutal nature of politics in the Republic was cruelly exposed in a remarkable week in October 2001 that also demonstrated the changing nature of Fianna Fáil. The leader of the party, Bertie Ahern, once the Modern Prince's most trusted lieutenant, appeared to be the Janus figure of modern Irish politics. Snubbed by Lynch's family and friends when the former Progressive Democrats leader, Desmond O'Malley, was asked to give the oration at the former Fianna Fáil leader's funeral in 1999, Ahern used a high-profile book launch to endorse the principle of unity by consent. At the same time he was preparing to officiate at the reburial of ten IRA volunteers executed and interred during the War of Independence within the confines of Mountjoy prison in central Dublin. The reburial, following a state funeral, would represent the biggest display of officially sanctioned republicanism in a generation. It represented a debt of honour, but it also risked providing a retrospective justification for the use of armed force. As such it prompted widespread negative comment at a time when the Taoiseach found his party under electoral threat from allegations of corruption. And all the time, Haughey, like Banquo's ghost, dominated proceedings.

On Wednesday, 10 October, the Taoiseach attended a glittering ceremony at the National Library to launch Bruce Arnold's *Jack Lynch: Hero in Crisis*, a signal of a rapprochement between Fianna Fáil and the supporters of its erstwhile leader. It was also a gesture of reconciliation between Fianna Fáil and Arnold, who, along with journalist Geraldine Kennedy, was a victim of the 1982 telephone tapping scandal initiated by the then Minister for Justice, Sean Doherty.[1] A decade after the scandal broke, Doherty caused a political sensation when he alleged that Haughey had sight of transcripts of the taps, in the process implying that the Modern Prince had authorised them by default.[2] The admission has long been held, erroneously, as this book has demonstrated, to have precipitated Haughey's final downfall.

The Taoiseach used the occasion of the book launch to apologise publicly to the political correspondents for what he termed an 'inappropriate invasion of their privacy and interference by the State with their roles as journalists'.[3] Ahern

1 Ahern also apologised to Vincent Browne for a tap ordered on his phone by the Fine Gael-led coalition government because of his contacts with the Official IRA in the mid-1970s.

2 *Irish Times*, 22 January 1992. See above, pp. 135–136.

3 *Irish Times*, 11 October 2001.

was reclaiming Lynch for Fianna Fáil and attempting to neutralise perceived journalistic opponents in one swoop. He was also fireproofing himself against allegations that in organising a State funeral for IRA volunteers he risked giving legitimacy to those responsible for thirty years of carnage in Northern Ireland.

Lynch's principle of unity by consent might still be reflected in official government thinking but the whiff of cordite and association with the military vanguard allows the party to tap into a still-powerful republican impulse within the wider Fianna Fáil constituency, particularly in the west of the country. The State reburials of the republican icon Kevin Barry and nine other IRA men executed during the War of Independence the following Sunday, coinciding with a rescheduled Fianna Fáil Árd Fheis, reflected the estimation of current strategists that the time had come to partially lift the veil. Far from the Good Friday Agreement providing evidence that the Republic was truly a post-nationalist State, the guiding force of traditionally expressed ideology was being used to resurrect the party's standing and, in the process, energise a disillusioned and cynical electorate.

Martin Mansergh, by far the most important strategic thinker within Fianna Fáil and a close advisor to each party leader since Haughey, oversaw the ideological project to exhume the bodies of the ten patriots from Mountjoy jail. In an interview with the author he made clear the rationale behind the decision. 'I think it's very important that the State should not make a present of the various elements that went to make it up; it shouldn't make a present of all that to radical or militant republicanism.'[4] Crucially, in a startling admission for a Fianna Fáil strategist, he delimited the scale of the War of Independence: an indication of the strategic electoral considerations now applying in the twenty-six county State.

> I think the State is the heir to the War of Independence. At that point the then Sinn Féin was a united broad-based movement. The principle that they were fighting [over] – and it was used in the debates at the time – was actually the principle of government by consent and the fact that the British government weren't actually prepared to accept that as it applied to the south of Ireland.[5]

The parading of the ten coffins draped in tricolours through the streets of Dublin on October 14 2001 was a spectacle to behold, rivalled only by the celebrations that accompanied the fiftieth anniversary of the Easter Rising in 1966. As light rain fell on the massed ranks of the army, air corps and naval service, a lone piper played a lament for the IRA volunteers, now formally incorporated into the ranks of the army of the State. Soon the cortège passed into the hallowed confines of the Pro-Cathedral. The State-sponsored requiem

---

4 Martin Mansergh, interviewed for 'Exhuming Republicanism', *Insight*, UTV, broadcast on 2 October 2001. Full transcript available at http://www.utv.ie/insight.

5 *Ibid.*

mass recalled previous occasions when more exalted leaders of the revolution, including O'Donovan Rossa, Griffith, Collins, Casement and de Valera, were afforded exaltation. This time the power of the proceedings was magnified by the presence of the television cameras and the sombre intonation of the RTÉ announcers. The decision to co-opt the leaders of the main religious denominations in multi-cultural Ireland in the service of the revolution was deliberately designed to break the once-exclusivist linkage between Catholicism and nationalism. On one level it reflected an attempt by the Fianna Fáil government to return to the politics of nostalgia, but a deeper, more subtle and fundamental shift in the body politic could also be observed at work.

The Celtic Tiger boom, replete with its vulgar consumerism, is a world away from the reality of the hanging rooms at Mountjoy and Pentonville, and the execution yard at Kilmainham, where those imprisoned scrawled the words of Padraig Pearse on the prison walls: 'Beware ye the Risen people.' With the economy showing signs of a downturn, the budget surplus forecasts heavily discounted and the political system under sustained threat from allegations of systemic corruption, Fianna Fáil was in desperate need to display tangible evidence that it held dear the three sacred goals of the revolution: social justice, economic dynamism and unity. Bertie Ahern exhorted the delegates the night before the reburial that 'not only Fianna Fáil but the people of Ireland have a destiny to fulfil'.[6] But providing continuity with the past carries its own set of problems.

Risking enhancing the cult of the gunman was always going to be problematic for the southern establishment. The descent into the chaos of violence which has scarred Northern Ireland since 1969 has had little demonstrable effect across the border, with the exceptions of the Dublin and Monaghan bombings in 1974 and a small number of assassinations. The Northern problems have caused a profound questioning of the conflicting balance of forces that resulted in the freedom of the truncated State. There has been strident criticism of the nostalgia associated with all brands of republicanism, including that sparked in 1916 which eventually liberated the State. Central to the revisionist argument is the belief that the commemoration of unconstitutional methods demonstrates, at best, moral ambivalence towards contemporary manifestations of that republican heritage. According to this paradigm, the modern IRA – including its schismatic dissidents – has a deep-rooted connection with the original revolution and its

---

[6] Bertie Ahern address to seventy-fifth Fianna Fáil Árd Fheis, City West Hotel, Dublin, 13 October 2001. In a key section he outlined how Fianna Fáil was going to underwrite change.

> Integrity is not a quality patented by any particular party. Fianna Fáil remains deeply committed to integrity in politics, notwithstanding individual lapses. The highest standards are rightly demanded of Fianna Fáil, because we are central to the political life of this nation. This Government is the first to be subject to new tough ethical rules and to freedom of information. Fianna Fáil and the Government, under my leadership, have shown our absolute determination to clean up politics and remove any demonstrable abuse that could diminish the reputation of our democracy or cloud our achievements.

use of violence is, in effect, justified as a legitimate method in pursuit of its goal of a united Ireland, irrespective of the democratic will. [7]

Added to the substantive argument about the wisdom of venerating gunmen, especially in the absence of a comprehensive settlement to the 'Irish question', was a scathing assessment of the political opportunism of Fianna Fáil. The timing of the Kevin Barry rehabilitation ceremony, coinciding with a rescheduled Fianna Fáil ard fheis, was widely seen as a blatant attempt by the Soldiers of Destiny to resurrect their standing. By providing continuity with the self-sacrifice of the past, the party would simultaneously lay to rest any suspicion that it had relegated principle to pragmatism. What better manifestation of that than according the executed men posthumous membership of Fianna Fáil?

This repositioning of the party's ideological goalposts has been an ongoing project within Fianna Fail for some time. Its intellectual roots can be traced to a speech by Martin Mansergh to mark the seventy-fifth anniversary of Fianna Fáil in May 2001. Mansergh took issue with the suggestion that there had been an apostolic succession from 1916 to the Provisionals, while at the same time asserting that Fianna Fáil retained the true mantle of heirs to the nation. Mansergh poured scorn on a political marriage of convenience between 'Republican fundamentalists' aided and abetted by the 'revisionist school of history' to view 'the modern and mainly Northern-based Republican movement as the sole legitimist heirs of 1916'.[8]

The Fianna Fáil strategist effectively accepted the Gramscian argument that a retreat to ideological purity alone meant 'political marginalisation, and also that pressing economic and social problems would not be properly attended to'. Yet he cloaked Fianna Fáil's claim to be the true inheritors of the republican spirit in the same terms that he denigrated 'the preposterous nonsense concocted of a pseudo-apostolic succession'. For Mansergh, then, not only did Fianna Fáil always represent the 'slightly, then fully constitutional embodiment of the mainstream Republican tradition, south of the border, [but it] attracted many of those associated with 1916'. He cited approvingly the defection of many pro-Treaty supporters, including 'Liam Tobin, who had been Collins's right-hand man, and Senator Jenny Wyse-Power, in whose home the 1916 proclamation had been signed'. The entire rationale behind the speech became clear with the following passage.

> One of our greatest services to the peace process has been to help build the

---

[7] See 'Exhuming Republicanism', *Insight*, UTV, broadcast on 2 October 2001. Transcript available at http://www.utv.ie/insight. See also Fintan O'Toole, 'A grotesque denial of bloodshed', *Irish Times*, 2 October 2001, and Kevin Myers, 'Ireland celebrates its murderous dead', *Sunday Telegraph*, 7 October 2001. For a vigorous response see Tom McGurk, 'A war worth remembering', *Sunday Business Post*, 7 October 2001. See also David Andrews, 'No shame in mourning Kevin Barry', *Irish Times*, 6 October 2001.

[8] Martin Mansergh, 'Reflections on the History of Fianna Fáil', speech given in Dublin, 16 May 2001.

> ideological bridge for armed republicanism to transform them into a purely political and democratic force... I do strongly believe that the sooner Republicans, who are now part of mainstream politics in the North, can safely consign the armed side of the movement to history the better, and I accept that is the desired direction.

In an interview with the author he explained the meaning behind this enigmatic statement that appeared to contradict his approval of the revolutionaries. He argued that within the modern Fianna Fáil organisation 'we would be very conscious that militant republicanism – even in the strictly political sense – has not been particularly successful, to put it mildly, in advancing the unity of the country'.[9] After a generation in which Fianna Fáil had effectively downplayed its republican roots, the time had come to reclaim a wider sense of purpose. This received tangible expression in a motion put forward by the Éamon de Valera Cumann in Dublin South Central to the October Árd Fheis: 'That this Árd Fheis reaffirms our position as the voice of Irish republicanism.'[10]

Despite misgivings by the Labour leader, Ruairi Quinn, and Fine Gael's Michael Noonan that the Kevin Barry ceremony was deliberately designed to buttress Fianna Fáil, the political pressure to partake was immense. And in the end they did so. Not to attend a State funeral officiated by the former leader of the Catholic Church in Ireland, Cardinal Cathal Daly, and which included the President as guest of honour, would be a slight to the historical underpinnings of the State, even in its truncated form. With the opposition caught in an ideological trap, Fianna Fáil sought to reassert its primacy as the guardian of the Irish national interest despite serious questions as to who actually owned the legacy of the executed men. It was a key point neatly encapsulated by Dublin historian Professor Eunan O'Halpin, the grandnephew of the most famous martyr and a pallbearer for the removal from Mountjoy.

> My grandmother Kitty Barry was Kevin Barry's eldest sister and she was a very active republican herself both before and after Kevin Barry's death and she remained a true blue, or true green, republican till the end of her days in that she would have been very anti say, claimed the Free State was illegitimate and she would have been very anti de Valera, curiously much more anti de Valera than anti Collins.[11]

The public veneration of Barry and his compatriots was a clear war of position in Gramscian terms within the wider republican movement, particularly dangerous given the fact that Fianna Fáil was claiming, as one of their own, someone who killed for a cause that did not initially succeed. Mansergh remained convinced

---

9 Martin Mansergh, interview with author, Dublin, September 2001.

10 *Irish Times*, 12 October 2001.

11 Eunan O'Halpin, interviewed for 'Exhuming Republicanism', *Insight*, UTV, broadcast on 2 October 2001. Transcript available at http://www.utv.ie/insight

that the exercise would extricate the republican ideal from the clutches of what he disparagingly referred to as the 'northern leadership of the republican movement'.[12] It was a point reinforced by Willie O'Dea, the Minister of State at the Department of Education. Writing in the *Irish Times,* two days before the re-interments, O'Dea noted:

> Throughout its history, Fianna Fáil has endured a fair amount of turmoil and upheaval. Some found its origins within the party, but mostly it was the party reflecting the turmoil within the greater Irish body politic. Seventy-five years on, we can ask ourselves: would the founders of Fianna Fáil be happy with the party today? I believe the answer is a resounding Yes.
>
> They would have felt at home with the policy of social partnership. They would approve of a party and a country taking their places in Europe. De Valera was a strong advocate of internationalism. Lemass urged greater participation in Europe long before EU membership was viable.
>
> Not everything about modern-day Ireland would have pleased them, however. They would be appalled to see some self-proclaimed republicans engaging in meaningless doublespeak and hypocrisy. They saw Republicanism as an inclusive philosophy, not an exclusive, ethno-centric one. [13]

The ideological claim and counterclaim within the republican movement therefore formed a subtext to the complex manoeuvrings played out on a wet October afternoon at Glasnevin among the pantheon of dead patriots. It is here that notions of 'blood sacrifice' and 'nationhood denied' are expressed in rhetorical flights etched on tombstones, the only tangible evidence remaining of fiery orations once delivered to thousands of followers.

This reclaiming of the ideological roots of republicanism had also been the hidden architectural framework for Ahern's address at the Fianna Fáil Árd Fheis the night before, where he delivered a well-aimed swipe at Sinn Féin's attempts to capitalise on disaffection in working class areas. The party's ambivalence towards summary justice in order to bolster its standing in the Republic, he said, would not be tolerated.

> There is no place in modern Irish society for physical force vigilantes, with their contempt for human rights. In this Republic, there is only one army and one police service. They are out there putting their safety – and lives – on the line every day. Fianna Fáil will keep law and order at the top of the agenda. The war on crime will go on relentlessly.[14]

Bertie Ahern was at pains to praise the SDLP's 'courageous stance' in accepting

---

[12] Martin Mansergh, interview with author, Dublin, September 2001.

[13] Willie O'Dea, 'Forging ahead with a modern policy of social partnership', *Irish Times*, 12 October 2001.

[14] Bertie Ahern, Presidential Address, Fianna Fáil Árd Fheis, Dublin, 13 October 2001. Full text available at http://www.fiannafail.ie

the challenge of policing Northern Ireland, a de facto acceptance by constitutional nationalism that its future lay within Northern Ireland.

> Any future constitutional change will occur only in accordance with the terms of the Good Friday Agreement. No actions by small splinter groups will ever alter that. It is time for all shades of Irish Republicanism to accept publicly that unity will only come about by free democratic persuasion and agreement, never by force. The vast majority of us would not want it otherwise. For a long time, the system of Government in Northern Ireland and the exercise of power was unjust, undemocratic, and oppressive to Nationalists. But today, there is a new way forward, endorsed by the people North and South, capable of bringing about justice and equality for all...
>
> We in Fianna Fáil represent the honourable, living and inclusive Republican tradition of this State. We have a particular responsibility, which we have been exercising since the peace process began, to give leadership to those in Northern Ireland who share our sense of nationhood, our outlook and our values. But our most urgent task is to strengthen the accommodation and co-operation between our two main traditions on this island. . .
>
> The issue of political legitimacy, for the future at least, because the past cannot be altered, has been settled by the Good Friday Agreement. We will work with the new Northern Ireland, not against it. Indeed, there would be nothing to prevent the new institutions with their strong safeguards for both communities from continuing, even in the event of agreed constitutional change.
>
> But the present has to be our priority now. We can and must build on what we have achieved in this generation in bringing the people of the island of Ireland and of these islands closer together. We should measure the advance, not how far we fall short of the ideal.[15]

But the SDLP is now the minority party representing Catholic opinion north of the border. The real challenge – and Ahern knew it as he walked into the Pro-Cathedral – was securing a similar commitment from Sinn Féin that the Good Friday Agreement represented the best way of securing an agreed united Ireland. While politicians from other parties arrived separately, Sinn Féin, never slow in spotting a media opportunity, paraded their entire leadership at the State's veneration of IRA activity. Making up the retinue were: Joe Cahill, the legendary gunrunner and founding father of the provisional movement; Martin McGuinness, its former chief of staff, now responsible for educating the children of the North; Bairbre de Brún, the Minister for Health in the Stormont government; Pat Doherty and Michelle Gildernew, the victorious Sinn Féin candidates responsible for the 'greening of the west' in the May 2001 Westminster general election; Gerry Kelly, who once attempted to blow up the Old Bailey; and Mitchel McLaughlin, the party's spokesperson for justice. The gathering was a tangible

[15] *Ibid.*

expression of the continued validity of the Provisional campaign of the Armalite and the ballot box: tangible expression, too, of the Provisional justification to take up arms to safeguard the revolution.

It was perhaps fitting that the cant surrounding both parties' attempts to justify their existence by reference to their ability to deliver a transformed Ireland was exposed by Cardinal Daly. In a highly political sermon, the former leader of the Catholic Church in Ireland exposed just how short of the ideal both had fallen. Still, he buttressed Fianna Fáil indirectly with this devastating assault on Sinn Féin's attempts to claim the rights to Kevin Barry's legacy:

> A United Ireland remains a legitimate and a noble ideal. But the people of this island have repudiated physical force or coercion as a means to attain it. It can be attained only by persuasion, not by force; only by consent, not by constraint; only by creating conditions and building relationships which make its attainment no longer repellent for unionists but acceptable and even attractive for them. Reunification is now seen as inseparably linked with two balancing concepts, namely, Unionist consent in the future, and a genuinely new Northern Ireland of equality and partnership in the present.
>
> Indeed, the possibilities of an agreed United Ireland in the future are actually being tested now by the willingness of both political communities to create together in equal partnership an agreed Northern Ireland in the present.
>
> The true inheritors today of the ideals of the men and women of 1916 to 1922 are those who are explicitly and visibly committed to leaving the physical force tradition behind, and who are committed to implementing all aspects of the Good Friday Agreement. This means being prepared to work for a reconciled Northern Ireland of equality between traditions and justice for all; a Northern Ireland freed from the scandal of sectarianism, at peace within its borders but in structured partnership with its neighbours south of its borders; a Northern Ireland where the allegiance of its unionist inhabitants to their British identity and of its nationalist inhabitants to their Irish identity are freely and fully respected.[16]

Fianna Fáil might have claimed the Barry legacy for the State and received important backing from the Catholic Church but Sinn Féin was determined to challenge that claim. As the Sinn Féin leadership arrived at Glasnevin cemetery, significant sections of the crowd roared their approval. The unity of purpose within the wider body politic was momentarily threatened by the one-fisted salute from Joe Cahill, a gesture of defiance and a gesture, too, of ownership. It was also an indication that, as with the initial response to the turmoil in Northern Ireland in 1969, the burning of the British Embassy in 1972, and again with the 1981 hunger strike rallies, the republican tradition is one that can be fought over

[16] Cardinal Cahal Daly, homily at funeral Mass for the executed volunteers at Mountjoy, Pro-Cathedral Dublin, 14 October 2001. Full text available at http://www.ireland.com/newspaper/special

within the confines of the twenty-six-county State. Therefore, despite the scattering of Fine Gael and Labour politicians at Glasnevin, the ideological war can be reduced to a straight fight between Fianna Fáil and Sinn Féin, who, despite the alien status conferred upon them by the Soldiers of Destiny, have succeeded in carving out ideological space in the State itself. As Sean Crowe, a key party functionary from Dublin, made clear, Sinn Féin views the republicanism of Fianna Fáil with ill-disguised derision.

> I think it takes a lot to convince people whether people are genuine or not and the fact that people are organising one commemoration, every year they organise a commemoration to Wolfe Tone which a handful of parliamentary TDs from Fianna Fáil turn up at, that doesn't make you a republican party. You need to be working towards fulfilling the ideas of the republic to bring about the unity of the Irish people. That's what Sinn Féin is about. We are an all-Ireland party. Fianna Fáil isn't.[17]

The significance of the reburial ceremony was its overt statement that a new paradigmatic construct was now in place, rendering meaningless arguments such as that of Sean Crowe. So it was that, among the tombstones at Glasnevin, Bertie Ahern sought to bury the Irish revolution. His mechanism was to challenge the Provisionals' claim to the ownership of the revolution on the contested, hallowed funereal turf. He wrapped the green flag around himself, his party and the State just yards from where Padraig Pearse had electrified the mourners at the O'Donovan Rossa funeral in 1915 with his panegyric: 'they cannot undo the miracles of God who ripens in the hearts of young men the seeds sown by the young men of a former generation… Life springs from death; and from the graves of patriot men and women spring living nations.' Ahern had an altogether different message. The Irish nation was not only delivered but its capacity for growth was finally delineated by a de facto unionist veto within Northern Ireland. The subtleties may have been lost on the Fianna Fáil faithful, content to perceive that the party was reasserting its past, but its significance cannot be over-estimated.

Ahern maintained the government was 'discharging a debt of honour'. Those executed were true to the revolution and had a mandate from the people, an assertion drawn from the 1918 general election. The Fianna Fáil leader was seemingly unaffected by the fact that Barry, Flood and Traynor were highly experienced operatives whose use of force predated any peaceful democratic mandate. The Taoiseach made clear, however, that in his view contemporary violence could not be justified.

> [I]t would be quite wrong to apply without distinction any such presumption to other times and circumstances, and to a quite different situation, or to stretch

[17] Sean Crowe, interviewed for 'Exhuming Republicanism', *Insight*, UTV, broadcast on 2 October 2001. Transcript available at http://www.utv.ie/insight

> the democratic mandate of 1918 far beyond its natural term. Conversely, the memory of the Volunteers of 1920 and 1921 does not deserve to be burdened with responsibility for terrible deeds or the actions of tiny minorities that happened long after their deaths.[18]

This was a deliberate, but subtle, rebuke to Adams's attempt to provide historical justification for those who fought for the Provisionals throughout the Troubles. At the 29 September 2001 Sinn Féin Árd Fheis, Adams had declared the Irish nation should not apologise for 'Wolfe Tone, or Padraig Pearse, or James Connolly, or Maire Drumm, or Mairead Farrell, or Bobby Sands or Kevin Barry'. According to Ahern, the past was the past. With the finality of State burials for those who had fought in the War of Independence, the debt had been paid and a new framework agreed. For the Fianna Fáil leader a profound shift had occurred, which, while moving 'us to a new stage in our history… certainly does not mean we forget or repudiate those who founded our State'.[19]

Ahern succeeded in breaking the monopoly of Sinn Féin's claim to the republican movement. The spectacle of the Irish army firing shots over the nine undraped coffins[20] made it abundantly clear that Fianna Fáil was determined to reclaim sole ownership of the republican heritage, but only insofar as it safeguarded the twenty-six county State. Against expectations, Ahern had succeeded in providing a renewed definition of republicanism that has the potential to set to rest the ghosts of 1970 once and for all. The consternation felt by some commentators that Fianna Fáil risked legitimising Sinn Féin was comprehensively undermined by a superb ideological performance.

This ideological repositioning has been accompanied by a determined effort to depoliticise the impact of the corruption allegations which have dogged the party since the McCracken Tribunal. The current leadership of Fianna Fáil has made concerted efforts to distance itself from the tarnished leadership of the Haughey years, of which the public apology to Lynch's biographer is only the latest manifestation. Writing in the *Irish Times* in December 2000, Bertie Ahern promised to root out any semblance of corruption. He declared his determination to 'to find the truth, whatever it is. We are determined to deal with all the issues that arise from all the enquiries, however many and complex'. Ahern pledged to lead on the basis of a brand of republicanism centred on the institutionalisation of the twenty-six-county State.

> We are a country of unprecedented opportunity. We can for the first time in our history create a country at peace, in a land where the basic needs of all our people can be met. Republicanism stands for equality as well as freedom. Now

---

[18] Bertie Ahern, oration at the reinterment of the remains of Volunteers executed during the War of Independence, 14 October 2001. Full text available at http://www.ireland.com/newspaper/special

[19] Bertie Ahern's oration at Glasnevin, 'Remembering the sacrifice of all Volunteers', *Irish Times*, 15 October 2001.

[20] The tenth reburial occurred at a family plot in the west of Ireland.

> is our challenge and opportunity to translate political freedom and economic progress into a decent quality of life for every community as well as a fair chance in life for every citizen.[21]

The strategy adopted by Ahern is deceptively simple and rooted in the premise that the past is a different place; they do things differently there. In the *Irish Times* article, Mr Ahern proclaimed the importance of a narrowly defined patriotism.

> Politics is about public service. It is about what can be done for others and about giving leadership. In getting elected, a politician is given the trust of his or her community. That trust is the most important thing a politician has... If this generation of politicians can show that we are in politics for what we can give and not what we can get, then I think real progress will have been achieved... Realising the historic opportunity that is now before us will require the rising generation to give of their talent and idealism. My greatest fear is that this, our country's greatest opportunity, will be squandered in cynicism.

The problem for the current Fianna Fáil leader is that he played a central role in prolonging the tenure of Haughey, staying loyal right to the end. Haughey once famously described him as 'the most skilful, the most devious and the most cunning of them all,' a reference to Ahern's loyalty and ability to withstand opposition within the party to the Modern Prince's leadership.[22] He played a key role in the administration of Fianna Fáil since the late 1970s and carelessly signed blank cheques that were later used to pay the exorbitant expense account the leader clocked up at Dublin's most exclusive restaurant, Le Coq Hardi.[23] Although there is no suggestion that Mr Ahern in any way personally benefited from the Haughey tenure, his tone of injured pride in the loss of faith and idealism carries little credence, particularly given his reticence to ban corporate funding, which remains the mainstay of contemporary Fianna Fáil.The perception, if not the reality, that politicians can be bought in Ireland remains undiminished.[24]

---

21 Bertie Ahern, 'Politics and politicians must be credible and clearly accountable', *Irish Times*, 4 December 2000. See also Ruairi Quinn's rebuttal, 'Banning of corporate funding essential', *Irish Times*, 8 December 2000.

22 Quoted in Stephen Collins, *The Power Game: Fianna Fáil since Lemass* (Dublin, 2000), p. 213.

23 The restaurant went on the market in March 2001 with a guide price of £2.5m. Its demise was mourned by the critic Kevin Myers, who regarded the restaurant as standing in the first rank. Its proprietor, John Howard, held 'a magisterial position... Cuisine in Dublin is infinitely better for his doing, infinitely poorer for his going': Commercial Property Supplement, *Irish Times*, 21 March 2001.

24 A similar imperative surrounds the funding of Fine Gael. See Vincent Browne, 'Source of Fine Gael wealth must be scrutinised', *Irish Times*, 14 March 2001 and a rebuttal of the allegation in John Bruton, 'Bruton rejects claim of impropriety in fine Gael fundraising campaigns', *Irish Times*, 16 March 2001. Whether state funding of parties can, of itself, root out corruption is of course debatable. For a comparison with Italy and Germany, which suggests that banning corporate donations cannot alone provide a panacea in the Republic, see Neil Collins and Mary O'Shea, *Understanding Corruption in Irish Politics* (Cork, 2000), pp. 49–53.

Ahern's failure to reform party funding rules following the excesses associated with the Haughey years raised serious questions about how serious the project to clean up Irish politics could be. This doubt was underscored by the massive expenditure in billboard advertising by both parties prior to the calling of the general election campaign in 2002, which neatly circumvented strict new rules on the amounts that could be spent *during* the campaign.

The 2002 general election demonstrated that Ahern had successfully read the mood of the electorate in emphasising pragmatic concerns. However, his decision to depoliticise the allegations of corruption by establishing the tribunals could well return to haunt him in the next Dáil, if the economic boom which characterised the late 1990s proves to be unsustainable. Fianna Fáil at the dawn of the twenty-first century offers economic probity alone as a justification for its existence. The unexpected success of the Progressive Democrats in doubling their representation and denying Fianna Fáil an outright majority resulted largely from the fear within the southern electorate of the consequences of allowing the Soldiers of Destiny untrammelled power. The Progressive Democrats' most important strategist, the former Attorney General Michael McDowell, now ensconced as Minister for Justice, deployed the mantra that Fianna Fáil was as yet unfit to govern alone with particular effect. The decision by Ahern to seek political stability by entering into an unforced coalition serves only to give credence to such a view. The political marriage with the Progressive Democrats, ceded by Haughey to remain in power and derided as a temporary little arrangement by Albert Reynolds, has now been consummated.

Within the truncated State itself, the fruits of the boom have served to further to make more obvious the gap between rich and poor in contemporary Ireland. Paying the price of stringent spending cuts may well carry a heavy political price in the medium term. The hegemonic construct has been comprehensively shunned in pursuit of short-term gain. Even the planned national stadium to commemorate the Celtic Tiger, derided by McDowell as a throwback to the grandiosity of Ceaucescu,[25] is a fading prospect. The absence of vision at the heart of politics leaves Fianna Fáil more susceptible to the vagaries of the political marketplace than other parties who never had such an ideology to live up to. When the tribunals eventually report their findings, the questions surrounding the probity of Fianna Fáil and what it stands for in modern Ireland will move centre-stage.

The coming difficulties for the party are magnified by the apparent instability of the Good Friday Agreement and the worsening crisis in public finances. When Haughey advocated the reining in of public expenditure in 1982 and again in 1987, he had at least the cover of the national question. That defence

[25] According to political commentator Sam Smyth, 'the personal nature of Mr McDowell's criticism – he spoke of a "Ceaucescu-style Olympic campus on a single site" – has shattered what had proved to be a very good working relationship between the Taoiseach and his chief legal adviser': 'I won't let Mac back vows angry Ahern', *Irish Independent*, 2 May 2002.

has gone in view of the compromises on the nature of Irish nationalism, traded for the illusion of a peace process which, in effect, has degenerated into a form of crisis management devoid of principle or long-term strategic purpose.

These are a far cry from the ideological firefights that characterised the political career of Ahern's mentor. Watching developments from Abbeville, the Modern Prince has opined that 'the outlook for the party is bleak' and that it 'now stands for nothing',[26] the permanent embrace of the Progressive Democrats taking it further from its roots. While the sense of personal betrayal undoubtedly felt by Haughey at his treatment by the party may lead one to discount the charge, it is undeniable that there is much truth in this caustic observation. In eventually concluding the ideological war at the republican plot at Glasnevin, the very thing that differentiated Ahern's Fianna Fáil from the other political parties was also buried, serving only to highlight that the emperor wears no clothes.

[26] Confidential source, interview with the author, Dublin, 24 July 2002.

Appendix

Reconstructing Fianna Fáil

The issue of ideological power is central to an understanding of the internal dynamics of Fianna Fáil, yet it is one that is curiously overlooked within Irish political science. Analysts O'Mahony and Delanty suggest this state of affairs emanates from two inter-linked rationales: an academic culture that does not question the culpability of the ideology underpinning the State as itself or credit it as potentially a destabilising factor and a distrust of Marxist analysis based on structural inequalities that explain cultural interpretations.[1] Far from being a superfluous extravagance, the use of nationalist symbols are key to what Schöpflin terms the centrality of 'cultural reproduction'. By this he means that paradigms that posit a qualitative difference between rationality and nationalism, reason and identity, are based on a false dichotomy:

> It is by looking at the role of symbols, myths and rituals and taking on board the implicit processes in which human societies are involved that the full rationality of cultural reproduction becomes clear and the apparent contradiction between reason and identity is resolved... [I]dentities are created at both the institutional and symbolic levels and the two should be seen as functioning reciprocally. An institution creates its symbolic dimension and is reproduced in part by reference to those symbols. Thus the use of symbols – flags, monuments, ceremonies and so on – is not a superfluous extravagance, a throw-back to a pre-rational age, but a central component of identity creation and maintenance. They are neglected at one's peril. [2]

Fianna Fáil was so successful precisely because it managed to achieve political, economic and social dominance, each serving to reinforce the other, cementing a hegemonic construct that defined the nation. Traditionally, Fianna Fáil made significant use of the tools of modern nationalism, using the establishment of the *Irish Press*, for example, in a way that mirrors the analysis put forward by the political scientist Benedict Anderson. 'These fellow readers, to whom they were connected through print, formed in their secular, particular, visible invisibility, the embryo of the nationally imagined community.'[3] It is useful to assess just

[1] Patrick O'Mahony and Gerard Delanty, *Rethinking Irish History: Nationalism, Identity and Ideology* (Basingstoke, 1998), p. 16.

[2] George Schöpflin, *Nations Identity Power: The New Politics of Europe* (London, 2000), pp. 28–29.

[3] Benedict Anderson, *Imagined Communities: Reflections on the Origin and Spread of Nationalism* (London, 1991), p. 44.

how far departed from the nationalist construct contemporary Ireland has become, and to chart, in particular, the consequences for Fianna Fáil, its chief ideological architect.

Fianna Fáil was formed out of a realisation that republican moralism of itself was not a panacea for Ireland's problems. The defeat of the Republican side after the Civil War left it with a stark choice: adapt the fundamentalist precepts of the revolution or retreat into obscurity. Long-term strategic thinking created a new template that successfully disarmed any attempts by sectional interest groups to assert their own agenda over the party. This strategy fundamentally transformed the politics of modern Ireland but it is one that has been curiously underplayed in most academic studies of Fianna Fáil.

A notable exception has been the work of Marxist scholar Richard Dunphy, who provided the first authoritative account of the dynamics of that strategy.[4] In the process he developed a conceptual framework which suggested that the root of Fianna Fáil's success can be traced to its ability to harness ideological ownership of the revolutionary tradition in conjunction with a programme for social and economic change. Repositioning the debate to focus on key interlocking determinants provides crucial insights into the social and economic bases for Fianna Fáil's hegemony. That hegemony had little to do with the national question *per se* and everything to do with the skilful manipulation of interest groups whose needs were clothed in the respectability of being championed by a national movement rather than a mere political party: the Soldiers of Destiny – the Republican Party.[5]

Using a deterministic Marxist approach, heavily indebted to Gramsci, he stresses instead how change in the superstructure (the ideological re-conception of the nation) was informed by economic priorities from the very beginning which in turn created an economic and social dependence on Fianna Fáil, reinforcing the hegemonic outcome.[6]

A central tenet in Gramsci's political writing is the acknowledgement that political success rests not on an individual but through a political party harnessing the collective will and becoming, in effect, the basis of modern laity. For Gramsci, however, such hegemony can only be achieved through combining the economic with the political. In a key passage, this updating of Machiavellian assumptions surrounding 'the Modern Prince' is spelt out.

> Intellectual and moral reform must be tied to a programme of economic reform; moreover, the programme of economic reform is precisely the concrete way in which every intellectual and moral reform is presented. The Modern Prince, in

---

4 Richard Dunphy, *The Making of Fianna Fáil Power in Ireland 1923–1948* (Oxford, 1995).

5 For an astute analysis using the Gramscian concept of hegemony to discuss the political geography of Ireland see Jim MacLoughlin, *Reimagining the Nation-State: The Contested Terrains of Nation-building*, pp. 37–42.

6 See Quintin Hoare and Geoffrey Nowell Smith, eds, *Selections from the Prison Notebooks of Antonio Gramsci* (London, 1971; 1998).

> developing itself, changes the system of intellectual and moral relations, since its development means precisely that every act is conceived as useful or harmful, as virtuous or wicked, only in as far as it has the Modern Prince itself as a point of reference and helps to increase its power or oppose it.[7]

As David McLellan points out, the key innovation associated with Gramsci rests on his explanation of how the bourgeoisie thwarted the classical Marxist notion of the inevitability of economic determinism in ushering in a revolution. By focusing on the complex symbiotic relationship between 'the base' and 'the superstructure', he demonstrated that 'a necessary part of the ideological hegemony of the capitalists was their ability to represent their own interests as those of society as a whole.'[8] This is precisely what Fianna Fáil achieved and forms an important theoretical undercurrent running through Dunphy's critique of party organisation, ideology and the relationship between party and state.

Within carefully defined limits, economic populism was combined with an assertive patriotism that conflated support for Fianna Fáil with moral certitude. As a mobilising strategy it not only created a strong electoral base but also redefined the nature of the Irish State. Support for Fianna Fáil became synonymous with support for the nation. Dunphy emphasised the 'strategic importance of the political choices of parties – to the field of tactical and strategic possibilities present in any historical situation'.[9] The explication of this thesis has important comparative consequences. It places Fianna Fáil success not as an anomaly in European politics,[10] but as a particularly adroit member of the same family whose strategic logic long predated similar shifts towards what Otto Kirchheimer has termed the 'catch-all' imperative.[11]

De Valera recognised that once the political state had been established – and its legitimacy solidified by successive elections – staying outside the structures of power would lead only to obscurity. By 1926 de Valera realised that unless Republicans embraced the parliamentary system, a new political order would be firmly established which had the potential to permanently exclude them. His

---

[7] *Ibid.*, p. 133.

[8] David McLellan, *Marxism after Marx* (Boston, 1981), p. 186.

[9] Richard Dunphy, *The Making of Fianna Fáil Power in Ireland 1923–1948* (Oxford, 1995), p. 25.

[10] See Peter Mair, 'Continuity, Change and Vulnerability of Party' in *West European Politics*, October 1989, pp. 169–187. Mair argued that in the Republic 'party identities are such that even the most conscientious comparativists find difficulty in locating the parties within the terms of reference of the broader European political families' (p. 171).

[11] Otto Kirchheimer, 'The Transformation of the Western European Party Systems', in LaPalombara, Joseph and Weiner, Myron, eds, *Political Parties and Political Development* (Princeton, 1966), pp. 177–200. In this sense, Fianna Fáil has remarkable latitude in constructing cross-class linkages comparable to the National Republican Union in France under de Gaulle's stewardship and superseding the Christian Democrats in Italy. Richard Dunphy himself explicitly states that there are strong grounds for comparison between the Christian Democrats and Fianna Fáil: *The Making of Fianna Fáil Power in Ireland 1923–1948* (Oxford, 1995), p. 2.

chief lieutenant, Seán Lemass, a founding member of Fianna Fáil, put the position succinctly in a series of articles for *An Phoblacht* in 1926. Lemass warned:

> We must forget all the petty conceits and formulae which bedeck us, like rouge on the face of a corpse, and face the facts, the hard factswhich we must overcome.[12]

Here was an acceptance that an appeal to mythical republicanism alone had rendered Sinn Féin obsolete. The strategists realised that it was necessary to create a political machine that could exploit the very obvious weaknesses presented by Cumann na nGaedhael's structural base.

In many ways the 1937 Constitution marked a defining moment in Fianna Fáil's successful attempt to cement its centrality in Irish politics. An astutely mixed cocktail of Catholic thinking and paternalism, it successfully managed to keep the dream of unfinished business alive while ensuring that nothing was done about it. Northern Ireland was claimed; a Republic was not. Declaring a Republic had the potential to undermine the cohesive identity of the party and potentially 'fuel the fires of disillusionment; far better to go on holding out the promise of a better and brighter future – by keeping the myth of the "real Republic alive, with talk of unfinished business'.[13] In this devastating aside, Dunphy captured the ideological imperative underpinning Fianna Fáil. Designed specifically with southern consumption in mind, for de Valera – as for most of Ireland – there was now no justification, whatsoever, for IRA violence.[14]

In short, no alternate vision was able to compete. The Republican movement found itself out of kilter with de Valera's assessment of an Ireland at peace with itself, of comely maidens dancing at the crossroads. Fianna Fáil's careful wielding of State power while paying lip service to the republican ideal placed the Republican Left at a severe disadvantage. The Labour movement was equally marginalized, unable to capitalise on the inherent weaknesses of Fianna Fáil's socio-economic policies because of the latter's astute handling of the inner-

---

[12] Quoted in Richard Dunphy, *ibid.*, p. 68. Lemass's dictum was to be a guiding principle throughout his career. As Taoiseach his pragmatic acceptance of Northern Ireland with its concomitant rejection of traditional Fianna Fáil policy typified this. See Henry Patterson, 'Seán Lemass and the Ulster Question, 1959-65' in *Journal of Contemporary History* Vol. 34(1), pp. 145–159. Patterson argued that 'we can see anti-partitionism in this period primarily as an ideology of consolation for a nationalist project whose central material dimension had just been unceremoniously jettisoned' (p. 159). The Arms Crisis of 1969–1970 served to demonstrate the fragility of such a move. The violence in the north coupled with an intense leadership struggle led to an imbalance that saw the reassertion of the primacy of ideology with devastating consequences for Fianna Fáil. See Justin O'Brien, *Patriot Games: Fianna Fáil, Northern Radicals and the Birth of the Troubles* (Unpublished MA Dissertation, Queen's University, Belfast, 1999) and a fuller explanation in Justin O'Brien, *The Arms Trial* (Dublin, 2000), pp. 33–95.

[13] Richard Dunphy, *The Making of Fianna Fáil Power in Ireland* (Oxford, 1995), pp. 206–207.

[14] Dunphy made the interesting point that the redefinition of the State as 'Eire' allowed de Valera the freedom to 'go after the IRA' in a way precluded by the Free State Constitution (*ibid.*, p. 210).

city constituencies, particularly in Dublin.[15] A new twenty-six county State had been delivered into the hands of the national bourgeoisie that owed its very existence to Fianna Fáil and its continued perseverance with protectionism, thus limiting the appeal of Fine Gael.

In essence, the threat to Fianna Fáil came from within and it is by delineating the consequences for Fianna Fáil that the conceptual vehicle of hegemony comes into its own. This mechanism explains not only the interconnection between base and superstructure but also the fragility of political power in the absence of either economic growth, or, more importantly, in the absence of the perception that only a particular party can provide it.[16] Intellectual and strategic torpor caught unawares an organisation that prided itself on its organisational abilities. The emergence of Clann na Talmhan in 1938 galvanising the rural vote and Clann na Poblachta in 1946 targeting the working class fit in with this analysis. The dissatisfaction within the rural and urban sectors demonstrated that a valid alternative to Fianna Fáil could be fashioned. The unified constituency, which Fianna Fáil had so carefully built up, was wilting before its eyes and the party had no answers. Dunphy observed pertinently that appeals to stability, to ideology, to ending partition, although central to Fianna Fáil's conception of itself as the guardian of the nation, were not sufficient to keep its cross-class appeal.[17]

It was this lapse of purpose more than any other reason that created the conditions for Fianna Fáil's loss of power in the 1948 election and the beginning of a renewed attempt to reconstruct a hegemonic construct. Following the declaration of the Republic, the first salvo in the battle to re-invigorate Fianna Fáil was detectable in the manoeuvring surrounding the Anti-Partition Campaign. Patterson is undoubtedly correct in describing both episodes as evidence of little more than a 'self-interested scramble' to determine nationalist credentials.[18] For its part, the remnants of the Republican movement misinterpreted the Anti-Partition Campaign, in particular, as a signal that the political establishment in Dublin was prepared to step beyond rhetoric. This was one factor in precipitating the re-arming of the IRA.[19]

Policy revolved around re-creating the dichotomy between Fianna Fáil as guardian of the national interest, operating beyond the petty conceits of class, and Coalition politics aimed at breaking that model. Despite the obvious weaknesses, as a strategy it proved remarkably successful until communal disturbances in Northern Ireland in August 1969 once again brought the issue of 'unfinished business' to the top of the agenda, exposing in the process an ideological deceit at the heart of Fianna Fáil hegemonic pretensions.

---

15 Richard English, *Radicals and The Republic: Social Republicanism in the Irish Free State* (Oxford, 1994), p. 265.

16 See Richard Dunphy, *The Making of Fianna Fáil Power in Ireland 1923–1948* (Oxford, 1995), pp. 297–309.

17 *Ibid.*, p. 304.

18 Henry Patterson, *The Politics of Illusion: A Political History of the IRA* (London, 1997), p. 85.

19 See Sean MacStiofain, *Memoirs of a Revolutionary* (Edinburgh, 1975).

This was the case because of the introduction of three crucial variables that had profound consequences: first, the implications of the transfer of power to the post-revolutionary generation; secondly, the emergence of factional conflict within Fianna Fáil; and, thirdly, the role of nationalist ideology as a weapon in those disputes. The conjunction of these three variables and, crucially, the impact of the Arms Crisis in redefining the nature and limits of Fianna Fáil nationalism necessitate that explanations of the mechanics of modern internal Fianna Fáil politics take into account the role played by ideology as a mechanism for securing control over both government and party.[20]

The analysis of political power has to take into account not only its inherent instability, but also the mechanisms by which those who use it seek also to persuade the populace of the efficacy and essential truth of a particular approach.[21] Indeed, as Ernesto Laclau has pointed out: '"hegemony" is more than a useful category: it defines the very terrain in which a political relation is actually constituted.'[22] This, according to Laclau, represents the singular achievement of Gramsci's theory of hegemony in that 'universal emancipation is achieved only through its transient identification with the aims of a particular social sector – which means that it is a *contingent* universality constitutively requiring political mediation and relations of representation'.[23] The implications of this for traditional Marxist theory are considerable as Gramsci's theory identifies the crucial lever of change as 'a laborious political construction, not of the automatic and necessary movements of any infrastructure'.[24]

There is considerable merit in using the logic of hegemony to identify the salient features of the politics of Fianna Fáil. It was the crucial husbandry of the resources of the State along with wider society that primarily allowed Fianna Fáil to assert its dominance. The aims of Fianna Fáil became entwined with the

---

[20] As Ian Lustick has pointed out, wars of position, in Gramscian terms, are fought over the beliefs and expectations that can enshrine and protect the legality of regimes and the governing coalitions that rise to power within them. These wars are fought around the threshold of ideological hegemony. According to Lustick, these require the following criteria:

> a): a stubborn contradiction between the conception advanced as hegemonic and the stubborn realities it purports to describe; b): an appropriately fashioned alternative interpretation of political reality capable of reorganising competition to the advantage of particular groups; c): dedicated political ideological entrepreneurs who can operate successfully where fundamental assumptions of political life have been thrown open to question, and who see better opportunities in competition over the basic rules of the game than in competition for marginal advantage according to existing rules.

See Lustick, *Unsettled States, Disputed Lands: Britain and Ireland, France and Algeria, Israel and the West Bank-Gaza* (Ithaca, 1993), pp. 123–124. All three mechanisms were present as the Fianna Fáil parliamentary party revolt took shape in the autumn of 1979.

[21] Alan Finlayson, 'Power' in *Contemporary Social and Political Theory* (Buckingham, 1999), p. 42.

[22] Ernesto Laclau, 'Identity and Hegemony: The Role of Universality in the Constitution of Political Logics' in Judith Butler, Ernesto Laclau and Slavoj Zizek, *Contingency, Hegemony, Universality: Contemporary Dialogues on the Left* (London, 2000), p. 44.

[23] *Ibid.*, p. 51. Emphasis in original.

[24] *Ibid.*, p. 52.

needs of the nation. One unintended consequence was to highlight the inherent instability of elevating an originally subversive doctrine into 'the legitimising rhetoric of a new political establishment.'[25]

The efficacy of the approach adopted becomes apparent when comparing the positions taken by Fianna Fáil at the Arms Trial with the ideological response to further pivotal developments, particularly the hunger strikes in Belfast's Maze prison (1980–1981), the Anglo-Irish Agreement (1985) and the Belfast Agreement (1998, also called the Good Friday Agreement). Such a comparison across time, a key conceptual comparative tool within the context of a single case study, provides the opportunity to assess the changing nature of Fianna Fáil and by extension of Irish society in general. By critically examining Haughey's tenure as leader of Fianna Fáil, it is demonstrated that, despite his continued antipathy to Britain, the move from militant rhetoric to potential military involvement represented an aberration. By the time he could exercise unbridled power, the institutionalisation of the twenty-six-county State as the nation was complete.

The failure of Haughey to capture the initiative in the 1981 general election is indicative of the distancing of the concerns of the south from the north. For critics, it was evidence of Haughey's lack of political acumen and the distrust of the electorate in the leader (notwithstanding that the campaign tune, 'Arise and Follow Charlie', rode high in the pop charts). In reality, the prison hunger strikes touched a sentimental nerve, particularly with Fianna Fáil supporters who voted tactically to pressurise London into changing its policy by denying Haughey the hold over government that he required. Throughout the campaign Haughey made clear his view that the hunger strike laid bare any pretension that Northern Ireland represented anything more than a failed political entity.

> I believe there is always in the general, in the mind, the Irish public mind a wish for a solution of this problem, a wish for ultimate Irish unity. I believe that's as present today as it ever was. And I would perhaps suggest that at the present time because of the particular tragedies of Northern Ireland, the violence and the bloodshed and all the terrible, all the deaths and all the terrible things that are happening – that perhaps the wish for Irish unity and for solution of the Northern problem that's always there is probably more intense now than it would be at another time.[26]

In this context, the impact of the Belfast Agreement with its concomitant dismantling of the de Valera constitutional claim on Northern Ireland is of critical importance for the future evolution of Fianna Fáil policy. The final institutional acceptance of the principle of consent articulated by Taoiseach Jack Lynch as early as October 1969 demonstrates not only Lynch's final victory over Haughey,

---

[25] Tom Garvin, 'Theory, Culture and Fianna Fáil: A Review', in Mary Kelly, Liam O'Dowd and James Whickham, eds, *Power, Conflict and Inequality* (Dublin, 1982), p. 184.

[26] Quoted in 'The Hunger Strike: Dying For Ireland', *Insight*, UTV, 27 February 2001. Transcript available at http://www.utv.co.uk/insight

but also the demise of the Irish revolution as a key ideological imperative. This in turn has profound, if as yet unacknowledged, consequences for future policy directions – and not only in relation to the Northern question.

Bibliography

Official Documents

'The Arms Trial: Changes Made to Colonel Hefferon's Statement', Report by the Minister for Justice, Equality and Law Reform, Department of Justice, Equality and Law Reform; http://www.irlgov.ie

Committee of Public Accounts Report 1968/69–1970, Government Publications.

Dáil Debates available at http://www.oireachtas-debates.gov.ie

Group of States against Corruption (GRECO), Evaluation Report on Ireland 17 December 2001; http://www.greco.coe.int

Hansard

Moriarty Tribunal Statements available at http://www.moriarty-tribunal.ie

Release of Documents on Arms Trial, 1970, Patrick Byrne, Commissioner of An Garda Síochána, 15 May 2001, Department of Justice, Equality and Law Reform; http://www.irlgov.ie

Report of the Attorney General on Questions Concerning the Prosecution of the Arms Trial in 1970, July 2001, Department of Justice, Equality and Law Reform; http://www.irlgov.ie

Report of the Inspectors Appointed to Enquire into the Affairs of Ansbacher (Cayman) Limited, Record Number: 1999/163 Cos, Government Publications, Dublin, 24 June 2002

Report of the Tribunal of Inquiry (Dunnes Payments), 1997, Government Publications

Archives

Department of Justice, S/7/70, National Archives

'Arrest and trial of former ministers of Republic of Ireland on charges of gun-running into Northern Ireland 1970 Jan 01–1970 Dec 31', FCO 33/1207, Public Records Office

Books

Allen, Kieran, *Fianna Fáil and Irish Labour, 1926 to the Present*, London, Pluto, 1997

Althusser, Louis, *Machiavelli and Us*, London, Verso, 1999

Anderson, Benedict, *Imagined Communities: Reflections on the Origins and Spread of Nationalism*, London, Verso, 1983; 1991

Anonymous, *Fianna Fáil and the IRA*, Undated

Arnold, Bruce, *Jack Lynch: Hero in Crisis*, Dublin, Merlin Publishing, 2001
Arnold, Bruce, *Haughey: His Life and Unlucky Deeds*, London, HarperCollins, 1993
Arnold, Bruce, *What Kind of Country: Modern Irish Politics, 1968–1983*, London, Jonathan Cape, 1984
Aristotle, *The Art of Rhetoric*, London, Penguin, 1991
Arthur, Paul, *Special Relationships, Britain, Ireland and the Northern Ireland Problem*, Belfast, Blackstaff, 2000
Arthur, Paul, *The People's Democracy 1968–1973*, Belfast, Blackstaff, 1974
Aughey, Arthur and Morrow Duncan, eds, *Northern Ireland Politics*, Harlow, Longman, 1996
Bardon, Jonathon, *A History of Ulster*, Belfast, Blackstaff, 1992
Barry, Sebastian, *Hinterland*, London, Faber and Faber, 2002
Bell, J. Bowyer, *The Irish Troubles: A Generation of Violence 1967–1992*, Dublin, Gill and Macmillan, 1993
Bell, J. Bowyer, *Back to the Future: The Protestants and a United Ireland*, Dublin, Poolbeg, 1996
Beresford, David, *Ten Men Dead*, London, HarperCollins, 1987; 1994
Bernstein, Carl, and Woodward, Bob, *All the President's Men*, London, Simon and Schuster, 1974; 1994
Bew, Paul, and Gillespie, Gordon, *Northern Ireland: A Chronology of the Troubles 1968–93*, Dublin, Gill and Macmillan, 1993
Bew, Paul, Hazelkorn, Ellen, and Patterson, Henry, *The Dynamics of Irish Politics*, London, Lawrence and Wishart, 1989
Bew, Paul, and Patterson, Henry, *Seán Lemass and the Making of Modern Ireland 1945–66*, Dublin, 1982
Bishop, Patrick, and Mallie, Eamon, *The Provisional IRA*, London, Corgi, 1987; 1998
Boland, Kevin, *Indivisible Faith*, Dublin, Self published, 1998
Bottomore, Tom, ed., *A Dictionary of Marxist Thought*, Oxford, Blackwell, 1983
Bowman, John, *De Valera and the Ulster Question 1917–73*, Oxford, University Press, 1990
Buckland, Patrick, *The Factory of Grievances: Devolved Government in Northern Ireland 1921–39*, Dublin, Gill and Macmillan, 1979
Butler, Judith, Laclau, Ernesto, and Zizek, Slavoj, *Contingency, Hegemony, Universality, Contemporary Dialogues on the Left*, London, Verso, 2000
Carty, R.K., *Electoral Politics in Ireland: Party and Parish Pump*, Dingle, Brandon, 1983
Chomsky, Noam, and Herman, Edward, *Manufacturing Consent: The Political Economy of the Mass Media*, London, Vintage, 1988
Chubb, Basil, *The Government and Politics of Ireland*, Stanford, Stanford University Press, 1970; 1982
Clarke, Liam, *Broadening the Battlefield: The H Blocks and the Rise of Sinn Féin*, Dublin, Gill and Macmillan, 1987

Clayton, Pamela, *Enemies and Passing Friends: Settler Ideologies in Twentieth Century Ulster*, London, Pluto, 1996
Cochrane, Feargal, *Unionist Politics and the Politics of Unionism since the Anglo-Irish Agreement*, Cork, Cork University Press, 1997
Cohen, Al, *The Irish Political Elite*, Dublin, Gill and Macmillan, 1972
Collins, Neil, ed., *Political issues in Ireland today*, Manchester, Manchester University Press, 2nd edition, 1999
Collins, Neil, and O'Shea, Mary, *Understanding Corruption in Irish Politics*, Cork, Cork University Press, 2000
Collins, Stephen, *The Haughey File: The Unprecedented Career and Last Years of The Boss*, Dublin, O'Brien, 1992
Collins, Stephen, *The Power Game: Fianna Fáil Since Lemass*, Dublin, O'Brien, 2000
Coogan, Tim Pat, *De Valera, Long Fellow, Long Shadow*, London, Hutchinson, 1993; 1995
Coogan, Tim Pat, *The Troubles: Ireland's Ordeal 1966–1995 and the Search for Peace*, London, Hutchinson, 1995
Cronin, Mike, *The Blueshirts and Irish Politics*, Dublin, Four Courts Press, 1997
Cullen, Paul, *With a Little Help from my Friends: Planning Corruption in Ireland*, Gill & Macmillan, Dublin, 2002
Daalder, Hans, ed., *Comparative European Politics*, London, Pinter, 1997
Della Porta, Donatella, and Mény, Yves, eds., *Democracy and Corruption in Europe*, London, Pinter, 1997
Devlin, Paddy, *Straight Left: An Autobiography*, Belfast, Blackstaff, 1983
Dogan, Mattei, and Pelassy, Dominique, *How to Compare Nations*, London, Chatham House, 1984; 1990
Doorly, Mary Rose, *Abbeville, The Family home of Charles J. Haughey*, Dublin, Townhouse, 1996
Downey, James, *Lenihan: His Life and Loyalties*, Dublin, New Island Books, 1998
Dunphy, Richard, *The Making of Fianna Fáil Power in Ireland 1923–1948*, Oxford, Clarendon, 1994
English, Richard, *Ernie O'Malley, IRA Intellectual*, Oxford, Clarendon, 1998
English, Richard, *Radicals and the Republic: Social Republicanism in the Irish Free State*, Oxford, Oxford University Press, 1994
English, Richard, and Skelly, John Morrison, eds., *Ideas Matter: Essays in Honour of Conor Cruise O'Brien*, Dublin, Poolbeg, 1998
Evans, Richard J., *In Defence of History*, London, Granta Books, 1997
Farrell, Brian, *Chairman or Chief, The Role of Taoiseach in Irish Government*, Dublin, Gill and Macmillan, 1971.
Farrell, Brian, *Seán Lemass*, Dublin, Gill and Macmillan, 1991
Farrell, Michael, *The Orange State*, London, Pluto, 1976; 1992
Feehan, John, *Operation Brogue: A Study of the Vilification of Charles Haughey*, Dublin, Mercier, 1984
Femia, Joseph, *Gramsci's Political Thought: Hegemony, Consciousness and the*

Revolutionary Process, Oxford, Oxford University Press, 1981

Fennell, Desmond, *Heresy, The Battle of Ideas in Modern Ireland*, Belfast, Blackstaff, 1993

FitzGerald, Garret, *All in a Life*, Dublin, Gill & Macmillan, 1991

Garvin, Tom, *1922: The Birth of Irish Democracy*, Dublin, Gill and Macmillan, 1996

Glenny, Misha, *The Balkans 1804–1999: Nationalism, War and the Great Powers*, London, Granta Books, 1999

Gramsci, Antonio, *Selections from the Prison Notebooks*, London, Lawrence and Wishart, 1971; 1998

Gramsci, Antonio, *The Modern Prince and Other Writings*, New York, International Publishers, 1968

Griffith, J.A.G., *The Politics of the Judiciary*, London, Fontana, 1977; 1997

Hall, John A., *The State of the Nation: Ernest Gellner and the Theory of Nationalism*, Cambridge, Cambridge University Press, 1998

Harnden, Toby, *Bandit Country, The IRA and South Armagh*, London, Coronet, 1999; Revised Edition, 2000

Hart, Peter, *The I.R.A. and its Enemies: Violence and Community in Cork 1916–1923*, Oxford, Oxford University Press, 1999

Hennessey, Thomas, *A History of Northern Ireland 1920–1996*, Dublin, Gill and Macmillan, 1997

Heywood, Paul, ed., *Political Corruption*, Oxford, Blackwell, 1997

Holland, Jack, *The American Connection, U.S. Guns, Money and Influence in Northern Ireland*, Boulder, Roberts Rinehart, 1987; 1999

Horgan, John, *Seán Lemass, The Enigmatic Patriot*, Dublin, Gill and Macmillan, 1997

Horgan, John, *Noël Browne: Passionate Outsider*, Dublin, Gill and Macmillan, 2000

Howe, Stephen, *Ireland and Empire, Colonial Legacies in Irish History and Culture*, Oxford, Oxford University Press, 2000

Ignatieff, Michael, *Blood and Belonging: Journey's into the New Nationalism*, London, Vintage, 1994

Joyce, Joe, and Murtagh, Peter, *The Boss: Charles J. Haughey in Government*, Dublin, Poolbeg, 1983

Keena, Colm, *Haughey's Millions: Charlie's Money Trail*, Dublin, Gill and Macmillan, 2001

Kelly, James, *Order For the Captain*, Dublin, 1971

Kelly, James, *The Thimble Riggers: The Dublin Arms Trials of 1970*, Dublin, 1999

Kelly, Mary, O'Dowd, Liam, and Whickham, James, eds., *Power, Conflict and Inequality*, Dublin, Turoe, 1982

Keogh, Dermot, *Twentieth Century Ireland: Nation and State*, Dublin, Gill and Macmillan, 1994

Kerrigan, Gene, and Speirs, Derek, *Goodbye to all that: A souvenir of the Haughey Era*, Dublin, Blackwater Press, 1992

Kuhn, Thomas, *The Structure of Scientific Revolutions*, London, University of Chicago Press, 1962; 1996

di Lampedusa, Giuseppe Tomasi, *The Leopard*, London, Harvill Press, 1960; 1996

LaPalombara, Joseph and Weiner, Myron, eds, *Political Parties and Political Development*, Princeton, 1966

Lawson, Kay, and Merkl, Peter, *When Parties Fail: Emerging Alternative Organisations*, Princeton, 1988

Lee, Joseph, *Ireland 1912–85 Politics and Society*, Cambridge, Cambridge University Press, 1989

Lustick, Ian, *Unsettled States, Disputed Lands: Britain and Ireland, France and Algeria, Israel and the West Bank-Gaza*, Ithaca, Cornell University Press, 1993

Machiavelli, Niccoló, *The Prince*, London, Penguin Books, new edition 1999

MacIntyre, Tom, *Through the Bridewell Gate: A Diary of the Dublin Arms Trial*, London, Faber and Faber, 1971

Mac Laughlin, Jim, *Re-imagining the Nation-State, The Contested Terrains of Nation-Building*, London, Pluto, 2001

MacSharry, Ray, and White, Padraic, *The Making of the Celtic Tiger: The Inside Story of Ireland's Boom Economy*, Dublin, Mercier Press, 2000

MacStiofain, Sean, *Memoirs of a Revolutionary*, London, Gordon Cremonesi, 1975

McCann, Eamon, *War and an Irish Town*, London, Pluto, 1989

McGarry, John, and O'Leary, Brendan, *Explaining Northern Ireland, Broken Images*, Oxford, Blackwell, 1995

McKittrick, David, Kelters, Seamus, Feeney, Brian, Thornton, Chris, *Lost Lives: The stories of the men, women and children who died as a result of the Northern Ireland troubles*, Edinburgh, Mainstream, 1999

McLlellan, David, *Marxism after Marx*, Boston, Houghton, 1981

Mair, Peter, *The Changing Irish Party System*, London, Pinter, 1987

Mallie, Eamon, and McKittrick, David, *The Fight For Peace: The Secret Story Behind the Irish Peace Process*, London, Heinemann, 1996

Mallie, Eamon, and McKittrick, David, *Endgame in Ireland*, London, Hodder and Stoughton, 2001

Manning, Maurice, *James Dillon: A Biography*, Dublin, Wolfhound Press, 1999

Mansergh, Martin, ed., *The Spirit of the Nation: The Speeches and Statements of Charles J. Haughey (1957–1986)*, Cork, Mercier Press, 1986

Nairn, Tom, *After Britain: New Labour and the Return of Scotland*, London, Granta, 2000

O'Brien, Brendan, *The Long War, The IRA and Sinn Féin, from Armed Struggle to Peace Talks*, Dublin, O'Brien, 1993; 1995

O'Brien, Conor Cruise, *States of Ireland*, London, Hutchinson, 1972

O'Brien, Conor Cruise, *Memoir*, Dublin, Poolbeg, 1999

O'Brien, Justin, *Patriot Games: Fianna Fáil, Northern Radicals and the Birth of the Troubles*, Unpublished MA Dissertation, Queen's University, Belfast, 1999

O'Brien, Justin, *The Arms Trial*, Dublin, Gill and Macmillan, 2000

O'Brien, Mark, *De Valera, Fianna Fáil and the* Irish Press: *The Truth in the News?*, Dublin, Irish Academic Press, 2001

O'Connor, Kevin, *Sweetie*: *How Haughey Spent The Money*, Dublin, K.O. Publications, 1999

O'Halloran, Clare, *Partition and the Limits of Irish Nationalism*, Dublin, Gill and Macmillan, 1987
O'Halpin, Eunan, *Defending Ireland: The Irish State and its Enemies since 1922*, Oxford, Oxford University Press, 1999
O'Higgins, Thomas, *A Double Life*, Dublin, Townhouse, 1996
O'Leary, Brendan, and McGarry, John, *The Politics of Antagonism: Understanding Northern Ireland*, London, Athlone, 1996
O'Mahony, Patrick, and Delanty, Gerard, *Rethinking Irish History, Nationalism, Identity and Ideology*, London, Macmillan, 1998
O'Toole, Fintan, *Meanwhile Back at the Ranch: The Politics of Irish Beef*, London, Vintage, 1995
Panebianco, Angelo, *Political Parties: Organisation and Power*, Cambridge, 1988
Patterson, Henry, *The Politics of Illusion: A Political History of the IRA*, London, Serif, 1997
Porter, Norman, ed., *The Republican Ideal: Current Perspectives*, Belfast, Blackstaff, 1998
Rose, Peter, *How the Troubles came to Northern Ireland*, Basingstoke, Macmillan, 1999
Ruane, Joseph, and Todd, Jennifer, *The Dynamics of Conflict in Northern Ireland*, Cambridge, Cambridge University Press, 1996
Ryle Dwyer, T., *Charlie: The Political Biography of Charles J. Haughey*, Dublin, Marino, 1987
Ryle Dwyer, T., *Short Fellow: A Biography of Charles J. Haughey*, Dublin, Marino, 1999
Sacks, Paul Martin, *The Donegal Mafia*, London, Yale University Press, 1976
Schöpflin, George, *Nations Identity Power: The New Politics of Europe*, London, Hurst & Co., 2000
Sharrock, David, and Devenport, Mark, *Man of War, Mean of Peace? The Unauthorised Biography of Gerry Adams*, London, Macmillan, 1997
Sinnott, Richard, *Irish Voters Decide: Voting Behaviour in Elections and referendums since 1918*, Manchester, University Press, 1995
Smith, Anthony, *Nationalism and Modernity*, London, Routledge, 1998.
Smith, Anthony D., *The Nation in History: Historiographical Debates about Ethnicity and Nationalism*, Cambridge, Polity, 2000
Smith, M.L.R., *Fighting For Ireland: The Military Strategy of the Irish Republican Movement*, London, Routledge, 1995
Smith, Raymond, *Haughey and O'Malley: The Quest for Power*, Naas, Aherlow, 1987
Smyth, Sam, *Thanks a Million, Big Fella*, Dublin, Blackwater Press, 1997
Starobin, Paul, 'A Generation of Vipers, Journalists and the New Cynicism', *Colombia Journalism Review*, March/April 1995
Stewart, A.T.Q., *The Ulster Crisis: Resistance to Home Rule 1912–1914*, Belfast, Blackstaff, 1967; 1997
Sweetman, Rosita, *On Our Knees: Ireland 1972*, London, Pan, 1972

Taylor, Peter, *Provos: The IRA and Sinn Féin*, London, Bloomsbury, 1997; 1998
Teague, Paul, ed., *Beyond the Rhetoric: Politics, the Economy and Social Policy in Northern Ireland*, London, Lawrence and Wishart, 1987
Thatcher, Margaret, *The Downing Street Years*, HarperCollins, London, 1993
Walsh, Dick, *Des O'Malley, A Political Profile*, Dingle, Brandon, 1986
Walsh, Dick, *The Party: Inside Fianna Fáil*, Dublin, Gill and Macmillan, 1986
White, Theodore, *Breach of Faith: The Fall of Richard Nixon*, London, Cape, 1975
Wilson, James, *Irish America and the Ulster Conflict*, Belfast, Blackstaff, 1996
Wolinetz, Steven, ed., *Political Parties*, Aldershot, Dartmouth, 1998
Wright, Frank, *Northern Ireland: A Comparative Analysis*, Dublin, Gill and Macmillan, 1987; 1992
Young, Hugo, *One of Us*, London, Macmillan, 1989

Principal Articles Cited

Adams, Gerry, Presidential address to Sinn Féin Árd Fheis, Royal Dublin Society, 29 September 2001. Full text available at http://www.sinnfein.ie
Ahern, Bertie, oration at Glasnevin, 'Remembering the sacrifice of all Volunteers', *Irish Times*, 15 October 2001
Ahern, Bertie, 'Politics and politicians must be credible and clearly accountable', *Irish Times*, 4 December 2000
Ahern, Bertie, Presidential address, Fianna Fáil Árd Fheis, City West Hotel, Dublin, 13 October 2001. Full text available at http://www.fiannafail.ie
Andrews, David, 'No shame in mourning Kevin Barry', *Irish Times*, 6 October 2001
Arnold, Bruce, 'Why they bugged me?' *The Times*, 23 January 1992
Arnold, Bruce, 'People's verdict awaited on Haughey culpability', *Irish Independent*, 23 January 1992
Arnold, Bruce, 'Captain James Kelly grievously wronged', *Irish Independent*, 14 April 2001
Arnold, Bruce, 'No need for another Arms Trial Inquiry', *Irish Independent*, 19 May 2001
Ball, Terence, 'From "Core" to "Sore" Concepts: Ideological Innovation and Conceptual Change', *Journal of Political Ideologies*, 1999, 4 (3), 391–396
Battersby, Eileen, 'Poor drama and bad manners', *Irish Times*, 9 February 2002
Boland, Kevin, 'The Tree We Planted is Rotten', *Magill*, March 1982
Brennan, Pat, 'A Short Measure?', *Magill*, April 1982
Brennock, Mark, 'From republican rhetoric to patient pragmatism', *Irish Times*, 31 January 1992
Brennock, Mark, 'Impeding Haughey's meant banking on trouble', *Irish Times*, 20 February 1999
Browne, Vincent, 'O'Malley's prospectives', *Magill*, December 1979
Browne, Vincent, 'The Making of a Taoiseach', *Magill*, January 1980
Browne, Vincent, 'The Berry Diaries', *Magill*, June, July, August 1980
Browne Vincent, 'Going Cool on Garret', *Magill*, February 1980

Browne, Vincent, 'Charlie McCreevy: An End to Political Hedonism', *Magill*, January 1982

Browne, Vincent, 'In the Shadow of a Gunman', *Magill*, April 1982

Browne, Vincent, 'The Secret World of SFWP', *Magill*, May 1982

Browne, Vincent, 'What's Bugging Haughey?', *Magill*, July 1982

Browne, Vincent, 'What has Haughey done to deserve disgrace', *Irish Times*, 30 December 1998

Browne, Vincent, 'Source of Fine Gael wealth must be scrutinised', *Irish Times*, 14 March 2001

Browne, Vincent, 'O'Malley series is a disgrace', *Irish Times*, 16 May 2001

Bruton, John, 'Bruton rejects claim of impropriety in Fine Gael fundraising campaigns', *Irish Times*, 16 March 2001

Collins, Liam, 'The indestructible exile, silent in face of betrayal', *Sunday Independent*, 23 May 1999

Coughlan, Denis, 'Haughey terminally damaged by Doherty, PDs conclude', *Irish Times*, 23 January 1992

Cruise O'Brien, Conor, 'A bug never flew on one wing', *Irish Times*, 15 February 1983

Cruise O'Brien, Conor, 'Don't write him off just yet', *Irish Independent*, 25 January 1992

Cruise O'Brien, Conor, 'The Rogue who ruled Ireland', *The Times*, 4 February 1992

Cruise O'Brien, Conor, 'How keeping Lynch saved Haughey', *Sunday Independent*, 22 April 2001

Daly, Cahal, 'Homily at funeral mass for the executed volunteers at Mountjoy', Pro-Cathedral Dublin, 14 October 2001. Full text available at http://www.ireland.com

de Rálaigh, Criostóir, 'Dublin debates the hunger strike', *An Phoblacht/Republican News*, 28 June 2001

Dowling, Brian, 'Time for Haughey to consider his position', *Irish Independent*, 28 September 2000

Dowling, Brian, 'You can always bank on CJH not being "improper"', *Irish Independent*, 29 September 2000

Downey, James, 'The hidden achievement of Fianna Fáil', *Irish Times*, 1 December 1982

Downey, James, 'MacSharry can't back Haughey's story', *Irish Independent*, 23 January 1992

Drapier, 'PDs have had enough but will the Club of 55 act?', *Irish Times*, 23 January 1992

Drennan, John, 'The Quick Buck and the Dead', *Magill*, October 2000

English, Richard, 'Library of the hard men', *Newsweek*, 31 July 2000

English, Richard, 'Left on the shelf', *Fortnight*, September 2000

Garvin, Tom, 'Political Cleavages, Party Politics and Urbanisation in Ireland – The Case of the Periphery Dominated Centre', *European Journal of Political Research*, 11/4 (1974)

Geoghegan Quinn, Maire, 'The by-line as brand name is journalistic personation', *Irish Times*, 22 May 1999

Germond, Jack, 'No sense of proportion', *Colombia Journalism Review*, November/December 1999; http://www.cjr.org/year/99

Gibbons, Fiachra, 'Ireland's villain recast in a new light: Satire based on Haughey's notorious career divides Dublin', *Guardian*, 16 February 2002

Glennon, Chris, 'The Final Days: A succession battle looms', *Irish Independent*, 28 January 1983

Harding, Ted, 'High-flying chopper pilot into low profile mode over Dunne affair', *Sunday Business Post*, 15 November 1998

Harding, Ted, 'The Unravelling of Haughey', *Sunday Business Post*, 23 July 2000

Harding, Ted, 'Generous friends who asked nothing in return', *Sunday Business Post*, 24 September 2000

Harding, Ted, 'Haughey, where to now?', *Sunday Business Post*, 3 June 2001

Harris, Eoghan, 'CJ more convincing but probably doomed', *Irish Independent*, 23 January 1992

Healy, John, 'Sounding off', *Irish Times*, 7 February 1983

Healy, John, 'The sleepers and the heave', *Irish Times*, 12 February 1983

Hennessy, Mark, 'Colley "feared phone taps on Cabinet"', *Irish Times*, 8 May 2001

Horgan, John, 'Vilification Once Again', *Magill*, January 1984

Judt, Tony, 'Counsels on Foreign Relations', *New York Review of Books*, 13 August 1998

Keena, Colm, 'Land deal not 'guise' to give money to Haughey', *Irish Times*, 22 May 1999

Keena, Colm, 'Revenue did not pursue Haughey for £300,000', *Irish Times*, 25 May 1999

Keena, Colm, 'Getting by with a little help from his friends', *Irish Times*, 30 September 2000

Kelly, John F., 'May the Source Be With You' an executive summary of the 1999 Watchdog Journalism Conference at the Nieman Foundation for Journalism, Harvard University; http://www.nieman.harvard.edu/events/conferences/watchdog2/index.html

Kerrigan, Gene, 'Pushing on the open door: How Haughey came to terms with the Gregory team', *Magill*, March 1982

Kerrigan, Gene, 'Charlie and the Press Gang' *Magill*, February 1983

Kerrigan, Gene, 'Time and Reality are all we need', *Sunday Independent*, 24 September 2000

Kirchheimer, Otto, 'The Transformation of the Western European Party Systems', in LaPalombara, Joseph and Weiner, Myron, eds, *Political Parties and Political Development* (Princeton, 1966), pp. 177–200

MacDonncha, Micheal, 'Looking after Number One', *An Phoblacht/Republican News*, 17 July 1997

Mair, Peter, 'Breaking the Nationalist Mould: The Irish Republic and the Anglo-

Irish Agreement', in Paul Teague, ed., *Beyond the Rhetoric: Politics, the Economy and Social Policy in Northern Ireland* (London, Lawrence and Wishart, 1987)

Mair, Peter, 'Continuity, Change and Vulnerability of Party' in *West European Politics*, October 1989, pp. 169–187

Mansergh, Martin, 'C.J. Haughey and the phone tapping saga', *Irish Independent*, 24 January 1992

Mansergh, Martin, 'Reflections on the History of Fianna Fáil', speech given in Dublin 16 May 2001. Full text available at http://www.fiannafail.ie

McCann, Eamon, 'Adams Removes Mandate of History', *Belfast Telegraph*, 25 October 2001

McDaid, Marguerite, 'Day the prize was snatched away', *Sunday Independent*, 25 November 2001

McDonald, Darach, 'Soldier of Destiny haunt Jack Lynch', *Hibernia*, 13 September 1979

McGurk, Tom, 'A war worth remembering' *Sunday Business Post*, 7 October 2001

Millar, Frank, 'The Man who looked most likely to succeed', *Irish Times*, 31 January 1992

Millar, Peter, 'Time and patience run out for Ireland's tainted "Boss"', *Sunday Times*, 26 January 1992

Mills, Michael, 'Kelly believed government authorised action', *Irish Times*, 30 April 1998

Muire Tynan, Maol, 'The Taoiseach's thoughts', *Sunday Business Post*, 30 December 2001

Mulcahy, John, 'The Making of a Leader', *Hibernia*, 13 December 1979

Murtagh, Peter, 'FF inquiry into phone tapping not to lay blame', *Irish Times*, 7 February 1983

Murtagh, Peter, 'Charlie warms to the media', *Irish Times*, 26 February 1983

Murtagh, Peter, 'Tightening belts for the chancer we knew so well'; http://www.ireland.com/newspaper/special/1999/eyeon20/

Myers, Kevin, 'Ireland celebrates its murderous dead' *Sunday Telegraph*, 7 October 2001

O'Connor, Alison, 'Arms Trial judge unaware statement withheld', *Irish Times*, 16 April 2001

O'Connor, Alison, 'Bertie: From the Inside Out', *Irish Times Magazine*, 19 May 2001

O'Dea, Willie, 'Forging ahead with a modern policy of social partnership', *Irish Times*, 12 October 2001

O Faolain, Nuala, 'Why shouldn't a free-born Irishman do exactly what he wants?', *Irish Times*, 31 January 1992

O'Leary, Olivia, 'Charles Haughey: Waiting, Watching and Waiting', *Magill*, December 1981

O'Leary, Olivia, 'The Winner Takes All', *Irish Times*, 26 February 1983

O'Leary, Olivia, 'Sun shone on Charlie's heaven', *Irish Times*, 28 February 1983

O'Leary, Olivia, 'The John Hume Show', *Magill*, March 1984
O'Leary, Olivia, 'Haughey at the Forum', *Magill*, May 1984
O'Malley, Desmond, Statement, released by Progressive Democrats headquarters, 9 May 2001. Full text available at http://www.ireland.com/newspaper/special/2001/omalley.htm
O'Molloy, J.J., 'Pioneers of Tough Adversary Political Journalism', *Magill*, January 1982
O'Reilly, Emily, 'Hapless Harney bitten by her own soundbite', *Sunday Business Post*, 4 June 2000
O'Reilly, Emily, 'Arms Trial report slipped in quietly', *Sunday Business Post*, 8 July 2001
O'Toole, Fintan, 'Respectable lose 'veneer of legitimacy'', *Irish Times*, 25 September 1999
O'Toole, Fintan, 'O'Malley blessed in his enemies', *Irish Times*, 22 May 2001
O'Toole, Fintan, 'A grotesque denial of bloodshed', *Irish Times*, 2 October 2001
O'Toole, Fintan, 'Portrait of Haughey as Macbeth at bay', *Irish Times*, 2 February 2002
Patterson, Henry, 'Seán Lemass and the Ulster Question, 1959-65' in *Journal of Contemporary History*, Vol. 34 (1), pp. 145–159
Pillars of society: 'Des O'Malley,' *The Phoenix*, 11 May 2001
Quinn, Ruairi, 'Banning of corporate funding essential', *Irish Times*, 8 December 2000
Riegel, Ralph, 'Haughey booed at funeral of Lynch', *Sunday Independent*, 24 October 1999
Rose, Richard, 'Comparing Forms of Comparative Analysis', in *Political Studies*, 39, 1991
Rosenthal, Daniel, 'Charles Haughey, I presume?', *The Independent*, 27 February 2002
Ryle Dwyer, T., 'Haughey's trial by media continues', *Irish Independent*, 23 January 1992
Ryle Dwyer, T., 'Lynch's biggest mistake was not ousting Jim Gibbons', *Irish Examiner*, 25 April 2001
Scott, Kirsty, 'Men of Letters, Men of Arms' *The Guardian*, 2 December 2000
Smyth, Sam, 'I won't let Mac back vows angry Ahern', *Irish Independent*, 2 May 2002
Starobin, Paul, 'A Generation of Vipers, Journalists and the New Cynicism', *Colombia Journalism Review*, March/April 1995; http://www.cjr.or/year/95
Toolis, Kevin, 'Troubles of a Taoiseach', *The Observer*, 3 September 2000
Walsh, Dick, 'Two sets of prints on the smoking gun', *Irish Times*, 25 January 1992
Walsh, Dick, 'Strongman Haughey looked after his interests', *Irish Times*, 22 May 1999
Walsh, Maurice, 'The word according to whom?', *Irish Times*, 1 February 1983
Waters, John, 'Personally Speaking', *Hot Press* Vol. 8, No. 24, December 1984

Waters, John, 'Nobody was spared – least of all himself', *Irish Times*, 22 January 1992
Waters, John, 'Exit our last leading character', *Irish Times*, 28 January 1992
Waters, John, 'Laying Bare the Secret behind the Celtic Tiger', *Irish Times*, 14 August 2000
Waters, John, 'Twelve reasons why Charlie should be forgiven', *Irish Times*, 23 October 2000

Principal Television Programmes Cited
'Charlie's Angles' *Spotlight*, BBC Northern Ireland, 26 October 1999
'Dying for Ireland', *Insight* UTV, 27 February 2001
'Evidence of the Colonel', *Prime Time*, RTÉ 1, 10 April 2001
'Exhuming Republicanism', *Insight*, UTV, 2 October 2001
'Licenced to Kill', *Insight*, UTV, 30 January 2001
'Patriot Games', *Spotlight*, BBC Northern Ireland, 10 March 1998
'Policing in the Dock', *Insight*, UTV, 4 December 2001
'Policing the Police, *Insight*, UTV, 17 April 2001
'The Sparks that Lit the Bonfire', *Timewatch*, BBC, 27 January 1993
Cabinet Confidential, BBC2, 17 November 2001
Charles Haughey's Ireland, Channel 4, 15 January 1985
Des O'Malley, A Public Life, RTÉ, 29 April, 6 May, 13 May, 20 May 2001
Hearts and Minds, BBC Northern Ireland, 10 May 2001
Nighthawks, RTÉ, 16 January 1992
Panorama, BBC, 3 September 1979
Panorama, BBC, 6 July 1970
Seven Ages, RTÉ, 27 March 2000

Newspapers and journals
An Phoblacht; Colombia Journalism Review; The Economist; Fortnight; Hibernia; Hot Press; Irish Independent; Irish News; Irish Times; London Review of Books; Magill; New Statesman; New York Review of Books; Newsweek; Sunday Business Post; Sunday Independent; Sunday Times; Sunday Tribune; The Times; The Voice of the North; This Week; United Irishman

Index